Jake's Take On the Lake

Learn To Become A Smarter Lake Fisherman

by

Jake Bussolini

Bloomington, IN Milton Keynes, UK

authorHOUSE®

AuthorHouse™
1663 Liberty Drive, Suite 200
Bloomington, IN 47403
www.authorhouse.com
Phone: 1-800-839-8640

AuthorHouse™ UK Ltd.
500 Avebury Boulevard
Central Milton Keynes, MK9 2BE
www.authorhouse.co.uk
Phone: 08001974150

First published by AuthorHouse 2/6/2007

ISBN: 978-1-4259-8080-1 (sc)

Printed in the United States of America
Bloomington, Indiana

This book is printed on acid-free paper.

Library of Congress Control Number: 2006911302

When it comes to fishing, luck is defined as the combination of knowledge, skill and persistence. This book hopes to address the element of knowledge. The reader needs to add the other two ingredients.

DEDICATION

Throughout my childhood I received constant advice on fishing technique, sportsmanship and wildlife conservation from my father. When I was six years old he trusted me enough to let me walk alone to the local fishing hole to develop my own fishing style at that early age. Even today I remember his advice given many years ago. Unfortunately, my father, Jake Sr. was taken at a fairly early stage of his life and never had the opportunity to watch me grow to a man and follow in his sportsmanlike footsteps. For that reason, I dedicate this book with love to him and hope that he continues to observe from above all of my fishing successes.

CONTENTS

Introduction.. xi

Having Fun Fishing 1

Getting Started—Your First Fishing Experience 5

The Instinct for Survival 16

Understanding the Waters that You Fish In......................19

The Water Temperature Effect 31

The Challenge Of Finding The Fish 36

The Flying Fish Finders 44

Other Indicators 52

Fishing and the Weather..55

The Bait Controversy 86

Some Simple Knots 104

The Element of Surprise 108

Different Fishing Techniques..113

The Right Equipment Without Going Broke 144

About the Many Different Types of Fish 175

Handling The Fish..241

Fishing Etiquette, Ethics & Safety..................................250

Some Devices Help Your Fishing Experience 258

Saving Your Trophies..279

Now it's Up to You 301

Acknowledgements...303

References...304

INTRODUCTION

It's an early May morning; the sun has not yet risen over the eastern shores. There is a gentle, seemingly lazy mist hanging over the water, wanting to escape the waters grasp and anxiously waiting for the warm rays of the rising sun to lift its blanket of white in the early warmth. Two loons come to life from nowhere starting their daily search for food. Far in the distance, I hear the lonely high-pitched screech of a gull and then another as I see two gulls begin their morning scout of the lake's shoreline for signs of the schooling bait fish which will provide their flock its daily meals. The lake's surface is calm and still as the warming rays of the sun have not yet created the gentle breeze that will soon kiss the waters surface. I hear the soft splash of a fish breaking the surface and at that time a quick shiver strikes my body reminding me that summer ahs not yet come and I too await the warming heat of the sun.

Then in the eastern sky I see the first light of the waking sunshine, seemingly grasping the tops of the distant trees and pulling itself up to peek over the tops and set the stage for the warming rays that will soon follow. As the light continues to grow and the distant shores of the lake come into clear view, a sudden calamity takes place as the entire world seems to come alive within minutes of the first suns rays. The water surface takes on a glimmering ripple of a gently breeze.

Suddenly there are thousands of gulls in the skies starting their individual quest for survival, they are now singing to each other in a form of communication that man does not understand. The loons seem unaffected by this waking motion and I hear a soft sound of a motor in the distance.

All of this beauty and awakening that is taking place around me and I can't help but think of a friend of mine last night that said that he didn't understand why I would get up a 5am to go fishing. I haven't touched a fishing rod, or baited a hook and I have already witnessed all of this beauty and it dawns on me that it is there every morning and has been there every morning of my life. And it is there for you and will be there for you for the rest of your life. It's the part of fishing that we never seem to talk about because our habits drive us to get out of the house, get the equipment and start fishing as fast as possible and before we know it, all of this beauty has gone right by us.

I'm a lucky man. I have served my time in the working world and now dedicate a good part of my life to the enjoyment of fishing and the thrill of catching. I have turned the fishing experience into a learning experience where I take every opportunity to try and make myself a better fisherman and a better "catcher". That process will end only when I see my last sunrise but in the meantime, I think it would be a waste to keep what I have learned to myself so I decided to write this book and share more than sixty years of fishing experience with those who are also interested in waking up with nature every morning and feeling the thrill of battling a fish against its natural instinct to survive.

In these days of mega stores and super-sized fishing supply stores, fishing has become a gigantic business which keeps its share of the economy rolling. I think that's fine, but I hate to see people wasting their time and money on equipment that they will probably never use. To avoid that, I think it is necessary for a fisherman, more specifically a starting fisherman or woman to understand the very basic facts about fishing so that they can make up their own mind about what kind of fishing they want to do and how they want to go about doing it. To accomplish what I think is necessary to take the major elements of the fishing experience and blend the science with the practical knowledge and common sense to create ones individual fishing strategy. There is no totally right or totally wrong way to fish for anyone. Fishing is an individual challenge and to enjoy the experience we should develop our own technique that permits us to get the maximum enjoyment out of the sport.

Much of the data presented in this book has been gathered from research conducted on Lake Norman, North Carolina, but most of the material that is presented is applicable to any fresh water body of water in North America. The book tries to reduce every category to its simplest terms so that the beginning fisherman or woman can gain the knowledge that they need. It also gets into slightly more detailed discussions so that even the more experienced fisherman can benefit from the information presented. I try to blend the science of a situation with the practical results that I have experienced so that you will understand why things happen when they happen and not just taking a chance to drop your line in and expect immediate results. I want to help you enjoy the sport of fishing as I do.

Remember, the only bad day of fishing is the day that you do not get on to the water. The worst day of fishing is better than the best day of working. I cannot have any effect on your working habits, but I hope that I can make your days of fishing better and more enjoyable for you.

Having Fun Fishing

Fishing is one of the greatest relaxation sports that was ever invented. Although it is indeed a sporting activity, most of us that fish are certainly not athletes in the truest sense but like athletes, we have to enjoy what we do in order to gain maximum benefit and more important we have to enjoy it to be good at it. There are indeed many professional fishermen and women that take the sport so seriously that they make a good living at it. There are thousands of others that wish that they could be that good or that lucky that spend far more money competing than they will every win in tournaments. This book is not intended for those people, they already know more about fishing than I could ever offer you. Those of us that simply love fishing or want to learn how to love it are the ones for whom I am writing this book.

To really enjoy this sport you have to look beyond the early rising times and the rain storms and the 100 degree heat of the summer months and recognize the pleasure of sitting on a large rock or perhaps your favorite lawn chair or on your boat as the sun rises to the sound of the terns and gulls and loons. You listen for the sounds of the gently waves washing against the rocks. You recognize the sound of a fish breaking the surface, or perhaps best of all, no sound at all as the sun slowly melts away the mist and the lake comes alive.

Without anything else, half the fun of fishing lies right here and not a fish has yet been caught. There have been many mornings that I just sat in my boat with no motors on just listening to the quiet. On other days after a few hours of working around the house, I take my boat out for a couple of hours and just relax with a beverage, just me and the lake. And then there are those special days when my wife and I go out in the lake in the late afternoon with some cheese and crackers and a bottle of fine wine and relax and catch a few fish as a bonus. That my friends is what life is all about.

BUT! I have never subscribed to the theory that it doesn't matter if you win as long as you play the game right. Any sport that I have ever participated in always made me feel better when we won that it did when we lost. Fishing is no different. I love the sport but I hate not to catch fish, that is not an acceptable outcome for me and it should not be one for you. If I spend an hour on the lake and I don't catch any fish, I feel that I am doing something wrong so I have made a study of my home lake in an attempt to get smarter than the fish so that I never get skunked. For the most part it has worked for me and it will work for you. Oh, I am not smarter than the fish; no human will ever be that smart.

Let's start with a promise to ourselves that fishing is not as good as catching. All of that great stuff that I just told you gets even better if you get the thrill of a fish battling you for survival. The catch involves four stages: finding the fish; making them like your food better than other food, setting the hook and making the retrieve, getting the fish into you net. Sounds easy doesn't it, but there are many ways to accomplish each of these stages and I am going to try to show you some, not all of them so that you can be a winner at the sport.

I get a laugh from reading or hearing interviews that are done with professional athletes who make their living at sports and for the most part make a bigger annual salary than any of us will ever dream of making. Almost without exception, somewhere in their interview they will say that all that counts for them is that they have fun doing what they do. Well, I don't know about that, if I was earning five million dollars a year I think I would want to be good at what I do and I certainly would want to keep my boss happy with my performance. I suppose that it's also nice to have fun at it but at those salary levels fun should be way down the list requirements.

Fishing however is different. Many of us work hard at this sport but we do it because we love it and indeed this is a sport that we should have fun taking part in, after all since we are not earning our living at it, what else will be our motivation?

This book can be read in several different ways. Unlike many books, you don't necessarily have to read every word of the book to benefit from it although I believe that a complete fisherman should be armed with all of the facts that he needs to be a success. I am starting with some of the very basic material that a beginner or advanced fisherman needs to know in order to develop his or her own fishing technique. Later in the book I get a little more advanced with descriptions of some of the more advanced equipment that is available as you progress with your fishing skills.

For this book, I have directed most of the information toward lake type fishing. My home lake is Lake Norman in North Carolina and many of the tests and information that I have collected come from this lake. However, I have tried to generalize the material so that it is applicable to nearly any North American lake. I have for the most part not included much information on stream or creek fishing simply because that is not my personal area of expertise.

I will start by discussing the waters in which you intend to fish. Most readers will not fish a large number of water bodies like I do but will concentrate their efforts on some water that is close to where they live or vacation. The lake is the environment in which the fish live so you need to know about that environment to make your experience more successful. Any fishing experience is affected by outside conditions like the weather so that will be presented as it affects the fish and the fisherman. Next I will describe several of the more popular methods of fishing so you can see which one best satisfies your needs. I will then discuss the fish that reside in these waters, where they live, what they eat, how they multiply. Next I will deal with the real problem of finding the fish and giving them a meal that is better than other meals that are available to them including some recommendations for the type of equipment that can be used without spending a fortune for it. There are also many other topics that I touch upon to help make your fishing experience a more pleasant one. That sounds like a lot to absorb and indeed it is so let's get on with it.

Getting Started—Your First Fishing Experience

Most people like me who know a subject and apply their knowledge in its implementation, usually start discussing the subject with others without considering that the other folks listening have little or no knowledge of the subject in question. This leads to a boring one-sided discussion and little if anything is retained. Haven't we all had a teacher or professor who fell into this category, how much did we really learn from him or her?

As I was writing this book I fell victim to this same condition rapidly wanting to jump right into details and complex data that a good fisherman needs to become a better fisherman. Suddenly I realized that I was missing a big audience, the person who has never fished and wants to get started but doesn't know how. It doesn't make any difference what the age or intelligence of the person is, if he or she wants to learn about fishing, we have to start with the very basics in order to get a real solid understanding permitting us to go on to the more complicated stuff required for technique improvement.

I am going to get into your equipment needs but first I would like to discuss your reasons for wanting to learn about fishing. Well, I don't want to know, I want to make sure that you know what your motives are. The motive might be to be able to take your kids out for a nice day together using the fishing experience as the basis for that. Or, you may have just met the potential future love of your life and you want to impress her or him with your outdoor style or knowledge. Or perhaps you are planning a camping vacation with your family and you want to catch some fish to cook over an open fire. Or maybe you read the first couple pages of this book and you decided that you wanted a little slice of that life full of beauty and relaxation. The US Department Of The Interior data indicates that in 2005 more than 27 million people went fishing in this country that might indicate that there are millions of different reasons why people participate in this wonderful sport.

Why is it important for you to understand your motives? Because each of the above reasons dictates a different level of knowledge of the sport, different starting techniques and probably different types of equipment to get started. Well, I'm certainly not going to give you a test to make that determination but it is important for you to understand what you want to achieve from your fishing experience. The way I have structured this book, it is possible for the reader to pick and choose the specific areas where they want to develop more knowledge. You may want to skip some of the more complicated subjects if you are a beginner or hold them off until you acquire more experience. I believe however that if you truly want to learn the right way to fish, you have to acquire some basic knowledge to do it and understand some of the science of fish and fishing to become proficient. I hope that you find that this book provides all of that.

Let's start by developing a little knowledge and understanding about the fish itself. We humans often think of ourselves as the super species, put on earth to live our lives with some kind of superiority over all other living creatures who also reside on the same planet. If you think about it a bit you may recall that long before humans inhabited the earth, it was inhabited by several of what we now think of as sub species or living creatures. I certainly do not want to discuss or argue who was here first or who is superior to what, but I do want to introduce the subject by reminding my readers that fish are living things and they should be though of and treated as living things. They were born, they survived and grew to adulthood, they reproduced their species, they thrived and eventually they will die. In the earliest times man used fish as a source of food. In some parts of the world, that is still true today. Restaurants thrive on serving all types of eatable fish and other seafood items and we think nothing of using fish as our selected source of food either at home or when we dine out. Since fish are indeed important to our modern society in many ways, let's start by developing some degree of respect for this living creature in order to insure that as fishermen and women we never intentionally do anything to hurt or destroy this valuable commodity. Fishermen and women are one of the most valuable resources available to help protect this family of living creatures. In all of our fishing experiences we must take care to honor our obligation in this regard. If you are fishing to catch a fine meal, keep only what you need for that meal. If you are catching fish only as part of the learning experience, take care not to traumatize the fish and try to return them into the water as soon and as gently as possible.

Be sure when you fish that you understand the local fishing laws. If a license is required be sure to obtain one. Fishing license fees go a long way to fund the re stocking of many of our good fishing spots. Make sure you understand the size and quantity limits for the area in which you are fishing. There are few is any laws that were made to make the fishing experience difficult, most of these laws exist in order to help propagate the population of the fish in that area. Local Natural Resources Organizations keep constant vigilance on the quality of the fish populations in your area. Support their efforts by understanding and obeying their rules.

Most of all make you fishing experiences fun whether you fish alone or with your family or friends. Keep your fishing experiences affordable to you. Do not let the cost of equipment or a fishing trip be such that it causes stress or strain on your financial situation. If you stay within your means and your individual capability, you will have a much more enjoyable fishing experience.

For some people the thought of catching and hurting a fish is mean and cruel and this keeps them from participating in this wonderful sport. There is a great deal of information being presented today dealing with the age old argument as to weather or not fish feel pain from being hooked and returned to the water. The general consensus for many years was that no pain is felt if the catching and releasing process is properly done. I discuss proper fish handling later in this book. Many fish will bite again the next day or even in the next hour or two so the pain that is felt, if indeed it is felt must not be great enough to change the habits of the fish. In this regard all fishermen should take care to cause as little trauma as possible to the fish that they catch weather they release them or do otherwise.

Let's start getting into the actual fishing itself. In order to develop the proper sequence of discussion I must assume at this point that the reader has no fishing experience at all and wants to know how to get started. For those of you who have graduated from this category, you can skip this section and go on to more complicated subjects. Let's talk about equipment needed to get started.

Rule number one - if you are a starter, don't spend a lot of money on equipment.

Most decent sporting good stores have starter kits which actually contain everything that you need to get starter, a fishing rod and reel with line already spooled, hooks, weight, bobbers and even a few artificial lures. These started kits normally cost less than $20. Understand however that this type of equipment is perfectly adequate to start your fishing experience but as always you get what you pay for and you should be ready to make this a throw away item as soon as you begin to become proficient.

The rod that comes with this type of kit is probably a two piece, five foot long rod and the reel will most likely be a spincasting reel which already has 5 or 6 pound test line on it. This reel offers almost fool proof casting ability but it isn't fancy and does not come equipped with all of the bells and whistles of the more expensive type reels. The spincasting outfit comes with a pistol like grip and the reel in mounted on top of the rods handle. Line is released using the push button on the reel. This and other type rods and reels are described in the Equipment section of this book.

The design of the spincasting equipment was purposely made to feel very comfortable to your hand and you will almost immediately feel that it fits your grip perfectly.

Of course, armed with this starter kit you may think that the next step is to go out and find a pond, creek or lake and start fishing. Well that depend again on your motives but I believe that before you do that you may want to take at least a few minutes in your back yard to do a little practice with you new equipment.

I recommend that you start by running the line through the rod eyes as your directions will probably suggest. Then you should tie a small weight to the end of the line rather than a hook. Your kit will probably contain some small lead shot weights; one of these is fine for your practice session.

There are three type of casting techniques used in some manner by all fishermen: the overhand casting method, the sidearm casting method and the underhand casting method. I will not deal with the underhand method here because as a beginner you need not learn it yet.

To practice casting, go to an area that has no obstruction for 50 feet or more. If you have access to a small 3-foot piece of rope, lay it on the ground in a straight line where you will be standing. Get a ball, can or any small object and walk off about 30 paces perpendicular to the rope and put this object on the ground. Again make sure that there are no obstructions between the area where you will be standing and this target object. Your objective in this practice session is to get the weight as close to the target as possible but more important to get your movements coordinated so that no matter where the line goes, you are comfortable with the results. Distance for the first few casts is not important it is the control and comfort that you are trying to achieve.

Stand at the rope facing the target squarely. Make sure that the line and weight are free of the end of the rod. Holding the rod in the hand that feels most comfortable to you, keep you elbow next to your ribs and raise the rod straight up with your thumb firmly pressing on the trigger button. When the tip of the rod is slightly behind your shoulder, whip it forward releasing the button as the forward movement starts. Follow through and end up with the rod pointing at the target. If your first cast was perfect you were probably lucky but don't get discouraged it won't take long to get the weight exactly where you want it. The secret with this equipment is to keep the movements flowing smoothly and releasing the button as the forward movement starts. Your wrist should be doing most of the work on your initial casts. With practice you will begin to use your arm and wrist combination to get the weight further out away from you. This technique is the overhand casting method using the spincasting reel.

The side arm method using a spincaster is nearly the same. Stand facing the target with the rod parallel to the ground. Make sure the weight and line are free of the rod tip. Keeping the rod parallel to the ground, swing the rod back to your casting arm side just past your body and again whip it forward with your wrist releasing the button as the forward movement starts. Follow through using the rod movement to control the direction of the cast.

Practice these two casting methods for a while, not concerned about the distance of the cast but more with the accuracy of your control of where the weight lands. As you begin to feel that you are getting control of the drop zone and the casting movement starts to feel comfortable, you can start using your arm and wrist combination to get more distance with your cast. Keep in mind that you don't want to smack the weight into the ground but lay it down as gently as possible. As you begin to feel more comfortable with practice you will probably invent your own technique, which will most likely be a combination of the two methods just discussed.

This will be the start of you defining your own fishing style. No one will ever notice how awkward you look casting out your line, or how many body movement you invent, what they will see is that you lay your bait down where you want it and with the lightest possible landing in the water. With a spincasting rod and reel I expect that with less than one hour of practice, you will be good enough to hit the water.

Your starter kit probably included some plastic artificial bait. I do not recommend using that on your first day of fishing. Go to your local bait shop and buy a small cup of worms or night crawlers. These are the best bait for learning fishermen. I have been fishing for more than 60 years and on occasion I still use worms as my bait of choice.

Your first actual fishing experience will probably be from shore, at either a public fishing area, a friend's dock, a riverbank or a public dock or boat launch area. Try to select your first area as one that has few if any obstructions. You have learned how to cast but you don't need anything adding difficulty to your first fishing attempts. I suggest a late afternoon or early morning first experience, that's when many types of fish come closer to shore to eat.

Your started kit included a bobber, probably white and red. You should use this bobber on your early fishing attempts. The purpose of the bobber is to keep your bait off of the bottom and also to provide you a visual indication that something is after your bait. Assuming that you have taken the practice weight off of your line, tie on one of the hooks provided with your starter kit. The equipment section of this book describes several types of knots to use to tie the hook to the line. I recommend the modified cinch knot for beginners. Make sure the hook is firmly tied to the line and snip off the end of the tie as close to the hook as possible. Add a small lead shot weight about 6 inches above the hook. These weights are crimped on to the line and are very easy to attach and remove. The bobber should be hooked on to the line about three feet above the weight. There will probably be instructions in your started kit on how to attach the bobber depending on the type that the kit contains.

You will now of course notice something is different from your practice set up, there is a tree foot distance from your hook to the bobber and the bobber is as far in as the line can be taken. This means that you will be casting with several items hanging from your line and they will be moving as you make your casting movements. Don't fret, you will quickly realize that all you need do is make your motions more deliberate and smooth and everything will go well. Try a couple of practice casts before you put actual bait on the line. Hook a worm on your line and you are ready.

Hook the worm through the head end with the barb buried in the worm. Let the tail end dangle freely. If you are in an area where there are bream, you bay want to hook the worm several times so that there is no tail dangling, bream will often nip at he tail and not hook themselves. If you are using night crawlers, it is probably wise to cut it in half initially until you determine what type of fish are in the area.

Cast the line out as far as is comfortable, laying the hook and bobber in the water as quietly as possible. As the line settles and the bait sinks to its established level, the bobber is now your target of concentration. Keep your eye on the bobber after a few seconds and the water has calmed from the cast. If fish are in the area and start to get interested in your bait, you will see the bobber start to move. Be patient until the bobber is pulled beneath the surface and then it is your time to act.

If the bobber is under water, take up all of the slack on the line that may have been caused by wind, current of simply drifting of the bait. Take the slack up quickly but evenly. When the slack is out set the hook with a quick snap of the wrist and begin reeling immediately.

Since your first fish will probably not be a whale, you need not yank it up as thought you were in a tug of war. A hard hook set will often pull the hook out of the fish's mouth. If you feel the fish on the line, keep reeling the fish in insuring that no slack is ever established in the line. You probably do not need any net for the first few experiences unless the fish in the area normally large. If you followed my instructions you have not yet purchased a net.

You have now begun your fishing career, your first fish is caught and of course you took care to get it off the hook quickly and to get it back into the water if it is not a keeper. If your first fish was a small bream or other pan fish you are probably excited and ready to go at it again. If on your first day of fishing you manage to snag a whopper, which is often the case for beginners, you are now completely hooked on the sport, you are already thinking about the first boat that you will buy and you will rush home to read the rest of this book to find out how to be a smarter fresh water fisherman.

Some beginning tips to remember

- A set of polarized sunglasses will permit you to see more clearly through the water and also help prevent glare.

- As you become a better fisherman with time, you will want to upgrade your equipment but for now be patient and upgrade slowly.

- It is always wise to fish with a partner at least at the beginning. Things can happen and it is always better to have help if it is needed.

- Start your fishing experiences in shallow waters. If there are rocks or underwater structure or growth, aim your cast at that growth, that's where the fish are likely to be.

- Fish hooks and artificial lures can be dangerous weapons, be sure to look around you and know where others may be standing.

- If your casts are going in all directions and you have trouble with your control, move closer to the water and make shorter casts until you work out the problem.

- Try to make sure that the lure or bait lands in the water as smoothly and quietly as possible. If you see target fish in the water, cast past the fish and move your bait in front of them. Fish cannot see to the rear and are often frightened when a lure passes them from behind.

- Cast with your wrist, not with your arm. The arm motion will come naturally as you gain experience.

- Lower the lure a few inches below the tip of the rod before casting. This will provide additional momentum to the cast.

- If you have to spool your own line, spool it no further than 1/8 inch from the top of the spool. Overfilling the spool will cause backlashes.

- Learn to load your rod tip when casting. Loading means that you cause the tip to bend on your backward movement. This results in a smoother and longer cast and a lighter drop to the target zone.

- Browse around your local fishing supply store and do not be bashful to ask questions. Fishermen like to talk to other fishermen and they all like to give advice.

- Always practice fishing courtesy. Don't intrude on someone else's fishing territory and keep your fishing mood positive.

Shown below is Gianna Caminiti of Cornelius, North Carolina, the author's granddaughter who started with the basics while sitting on the boat tied to the dock. She is comfortable with her simple equipment and intent on what she is doing.

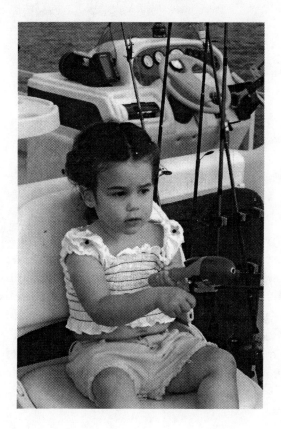

THE INSTINCT FOR SURVIVAL

All of Gods creatures, weather human or animal have the same basic objective, SURVIVAL. We all go about it differently but our basic purpose and instinct is to survive and thrive. Fish are exactly the same. Oh, we don't understand some things about fish like what they do with their leisure time? What their career objectives are? But we do know that a fish spends every moment of its life doing those things that will permit its survival and the survival of the species. In simplest terms this means that once a fish is born it attempts to stay alive and reproduce and these are the two things that drive all of the theories of fishing.

From the instant a fish is first born it becomes "the hunted". Nature's cycle of life creates the situation where the smaller fish are the food for the larger fish. It's not important for this book to understand the survival rate of new born fish but we can estimate that it is at or less than 10%. This means that for every 100 fish born, less than 10 will survive the first year of life. What this means is that a large part of a brain of a fish is probably dedicated to understanding how to hide or run away from the bigger fish. Remember, they are not wrapped in blankets and cuddled in cribs during the first months of their life. They are out there as the nice tender meal for those other fish and animals that are also trying to survive. Remember that to survive, all

16

creatures must eat and in the case of fish, it is the eating habits that we have to understand in order to learn how to "go catching" rather than "go fishing".

In an undistributed pond, lake or river fish roam in constant search for food. That food can be in the form of insects, bugs, plant life or other fish. Under different circumstances fish will prefer any or all of these food sources. What we try to do when we go fishing is to present to the fish something that looks more appetizing than other stuff that is around them. Waters are full of grass, weeds, plants, plankton (small fish), insects and other live life. What we have to do is make our bait look more tempting than the surrounding food. Scholars have indicated that humans have the brainpower to reason and rationalize and many animals and fish do not, in other words the fish are stupid. Well if the fish are stupid and we are not then we should all catch our limit all of the time and the term "going fishing" would disappear and would be replaced by "going catching". Obviously, then that theory is not correct.

Because we believe that all creatures were created somewhat equal does not mean that we are all equal in all aspects. Fish may not be able to think but they have a sharper power of instinct that we humans. They create much of the oxygen that they need to live and therefore can live under water and we cannot. Fish have sharper senses of smell, sound and vibration than humans. But like us humans fish are also affected by the heat that surrounds them the light that is created and the weather conditions that exist. So to become a good fisherman, we have to try and understand all of these factors and to put them together with the environment that surrounds us. If we do it right we will catch fish. If we do it wrong, we will be spending a lot of quiet time trying to understand why the fish are smarter than we are.

I remember many years ago traveling to Yellowstone National Park. In one section of the park there was a foot bridge that passed over a small river. The water was crystal clear and there were thousands of golden trout swimming gently under the bridge. Dozens of people were fishing from the bridge but no one could catch one of those fish. Why was that, well obviously the fish were smarter than the people.

I recently was at a local super sporting goods store where there were tens of thousands of different lures, baits, jigs, rigs and special equipment to bring man's fishing intellect up to the level of the fish or hopefully higher. It brought back my own memory of my earliest fishing days. I started fishing when I was about 6 years old. I had a simple telescoping rod and a real that didn't even have one gear in it. I dug worms from the neighbor's chicken yard and carried them to the pond in a canned food can, which I re-used every day. I would walk to the pond with one rod and one hook and maybe a small sinker. I would throw my line out as far as I could (no spinning rods at that time) and place the rod on a fork stick that I had stuck in the ground. I would then sit and wait, many days for hours for a trout to come along and want my worm more than other food that was in that pond. I would usually get two or three (five was the limit) and carry them home also on a fork stick that I had cut for that occasion. How different it is today. I don't ever remember spending much money on fishing gear since I used the same pole for many years. Today with thousands of dollars worth of gear, I am still trying to accomplish the same goal, to make the fish like my worm better than the other food in the lake. It doesn't make any difference what kind of fish I am after, brim, crappie, catfish, stripers, perch or bass, my goal is still the same, to present something that will make the fish want to eat my bait more than other food that is around it. That's as simple as it is so why can't we catch our limit every day, well let's see if we can figure it out.

Understanding the Waters that You Fish In

When I was planning this book I really struggled defining what the important contents should be that would prove most useful toward helping you develop your fishing talents. Each time I had doubts about a particular subject, I went back to my early days of fishing when I was a young man and all I cared about was the number and size of the fish that I caught. I knew that there were certain sections of my favorite fishing hole that no one fished in but I never really questioned why? As I grew older and wanted to develop my fishing skills to a higher level, I started wanting answers about these types of things like why do some areas of a water body house fish and other areas do not. Why are there some ponds and streams that have no fish at all? Why are there seasons for certain types of fish? As I began to research some of these topics (in those days there was no internet), I realized that every body of water is different but has certain common characteristics that I really had to know to become a good fisherman, or more important to help me not waste my time fishing where my chances of catching big fish were minimal.

Remembering this, I decided that this book needed a short tutorial on water bodies, specifically lakes and ponds in order to establish a starting point for an understanding of how the science of fishing effects this sport of fishing. The danger here is that some people spend their whole lives studying this subject and I do not want to make this book a boring science project so I am including only a single summary description of the important facts effecting the water that you fish in, not a scientific thesis.

Let's start by asking, what is a lake? Well it is a large body of water, usually fresh water for purposes of this book, which was formed by glaciers, river drainage, surface water run off or ground water seepage. In some cases, lakes are created by man rather than by nature. Every body of water exists in a complex balance, which is normally managed by Gods most amazing creation, Nature. In good waters this balance must be maintained and it consists of the balance of three elements, water, oxygen and energy. Each of these elements if changed will affect the other two. Nature's job is to keep everything balanced. As an example, in a small pond, if there is not much water in the hot months the water gets warmer and warm water holds less oxygen. Water that has low levels of oxygen will not support big fish. (There are a few exceptions) If the fish are not large enough, too many of the smaller living creatures and plants will survive and eventually create a nutrient imbalance. Why is this important to you since you probably can do nothing about it? Well to be a knowledgeable fisherman you have to understand the food web and the balances that affect it. The better you understand this, the better a fisherman you will become.

A lake or river by definition holds water. The amount of water it can hold and the temperature of that water will determine what type of fish will reside there. Large changes in the water level can have a significant effect on the food web and therefore a big effect on the fish that can survive. Lake levels are determined by several factors. Most lakes receive their water from the rains or via feeder streams. Water leaves a lake by seepage into the ground and mostly by evaporation into the air. In areas that are cold enough to have ice, the lake will loose water to the ice but gains most of it back from melting ice. To many lakes, specifically those that are used for electric power are governed by flood control - humans control the exiting water flow. The amount of water in a lake affects the fish in many ways but primarily its effect is from varying oxygen levels, temperature and acid balance. As a general rule, the bigger the lake the better the living conditions for the fish.

While the fish need water to swim in, what they really need is the oxygen for breathing. All water, no matter how stagnant it may appear, takes on oxygen from the water surface and atmosphere. Other sources of oxygen are the stream inflows and the aquatic plant life. All of these sources need to be in balance. If excess aquatic growth takes place and these plants rot and decompose in the winter, this decomposition eats up oxygen and starves the water. Nature normally manages this but in some lakes, primarily those that used for hydro electric power or for flood control, where water levels vary a great deal, the balance has to be managed by humans to prevent damaging the fish population. If a lake becomes water starved by natural or man-made causes the big fish (that need more oxygen) will die first.

Another item in the balance equation is the energy. The energy balance is influenced primarily by the sun. Every water body has tiers or levels, the highest tier being closest to the surface. These tiers affect the food web, which defines where the fish are. There are a couple of simple rules involving energy: the closer an item is to getting its food from the sun, the more food energy it produces when it is eaten. Secondly, the higher you are in the tiers or the closer to the surface, the greater the biomass that exists including a combination of all living organisms. Last, every body of water has an optimum balance in the biomass that exists at the various water depths. Simply stated, too little sun can kill the plants, which will starve the plankton, which starves the small minnows, which starves the bigger fish, etc. Water bodies that do not have the proper biomass will contain only the smaller fish.

The above factors explain why the larger, deeper cold water lakes in the northern regions have no problem with either the temperature or water depth and they contain a variety of large fish.

We can oversimplify the water depth science by defining a water body as having 6 tiers or levels. The first three levels closest to the surface are the same for almost every water body. They contain a variety of organisms such as crayfish and other crustaceans, large aquatic insects and larvae and the smaller species of fish. Level 4 is the first depth that hosts sport fish like sunfish, perch, small trout, suckers, and herring. Level 5 hosts most of the real large game fish like the bass, stripers, catfish and larger trout. Level 6 gets real interesting hosting the big ones like the Northern Pike, Muskie, Sturgeon and Lake Trout. The six tiers of a water body are illustrated below.

This tier concept explains somewhat more clearly the circle of life beneath the surface of a lake. The small fish at level 1, 2 and 3 eat the insect larvae, plant life, and plankton. The level 4 fish eat the level 1, 2 and 3 fish and some of the other living creatures that exist there. Level 5 fish eat the level 4 fish and so on down the food chain. As you read further on in this book where the various types of fish are described, this information may help you understand why certain fish spawn where they do, eat what they eat and live where they live. If you are going to consider yourself a complete fisherman, you should have a basic understanding of this information.

I have, of course, greatly abbreviated this lesson in water science. Having defined some of the basic of lake existence, we cannot go on and get more specific about your fishing hold, lake or pond and what you should look for when developing your fishing strategy.

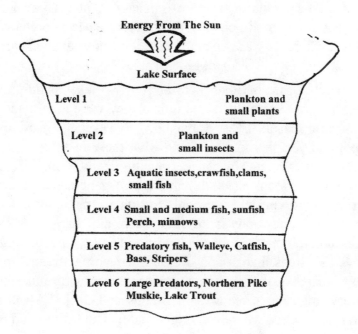

Note: Much of the specific information used in this section used internet source http://www.combat-fishing.com--Ecology of Lakes and Ponds for Anglers, as a reference.

If you apply this tiering concept to your favorite fishing spot you will, of course, realize that the various depths at which the tiers change will vary with the individual water location and overall water body depth. There is no real unchanging fixed set of depth measurements that you can apply to this theory and the various depths will change with the seasons and conditions but it can be a guide for your to determine what kinds of fish you can expect to catch and where they might be located.

Also keep in mind that a person that lives in a penthouse apartment has to travel through many floors to get to his or her home. Although a fish species may find it comfortable to live at level 5 or 6, they will certainly move through the upper tiers to feed and travel. This tiering concept will be put into sharper focus in later chapters as we describe the various water conditions that different fish species prefer, where they feed, where they spawn and what their seasonal habits area.

It's probably a safe bet that there are no two lakes or large water bodies that are exactly the same unless they were man made for a very specific reason. Every water body however has features that define it and you should understand what these features are. There are natural lakes created by glaciers or natural land formations. There are river lakes, many created years ago to generate hydroelectric power and there are lakes fed only by underground springs. Even though every water body is different, there are characteristics that are common to every one like the varying depths, surrounding land features like trees, banks and overhangs; feeding streams; points; shallow areas; aquatic vegetation; underwater structure like stumps and trees; man made features like dams and docks. All of these features help define where you might find fish and what kind of fish you can expect to catch.

If you have ever been a spectator at a professional fishing tournament you might have noticed that every professional fisherman has in his or her possession as many maps of the lake as they can put their hands on, even if they have fished the lake before. They study these maps and note in advance the areas that should produce fish. For good fishing lakes there is usually a map or two available at the local sporting store. That will give you some of the information that you need.

Of course talking to other fishermen is a great source of information. Don't ask them where the fish are because you really don't know what their answer will be and you could well be pointed in the wrong direction. I normally take a few minutes to hang around the local gas station and convenience store where the local boats stop to fill their tanks. Observing the types of gear being used or even the lures that are most popular can tell a lot about the fishing without even asking a question. If there is no place to buy live bait near your fishing spot then it's a pretty safe bet that there is no live bait being used.

Wherever I fish and I am not completely familiar with the waters, I try to spend a few quiet minutes at the dock at dusk or even early morning. This quiet time lets me get closer to the lake and by just looking around above the surface I can learn a lot about what is going on beneath it. I check the aquatic growth, is it hidden beneath the surface or has the water level pushed it through the surface. If it is visible, do I see any random movement of the weeds which would indicate the presence of fish or other underwater life. I look for signs of natural bait that is visible which may give me a clue of the type of bait or lure that I should use. I check the surface temperature, sometimes by simply putting my hand in the water. Cold water will make the fish move slower and tell me how to move my bait or lure. I look at the sky to determine how much sunlight I will have or whether it will be overcast. I look for bird activity, particularly any gulls or loons that may be in sight. These birds hang around where there are large concentrations of baitfish. I examine the water clarity, which will help me define the extent of the strike zone. I look for areas where there might be abnormally high plant growth, this might indicate an area where there is a water inflow or a small creek, this will attract fish because it is an area that brings in new food, nutrients and fresh oxygen.

By taking this time to just look around, I can start formulating my fishing strategy for that particular lake and I haven't spent an extra dime or taken any valuable fishing time. Simple but effective.

There was a famous book written a few years ago called "Managing by Walking Around." Its theory is that you can learn a lot about your environment by just walking around the workplace. The same concept applies to fishing except that it doesn't require walking but rather taking your boat and looking around as you make a short exploration of the fishing waters. It is not always possible to do this if time is not on your side but in any case, even on your first day of fishing in new waters, a lot of looking around will prove very valuable. What will you learn by observing? What is the direction of the prevailing winds? Erosion of certain banks and shorelines can point to a prevailing wind direction. Where are the steep drop offs?

Steep banks normally indicate steep drop offs. Where are the points and shoals? If they are not marked on any map you can find them by looking for land masses that protrude sharply into the water body. Shorelines that are rocky, point to a rocky water bottom. Overhanging trees and bushes provide the shade and hiding places for many types of fish. Any unusual amount of vegetation at a particular spot near the shoreline usually indicated that there is some kind of a feeding stream to the lake. This is always a good spot to try since fish know that inflowing water bring in new nutrients and food. Note the direction of the shorelines so you will know where the sun will rise and set. If you have a depth finder it is important to note the various water depths and to keep them in mind. If you can find stumps or other growth coming through the water surface that of course indicated underwater hiding places for the predator fish.

Maybe I have jumped ahead of myself a little for the basic or beginning fisherman that has never fished and simply wants to start by catching a few fish or maybe introducing a child to fishing. Here again it always helps to learn just a little about what is going on under the surface of the water because after all that is where you will try to catch fish. How about trying this learning experiment, if you are a beginner.

On a mid-week spring or summer day, go to your fishing water and find a friends dock or maybe a public dock where it is quiet and no one else is disturbing the water. Bring a few worms with you and maybe some bread, corn or other meat. I suggest a mid-week visit because you will avoid the weekend boating activity and by mid week the water should have calmed and cleared so that you have some water visibility. Find a place where you can clearly see the bottom in two or three feet of water and sit for a while. Soon you will probably see some sunfish or both bream swimming around. If you see a fish or two, throw in a small piece of bread or maybe two but make sure that they are small pieces, maybe the size of a kernel of corn. You will likely see the fish dash toward your bread and take it in but the fish will quickly spit it out, then take it again and again spit it out again. Eventually before the bread hits the bottom the fish will swallow it.

Now cut a small piece or worm, about the same size as the bread that you just threw in. Throw the piece of worm into the water and watch. The fish will react differently to the worm, he will quickly grab it but will not spit it out and you will soon see other fish arrive. This is the good stuff, their natural food. There is a communication that takes place when good food is found so if you cut the worm into many small pieces and throw them all in at the same time you will likely see many fish arrive and a feeding frenzy will start. You may even see the fish fighting each other for the worm parts. You should also observe that the fish probably do not hit the worm as soon as it hits the water but they watch it sink for a while before attacking it. This is a very common characteristic for fish to take food as it sinks to the bottom but before it actually hits and rests on the bottom.

If you then started throwing in bread pieces and worm parts, you will notice that only the worms are eaten and the bread will sink to the bottom. If you try kernels of corn with bread you will probably see them take the corn first as they did the worms. What has been learned from this simple experiment? Well I think you have learned more then you think you have learned.

- With the worm you gave the fish a food that was better than the other choices that they had available to them and they grabbed it first.

- You have witnessed the competition between fish that exists when it comes to feeding.

- You have witnessed the communication system that somehow exists when food is involved.

- You have probably seen the fish take the food on the way down and take it to the bottom to eat, then to again rise for the next morsel of food.

All fish will not behave in exactly the same manner but in general this is the way fish behave when it comes to eating.

Now let's try another learning experiment. Stop feeding the fish and wait quietly for a few minutes as the fish calm down and start swimming around normally. Find a small pebble and throw it into the water near the fish. The fish will probably scatter. Perhaps instead of the rock, you simply start waving your arms around to make your shadow move in the water, you will likely also spook the fish. Now wait a few minutes and again throw in a few pieces of worm. The fish will forget that they are scared or spooked and immediately go for the food because despite all other factors, the need to eat ranks above everything else for a fish.

If you have the time you might want to find another location and try these experiments again. It would not be unusual if your other location brought no fish toward you and the actual experiments could not be performed. This in itself is a learning experience since it points out that fish are not always where you think they are and they don't always behave in the same manner so the more you know about the habits and characteristics of the fish you are after, the better your odds of success and that is what this book is about, increasing your chances for a successful fishing experience.

My home lake is Lake Norman, North Caroline, and I have chosen this lake to use as an example in many areas of the book. Many of the map excerpts and test data that are included in this book were taken from Lake Norman but I have only used those that I feel are typical of other bodies of water throughout the country. I have fished many other lakes in the US and Canada and I have also used material from those experiences including many of the photos and data.

Lake Norman makes an interesting study base because it contains a large number of the fish that are common to other lakes. Many of the lake features of this lake are also common to nearly all other lakes. But there are also some very specific features of Lake Norman that are not common to many other lakes and I will not dwell on these differences other than to point them out or use the example to illustrate how the feature effects the ability to catch fish. A brief synopsis of Lake Norman will prove helpful.

Lake Norman is a man made river lake created in the 1950's to satisfy the need for more hydroelectric power for a rapidly growing population around Charlotte, North Carolina. One feature of this lake, which makes it ideal for fishing research, is that it contains a lot of water, nearly 3.5 billion gallons. The lake extends about 35 miles along the Catawba River and because of the land contours it contained more than 550 miles of shoreline. The surface area of the lake at full pond is more the 32,500 acres and that is a lot of water area to try to find and catch fish. Because of its size the configuration, it is important to understand those features that govern fish life. Because the lake is used for both the generation of hydroelectric power and as a flood control lake for the entire Catawba River basin, the water level can vary more than six feet throughout the year which makes the fishing challenge even greater. The lake is normally filled in the spring and stays near full pond until the fall. Lake Norman hosts many of the common game fish types including a wide variety of bream, carp, gar, white perch, largemouth bass, spotted bass, white bass, channel, flathead and blue catfish, crappie, striped bass and hybrids and an occasional yellow perch and sauger are rarely but sometimes caught. The Lake is most famous for its bass and striper fishing.

As a river lake, the maximum depth reaches 100 feet at some points along the main river channel and there are many creeks, channels and coves that provide for excellent fishing situations.

The one characteristic of the lake that is not common to many other lakes is that is has no natural bottom. When the lake was being constructed the land was cleared of all vegetation, trees and stumps to provide cleaner water for power generation. The result of this is that there is little or no underwater growth for attracting the fish so that all fish tend to be transient and move constantly around the lake. This makes the fishing challenge tougher. Because the lake has become widely developed first for the weekend leisure and now for full time living, there are massive numbers of piers and docks, which make excellent hiding places for those fish that like that, environment. The down side of the development however is the boating activity on the summer weekends, which makes summer daytime fishing difficult, if not impossible.

As is the case for many lakes, the striped bass population has grown significantly in recent years after stripers were introduced several years ago. Due to the lack of proper turbulence of the riverbed, stripers cannot reproduce in this lake but more than 300,000 are stocked each year and the population of mature fish is growing. Similarly the population of Largemouth Bass has been supplemented by a nice mix of Kentucky Spotted Bass so that Lake Norman has become a fine tournament lake for bass fishing.

As a southern lake, Lake Norman does not freeze over in the winter and its yearly water temperature variation is between 40 degrees and 90 degrees. This variation makes it more important to understand the effects of water temperature on fish behavior in order to have fine fishing all year round.

THE WATER TEMPERATURE EFFECT

I will talk about many factors that affect your fishing strategy in this book but one of the most important factors is the water temperature. I will discuss later in this book some of the biology of a fresh water fish but of great importance is the fact that fish are cold blooded meaning that the fish's internal body temperature and therefore its habits change with the water temperature. Like humans (though we are warm blooded) fish have favorite temperature ranges in which they like to live. If their surrounding gets too cold the fish slow down and eat less. If the water gets too warm and becomes oxygen starved, the fish get stressed and behave differently. The preferred temperatures therefore are important permitting us to predict the behavior of the fish and the changes in their behavior caused by the changes in the seasons. Listed in the chart below are the average temperature ranges preferred by many of the fish discussed in this book.

Freshwater Fish Preferred Water Temperatures	
Fish Type	Preferred Temp. Degrees F
Largemouth Bass	75---82
Smallmouth Bass	60---75
Spotted Bass	73---77
Striped Bass	65---70
White Bass	65---75
White Perch	60---80
Yellow Perch	55---78
Crappie	66---76
Bream	64---70
Sunfish	77---87
Channel Catfish	75---85
Blue Catfish	70---82
Flathead Catfish	75---85
Brown Bullhead	65---82
Carp	40---90
Walleye	55---68
Northern Pike	50---70
Muskellunge	50---78
Brown Trout	56---68
Brook Trout	48---60
Lake Trout	42---52
Sauger	65---70
Sturgeon	50---65
Whitefish	45---52
Gar	68---75
These preferred temperature ranges are average conditions which will vary slightly with different regions and different seasons.	

Another factor associated with temperature that effects fish behavior is the oxygen level of the water but that factor is not possible to measure by the average fisherman so we concentrate on the temperature and assume that the oxygen level will go along in a natural fashion.

Why is water temperature so important? Well obviously if the fish has a choice; it will seek the water temperature that is best suite to it.

The depth at which fish live in a body of water is therefore governed by the water temperature and energy and of course the oxygen level. All of these factors will vary with the seasons and the geographic location of the lake.

The temperature layering of a body of water is governed by its surrounding weather conditions and water clarity. Many shallow lakes in plains regions where there is a lot of wind have no layering because the high winds constantly mix the water. Even in these shallow lakes however the water temperature will vary, sometimes only slightly with the depth. I will address this more completely later in this book.

Despite all of the possible scenarios that may exist, the fact still remains that water temperature will vary with depth so if you are fishing for a fish that loves cool water and you are fishing in a shallow lake, expect to find that fish deeper in the water column or perhaps that lake has no large fish.

Deeper lakes in the summer are quite a different story. Early in the springtime the water temperature in a deep lake is quite uniform. However as summer approaches the surface water warms up and becomes less dense and at some point it will no longer mix well with the colder water below. This point is called the Thermocline level and it is important to understand the approximate depth where the thermocline resides because most fish will be at or above this level.

We have discussed the concept of tiering earlier in this book and it is also represented here. The warm, well-oxygenated water at the top varies in depth from a few feet down to levels as deep as 50 feet or so. Rooted plants, algae and insects thrive at the depths in the upper layer. At the bottom of the lake is the cold, somewhat stagnant layer that has no real contact with the surface and therefore is deprived of sufficient oxygen especially in the summer. Little light from the sun can penetrate the deeper water and therefore no plant life can thrive there. Fish will avoid these cold dark lower depths during the summer months.

Because of this temperature change factor, many if not most fish will seek the area around the thermocline during the summer months to feed. This does not mean that they are always at that level but it is a good indicator of where they might be. Later I will discuss some of the advanced equipment that can assist you in finding fish. A good fish finder will easily indicate the depth of the thermocline this is a very valuable tool especially in summer months.

In a deep lake the layers start to mix together in the late fall and maintain a rather constant temperature until the next spring. You may have heard of the saying that the "lake is turning." What does this mean? Most things expand or get a little bigger when they get warmer and they contract or get smaller when they get cold. Water however is a special kind of element. If you cool water it contracts until it reaches about 39 degrees F, then it starts to expand again as the temperature is lowered. At 32 degrees F the water really expands when it turns to ice. That is why ice floats to the surface. This also indicates that cold water will rise to the surface as it reaches 32 degrees.

Warm water however at a temperature of say 75 degrees F will float to the top of cooler water at 60 degrees F so in the summer all of the warmer water will be at the surface and the cooler water will be at the bottom. When the weather starts to cool as the winter approaches the temperature/depth relationships will remain stable until the surface water approaches 32 degrees. At this point the less cold water wants to rise to the surface and this is called "turning the lake."

Perhaps all of this is too complicated and you are certainly not going to go fishing with a computer to calculate all of it but you should remember that in the winter the water temperature is about 2 degrees warmer for every ten feet of depth and in the summer it is about 2 degrees cooler for every ten feet of depth. These numbers will of course be slightly different for lakes further north or south.

If you intend to fish all year round you really need to know the basics of the temperature effects on fish. If you are looking for Trout as an example, they are most comfortable at water temperatures between 50 and 70 degrees F. You will have to fish for them at greater depths in the late summer months and at or near the thermocline at other times.

Fish that like warmer water like bass that prefer water temperatures between 70 and 80 degrees F. You will have trouble finding active bass in shallow water in the winter and early spring. As the water heats to about 65 degrees F, the bass become much more active and will seek the warmer more shallow water to eat and to spawn. As summer approaches and the water warms beyond their comfort zone, the bass will head to the cooler deeper water during the daytime and come in to the shallow water to feed at night.

Now that I have provided this tutorial on temperature, I need to tell you that it all disappears when the fish are hungry and you pass good food into their strike zone. For food fish will go into water of almost any temperature unless the temperature is at a lethal level. In general however you stand a much better chance of getting nice fish if you pay attention to the temperature consideration.

THE CHALLENGE OF FINDING THE FISH

So far we have spent some time trying to understand the nature of the water that we are fishing in. That understanding is the first step in the process of developing a good fishing strategy. Now, having learned a little about lake structure and water life living conditions, we have to go about learning how to find the fish in the particular waters that you are fishing.

In a later section of this book I will get into some of the equipment that is available to assist you in the job of finding the fish. At this point however I want to concentrate on making you think about the water body you are fishing in, in terms of its features that are more or less likely to attract nice fish.

I have fished many waters and observed other people fishing those same waters and I believe that there are some common mistakes that people make that reduce their fishing fun. The first common mistake is to fish where it is comfortable for YOU to fish. You are out in your boat on a nice day and you want the sun shinning on you, you want a nice calm area out of the wind that is not too deep especially if you are going to anchor. More likely than not this will be absolutely the wrong place to fish on that lake. It may be a great place to have an enjoyable day on the water but not necessarily the best place to fish.

How then do you learn where the fish are located? Let's see if we can find that answer. I live on a large lake and when I first move to this location a local fishing guide told me that there were five hundred miles of shore line on this lake and if I tried to learn the whole lake I would just go crazy trying. I would spend the rest of my life trying to find the good fishing holes. He suggested that I break the lake into sections, possibly four sections, and pick one section at a time to learn. I should then fish the selected section until I knew every main channel, every deep hole, every point and shoal, every brush pile and every area where there were radical bottom changes. When I learned all of that about the selected section of the lake, I should pick seven or eight of my favorite spots and fish them regularly until I got tired of the scenery. At that point I could move on to the next section of the lake and do the same thing.

I described my home lake earlier in this book; it's a huge lake but is fairly easy to divide it into several pieces. I first divided it into two sections, the north end and the south end. The reason for this was because each end of the lake has similar features. Each has coves, bends in the main channel, many docks and bridges, stone and rip rap shores, some brush piles, submerged islands, old road beds and many other common features. In addition each end has a power generating station that exhausts hot water at times which changes the temperature and flow characteristics of the area. I live on the southern end of the lake so I picked eight creeks and channels on that end and learned them thoroughly. All of my initial learning concentrated first on the bottom structure of the area being studied. I believe that the bottom features tell the most about fish locations.

You can dissect your fishing water the same way and in the process of learning about the area, you will have fun catching fish. This is how I became hooked on trolling as my primary fishing technique on my home lake since it allowed me to move around the lake continuously while I always had lines in the water. Since I covered a great deal of area under varying conditions, I also kept a rather thorough log of my activities in order to develop a record for future reference.

As you are moving forward in the process of finding the fish in any waters, it will help if you keep in mind the survival issues that we discussed earlier in this book. Remember, eating is the most important survival issue for the fish so if you can find where the fish eat you will catch fish. Also important to the species survival problem is to have the game fish grow to full maturity so they can reproduce and grow their species. Nature and instinct tells the small fish that in order to survive they must escape the larger predator fish, which to them usually means hiding from the bigger fish who want to make them a fine meal. Fish do not know instinctively that we fishermen are a threat to their survival because fishermen are not a normal part of nature's survival cycle. This is probably the only advantage they we fishermen have over the fish. Think about the hiding process and think back to your childhood when you played hide and seek with your friends. Your life was not at stake but even so you didn't hide out in the open, you picked trees or houses or tall grass as your barrier to protect you. Fish do the same thing; they hide behind under water structure, trees, stumps, docks and brush piles. Fish will not hide near open flat bottom areas where there is no vegetation. You will occasionally find fish in the open flat areas but they are probably just passing through. What this sums up to it that we need to understand what is beneath the surface of the water, where the bottom is uneven and provide a hiding place, what the nature of the shoreline is, where the overhanging trees and bushed are, where there might be a sunken brush pile. All of these features represent areas where fish will consistently hide and therefore areas of good fishing.

One necessary tool for learning this basic information is a topographical map of the lake being fished. There are usually maps available that can be purchased at local fishing supply stores or at gas stations. Make sure the maps you choose have topographical lines on them or they are of little use to you for locating fish habitat. The "topo" lines will show you where the depth and bottom features change. A portion of a topographical map is shown below illustrating this.

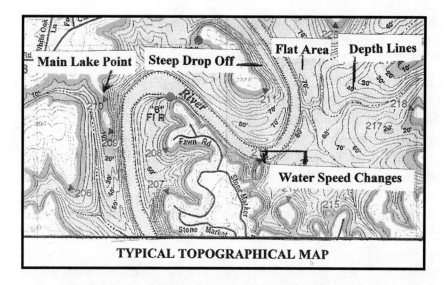

TYPICAL TOPOGRAPHICAL MAP

The numbers along side the lines tell you the depth of that line. Where the lines are close together, the depth changes rapidly Since Lake Norman which is shown here is a river lake and water flows in and out of the lake, the main channels have a mild current flow which is also affected by the contour of the lake bottom. Where the lines run close together, there is probably water flowing faster than in other areas along the main channel. Where the water flows fastest, it is most likely to wash the small bait fish up against the banks. You may have read or heard about small baitfish being washed up to the shallow banks of the shores, shoals and points. This is because the point or shoal is the area where the banks rise sharply and fall off sharply on the other side. Main points on a lake project out into the main water or water flow and are the most likely places to locate baitfish and therefore the best places to find the game fish feeding. As one person I recently heard describe this, "the main channels are like the super highways, when a sharp turn or bend occurs in the road, you slow down as a natural reaction". In a river lake, many of the larger fish swim the main channel and they will also slow down at the bends and they will work the shoals and points looking for food. This is why points and shoals are always good places to look for game fish. There are different kinds of points and they affect your fish finding capability differently. If for a moment we assume that the larger fish are using the main river channel as their regular route of travel and why not make this assumption, this is where the main current flow is located. Those points of land that protrude out into the main water of the lake are the primary points. These primary points are the areas where there is normally a fairly steep drop off on each side of the point. Since a land mass forms the point above the water, it is safe to assume that the bottom area under the water will continue this feature. As water flows down the main channels its speed changes at these underwater points and this causes a secondary current flow. Bait fish, not having the age and experience of the larger fish, think that having a protective wall at their backs makes them safe from the predator fish but indeed it has the opposite effect and causes a trap as the larger fish rush in to feed. The bait has nowhere to go. In many of the larger coves, channels or creeks, there are less dominant points of land that protrude out into the cove. These often also have sub surface drop offs that form shoals. These are considered secondary points. Although the river currents have no effect on these points, the drop off effect draws baitfish and therefore the predator fish so the secondary points are also good places to find fish. The map section below shows how primary and secondary points are depicted on a topographical map.

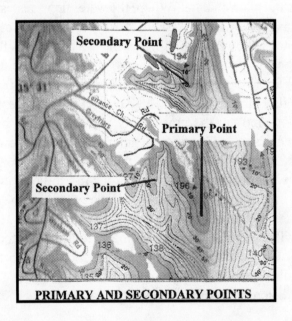

PRIMARY AND SECONDARY POINTS

Submerged islands and large bottom humps are also good places to find fish. Almost every lake has this type of underwater feature. A sunken island is simply a large mound or small hill that got completely covered when the lake was formed. These sunken islands are havens for baitfish because they normally have steep banks that fall off on more then one side. A map section showing a sunken island is shown below.

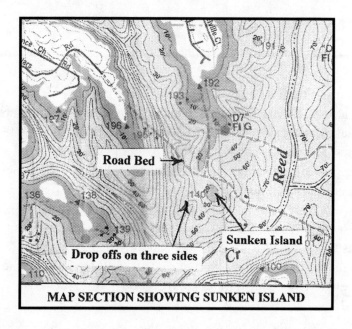

MAP SECTION SHOWING SUNKEN ISLAND

Old roadbeds are also great places to find fish. Most man made lakes will have underwater roadbeds that were actually roads before the lake was made. Roadbeds are normally marked on topographical maps by red or black dotted lines. The map section above illustrates old roadbeds.

Why are the old roadbeds good fishing areas? If you examine a good lake map closely you will notice that that the depth contour lines ripple slightly where the roadbed lines cross the contour line. This indicates that the road represents a flat area about twenty feet across with small gullies or ditches on either side. These uneven bottom areas are excellent areas for the small fish to hide. This is illustrated simply below.

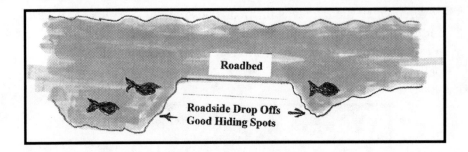

The main water flow on my home lake come from the Catawba River and it is very easy to follow the Main channel flow on any map. Like other lakes, there are also several other major creeks that also feed the lake but with much less water flow. Any and all of these secondary creeks provide good fishing at different times and the problem is that there is really no way to know which creek is best at a given time since there seems to be no repeated fish habit or pattern. As on many lakes there are fishing reports available to fishermen but these reports tell you where the fish were caught yesterday but that does not mean that the fish will be there today, we still have to use the basic knowledge that we have to locate the good spots.

As a general rule you can almost always look to the mouth of a major creek or the area where it meets the main channel as an area to start fishing. Why is that? We have already mentioned that the main channels and secondary creek channels are like the super highways for the bigger fish movements. The intersections of these highways therefore are often places where the fish change direction in their travels or slow down or stop to rest and feed. They will usually take the direction where they sense the bait fish are located. The points of land where major creeks meet are good starting points to look for other signs that I will soon discuss.

Within each major creek there are normally many coves and channels and some secondary creeks. These areas are also good fishing spots or at least areas to consider. The mouth of a cove or channel provides the same opportunity as the intersections discussed above.

Where you fish will also be influenced by the season of the year, which defines the water temperature. During the hot summer months the shallow coves and channels will not produce the bigger fish who are seeking the cooler spots. As we discuss the different species of fish later in this book we will further discuss which fish like which types of water and that will assist you in determining the best areas to search for the fish.

In simplest terms, the best way to determine your fishing strategy is to take the time to study the bottom features and depth conditions of the creeks and channels nearest your home of launching place. Look for uneven bottom structure, significant depth changes, point and shoal locations, rocks, sunken debris and water flow and wind conditions. Knowledge of these factors will increase your fishing success.

THE FLYING FISH FINDERS

Most fishermen never have the time to properly evaluate the waters that they are fishing. In most cases the opportunity to get a line in the water in a strange lake or pond is too inviting to permit a lengthy examination of the situation before the fishing starts. That's OK because there are many indicators that provide valuable information on fish locations that you can observe while you are fishing and you can adjust your fishing strategy as you go. One of the best indicators are the birds that are flying overhead, swimming on the surface, wading the shoreline or perched high above the water. These are nature's "fish finders" and you don't have to spend a penny to buy this source of information.

Depending on the area of the country that you are fishing, the specific breed of bird that you will see will vary and also will change with the season of the year. There are dozens if not hundreds of different birds that feed on fish. If the main food source for a bird is fish, then you can let those birds help point you to the best fish locations. Some of the more popular "fish finding" birds are the Loons, Gulls and Terns, Great Blue Herons, Egrets, Kingfishers, Ospreys and Eagles. Not only can these birds provide you with information about fish locations but on occasion they will provide you with a show of nature that will leave you in awe of their capability. Ospreys and Eagles as an example will catch their own fish by skimming low over the water and grasping the fish near the surface with their powerful talons. These two birds also pride themselves with their ability to steal fish from other birds that have made a successful catch. Watching this natural hunt is a fascinating display of predator fighting predator.

Gulls and Terns are perhaps the most popular flying fish finders and in my opinion they are the most reliable. Gulls seem to have a natural system for hunting and catching fish. In the southern regions where fishing is often best in the fall and winter months, the gulls migrate to the southern lakes from the frozen northern regions and they populate the southern lakes by the thousands. Their hunting process seems always to be the same. Soon after the run rises in the morning, small groups of "scouts" leave the nesting area and fly out to cover several areas of the lake. They fly near the shore lines and scout the points and shoals in the hunt for signs of food. These birds have some innate ability to see down into the water and spot both game fish and the small baitfish. When the scout finds a sign of food, normally a school of baitfish, there is some kind of signal that is sent out to the larger flock that brings a large group of the birds to this location. The group will often land on a nearby shoal, beach or rock pile and wait for another signal from the scouts. The scouts will continue to scan the waters for food. This food can be in the form of individual fish near the surface, wounded or dead fish floating on the surface or where there may be Stripers or other predator fish feeding off of a school of shad or herring, the birds will look for remains from this feeding frenzy that float to the surface. When this happens, the larger groups of gills and terns will begin diving to the water to grab the remains. For Striper fishermen, this is a wonderful sign since it is fool proof evidence that stripers are feeding in the waters below the diving birds. Circling these areas with bait or jigs will normally product a nice catch of Stripers.

Loons are another fish indicator. These birds spend most of their waking hours on the water looking for food. Their food is also small fish and they nearly always have their head down looking for signs of schools of small fish. When they spot these fish beneath the surface, they dive quickly to catch them. Loons normally do not work in groups but hunt alone or with a partner. If you see a Loon diving repeatedly, it is a good indicator that small baitfish are in the area and if the bait is there the game fish cannot be far behind. Sometimes however the Loons can be somewhat deceiving. They can dive deep and often come up at great distances from where they went down. You have to watch the pattern of the Loons hunt to determine the bait school locations.

I indicated above that there is sometimes fierce competition between different types of birds for food. I have also seen situations where there is cooperation between species to achieve a bigger catch. On several occasions I have watched Loons and Gulls and Terns seemingly working together in some kind of planned search. The Gulls would stand off 40 or 50 yards from the Loons in a group of maybe 10 birds, sitting on the water surface waiting. If the Loons remain on the surface the Gulls will remain stationary. Once the Loons dive for food, the Gulls fly over the area circling to spot fish. I have not verified scientifically that this teamwork is well known to aquatic biologists but I have witnessed it enough that I believe that it is a natural hunting maneuver for these birds.

Herons and Egrets are also popular fish eaters but these birds are shore hunters and slowly and persistently hunt the shallow waters for fish or other live food. I have found that where these birds hunt is normally an area where small baitfish have been washed to the shallow shore line. The presence of a Heron or Egret is not fool proof evidence that fish are in the area but remember they are not going to waste their time hunting in areas where they have not found food before.

The Kingfisher is the aquatic relative of the Woodpecker. The kingfisher will fly over water looking for food much like the Gulls. When they spot fish they will hover and dive to grab the fish in their bill.

My favorite show to watch is the Osprey. This large bird can often be seen perched on a pole, tree or other structure that sticks high above the water. The Osprey has often been called the "fish hawk" because it will watch for surface movement from its perch. When a surface indication is seen, the Osprey will fly high over the area and swoop down to grasp the surface fish with its talons. The final catch movement is slow and deliberate and yet swift, that if put to music would sound like a finely tuned concert. I have seen Ospreys grab fish that appeared to be bigger and heavier than the bird itself and find the power in their huge wings to fly away with their meal safely in their grasp.

I believe that the aquatic birds are the most reliable indicators that fish are in the area. I have had days when the fishing was slow and nothing seemed to be in the area to catch. I would catch a glimpse of a Gull circling high over a particular spot in the water, flying away and quickly returning to circle again and again without diving to snag its food. When I went to the area where the Gull was circling, I would nearly always get fish. This indicates tome that the Gulls can spot game fish from a long distance above the water even if those fish are deep in the water column but the Gull will not flutter and dive unless there is action close to the surface. These sightings provide no success for the bird getting food but they do provide success for the fisherman who is observant of the Gulls actions.

Gulls come in many varieties and often get their food from easier sources on land. The Gull is however a very reliable fish finder especially for spotting bait schools. Gulls and Terns are most often the fisherman's friend when other sources of finding fish are not available.

Loons are also a reliable indicator of the location of baitfish schools beneath the water surface. The howl of the Loon also provides an enchanting tune for an evening on the lake.

Herons and Egrets constantly search the shore line for small fish. If fish are not available as their food of choice both these birds will eat mice, crawfish and even other small birds and mammals.

The Osprey and the Bald Eagle are the kings of the aquatic birds. Their search for food is a sight to behold and their smooth but swift flight is a symphony of motion. The Eagle will perch high above a lake in constant search fro food in the water and on the ground. Both of these birds will not hesitate to take a fine catch away from another bird either during the capture or in flight. Nature being what it is, if there are no fish in a particular water, there will be no Osprey or Eagles.

The Kingfisher family of aquatic birds is not normally thought of as a fisherman's friend although it is widely populated in many areas of the country. It is considered part of the Woodpecker family but is the aquatic version. This bird feeds exclusively on aquatic life, mostly fish. Kingfisher's perch or hover high above the water and when they spot a fish they dive steeply and swiftly for the catch, securing the fish in their bill. This method of catching their food limits their prey to the smaller fish and the small baitfish and plankton that swim near the surface.

OTHER INDICATORS

One of the most obvious indicators of fish activity that is often neglected as an assist for finding fish is the water surface itself. I do not consider a smooth lake surface with a quiet wind to be a good condition for fishing. I would rather have a slight breeze which puts a constant ripple on the water surface. But there are days when the water surface is calm and the wind is down and at those times the lake is like a mirror or maybe more appropriately a picture that stretched for miles in every direction. Just think how far you can see in this condition and how much information is in that picture. You can probably see good detail for at least 100 yards in all directions, what a fine source of information as to what is going on beneath the surface.

Fish activity at the surface is a good indicator of fish activity beneath the surface. A calm surface permits you to see schools of small plankton that are not visible when the surface is rippled. A calm surface lets you see fish rolling or feeding near the surface that are not visible on windy days. I once thought that fish jumping meant that the fish were jumping out of the water to catch flies or other bugs that were floating on the surface. Although that is indeed sometimes the case, more often a jumping fish represents a nice game fish that came up to capture a smaller fish near the surface and it couldn't stop at the surface and appeared to jump out of the water. Jumping fish indicated fish presence.

During the spring spawn; Carp as an example will roll on the surface during the spawn. You can often observe these monster fish swimming along side your boat in the early morning. Don't plan on catching one at this time because they are very hard to catch under this condition but their habits sure let you know that they are there.

Gar are also a surface fish. During calm water days I have actually seen the dorsal fin of a Gar sticking up through the surface like a small Shark. Gar patrol the surface for food and if you put bait in front of them in this situation they will usually hit it with a fierce action. I have seen Gar hit a bobber at the surface and not let it go until they were in the boat. Gar are a wonderful fighting fish and will hit anything when they are feeding. They will give you a fierce fight but they are very hard to get into the boat. Gar are not often hooked because of their very bony head and mouth structure. They clamp down on the line or lure or bait without being hooked and they will not open their mouth until they see the boat and then they will let go. I estimate that the Gar catch rate is less than 50% for this reason. Gar sighting at the surface on a calm day is common in the hot summer months when the water is very warm.

Sun and shade are also good visual indicators of fish locations. In the early morning and in the late afternoon when the sun is rising or falling I find that the line between the sun and the shade is a good place to fish. In general under this condition the fish will be in the shady area. Fish will normally come closer to shore at night to feed.

When the sun begins to rise the fish will try to remain in the shady area as long as possible and when they can no longer see shade they will often head for the docks or other shady cover. In the late afternoon as the sun sets, the fish will start the movement toward the shore for the evening feeding. The shady side of a shade-sun line will often find fish.

As a pilot I was taught very early in my instruction that my eyes and my ears were two very important additional instruments that I would often depend on when everything else failed. I have had a few situations where that has proven very true in my aviation experiences and it is also true with fishing. During the peak Striper months of September through May, there are often situations where the lake is quiet and suddenly there is a rush of noise and as you look in the direction of the noise you see hundreds of fish boiling on the surface. This is the wonderful sight of a school of Stripers that have driven a school of baitfish to the surface and the birds have not yet spotted it. The noise is the baitfish being driven above the surface and the stripers also making their frenzied trip to the surface to secure the meal. This noise will not last for long; perhaps a minute or two and then it will be over. Hopefully during this few minutes you have managed to get a few Stripers in the boat. Shortly after you detect the activity the birds will likely arrive for their cleanup.

FISHING AND THE WEATHER

By this point in this book you are probably already getting the hint that there are many factors that play a role in determining your fishing strategy on a given day. If you had the opportunity to sit around a group of experienced fishermen who are telling their fishing tales you would certainly hear weather mentioned often as a major factor governing the success or failure of a fishing experience. Weather effects can be divided into two major categories; its effect on the fish and its effect on the fisherman. More often than not, the later of these two is the real issue because it will often be the determinant as to the length and quality of a fishing day, but every fisherman is different and responds differently to weather conditions especially if the weather is bad. Because of this it is impossible to make any conclusive judgment as to the effect of weather on the fisherman. The effect of weather on the fish however is another story and there are hundreds of expert opinions on how weather affects the fish and quite frankly I am not sure if there is any one of those opinions that should be considered the bible on the subject.

We have all heard the stories of how some cattle show strange behavior just before major weather events like hurricanes and earthquakes. I believe that is true but is apparently not convincing enough to have convinced the experts to determine exactly how this happens. Nature is a wonderful manager. Nature seems to have a way to keep things under its control. I'm sure that one of Natures control mechanisms is a special instinct that has been given to some animals to help achieve the required balance of the elements of Nature. Fish would certainly be included in this category.

Rather than making a broad statement about the effects of weather on fish behavior, I am going to dissect the various weather elements like wind, rain, pressure and temperature and examine each of these in summary form so that each reader can come to his or her own conclusion on the overall weather effect. Some factors are universally accepted such as the fact that rain brings oxygen to the water and fish like well oxygenated water. Does that however mean that fish will come to the surface when it is raining? No it does not.

I will also discuss in some detail the issue of barometric pressure because it is widely accepted by most fishermen except myself that changes in barometric pressure effects the behavior of fish. I will disprove this theory.

Included as part of any weather discussion has to be the subject of temperature. I have covered that subject earlier but I will address it again here as it relates to the seasonal effect on the fish.

One element that doesn't find its way into any category is the time of day. I find this subject quite interesting because again I seem to find myself in disagreement with the majority of experienced fishermen on this subject. Let's discuss that a little here.

Since my first fishing experiences as a six-year old, I was taught that to be a good fisherman I had to rise and shine very early in the morning, to get the bait in the water before sunrise. For years I held to that practice whenever possible but as I look back on that I realize that all it got me was more tired earlier in the evening and did not necessarily get me more or bigger fish. In recent years as I fished more, I sometimes still get out before sunrise but I have concluded that most of the good fishing that I have had and most of the big fish have been caught happened after 2pm in the afternoon and before 7pm in the evening. As you proceed in this book and learn about the habits of the different fish, I have to admit that certain fish behave differently at different times of the day but that does not mean that they are only caught during those times. Bass for example are known to be more aggressive in the early morning and early evening hours. Does that mean that they are not caught in the middle of the day? No it does not; it just means that the chances of finding a hungry bass is better during those hours. Catfish are known to also feed in the early morning and at night. Does that mean that they can't be caught at mid day? No it does not. Stripers feed all day whenever the opportunity presents itself and they are known to like to feed more aggressively at first sunlight. Most of the hundreds of Stripers that I have caught have been in the afternoon hours. Ironically I have caught many trophy fish that hang on my wall and not one of them was caught before 2pm. So what's the real story on the right time of the day, let's take a quick look at that.

I believe that one of the very important factors that finds its way into nearly every argument about weather is the effect of the sunlight. I discuss in other areas about the eyes of most fish that are located on the upper portion of the head and normally look up better than they do looking down. Many fish cannot look down. From this fact I conclude that the sunlight is what changes the behavior of fish more than other considerations. The reflectivity of the sunlight down through the water affects the comfort of the fish's eyesight; it affects their field of view and their ability to effectively find food. As a result the strike distance for seeing and catching food is greatly reduced when the sun is not deflected by either a rough water surface or shade from clouds of the angle of the sun. The angle of course is determined by the time of day. So! A cloudless day at noon with a calm water surface would not be the time to expect to catch fish near the surface. Does this mean that you should go in and take a nap at mid day? No it does not, it just means that you should expect to fish deeper at that time or fish in areas that provide shade where the fish will be hiding. This is why morning fishing appears to be the best time to fish since the angle of the sun is such that it creates no annoyance to the eyes of the fish. Similarly in late afternoon the same angle exist in the opposite direction and the annoyance again is reduced.

What all of this means is that you can fish all day and expect good results if you change your fishing technique as the sun angle and brightness changes. We have learned from our earliest school days learning about the suns power that we cannot live without the sun. It is responsible for sustaining all life, as we know it today. Well the same goes for fishing; the sun controls the fishing experience not only by its effect on the energy provided to plant life but also on the behavior of fish. This subject will be touched upon later.

THE EFFECT OF BAROMETRIC PRESSURE ON FISH BEHAVIOR

I may be a little early in this book to get into the somewhat complicated subject of the Barometric Pressure and the effect that it has on the behavior of fish. This is one of the subjects where I find it necessary to perhaps challenge the science in favor of common logic and we will look at examples of that later. Almost every serious fisherman will tell you that the barometric pressure effects the quality of the fishing on any particular day but if you ask them a serious question as to why that is true, you will either get no answer or you will get a variety of comical answers. The truth is that we really don't know why and most fishermen don't have the time or experience to find out and most scientists don't really care. I think the answer is rather simple but before I let you in on the secret I am bound by my honor to present the whole story and some of the many versions of it. You might want to draw your own conclusions on this subject but before you do you should hear the alternatives.

We have all heard of some of the weather related folklore that often guides our daily lives. There are a never-ending series of folklore facts about the weather and ho we are able to read the tealeaves based on the weather and how it effects our natural environment. Some of this folklore may seem questionable but usually there is some grain of truth in every story. As an example, some farmers believe that they should watch their sheep because "if the sheep huddle there will be a puddle". Some people believe that if cows lie down, rain is coming. And how about those who believe that if the humidity goes down, your cat will incessantly lick it skin? There are times when each and all of these are true but I for one would not bet money on any one, at any time.

We do know from experience that weather conditions overall do indeed effect the fishing but the level of the barometer is only one factor of the weather and it isn't always obvious whether it is a cause or an effect. It is controversial enough that it warrants some space in this book.

Nearly everything that happens in our environment in both the air and in the water has an effect on most freshwater game fish. Some species are affected more than others. Normally however when there is a fluctuation in an environmental effect there are several fluctuating conditions that are also in effect at that time. It does seem that everything that happened in the atmosphere eventually affects the watery world of fish. But is it really the barometric pressure that is the cause or is it one of the many other factors occurring at the same time.

To better understand barometric pressure we do have to understand at least the basic science of it but let's keep it simple. Barometric pressure is the measure of the weight of the atmosphere above the earth. This pressure is exerted on everything above the surface of the earth. The term comes from the instrument that is used to measure this pressure called a barometer. Without going into details, the earliest barometers measured the pressure by putting mercury into a glass tube holding a vacuum. As the pressure increased the mercury rose, as the pressure fell the mercury fell. The result was that the pressure was measured in terms of the inches of mercury that rose or fell above the surface of the earth, hence the term, inches of mercury. This is also often expressed in millibars where one inch of mercury equates to 33.864 millibars. When you listen for your local weatherman give you the barometric pressure he will normally give you the inches of mercury. There is really no normal here but we have become accustomed to allowing 30 inches of mercury to become the normal. The reason for the lack of a normal is that barometric pressure is itself affected by several factors. One factor is the altitude. The higher points have less atmosphere above them which exerts less pressure. It is also affected by air temperature because colder air weighs more than warm air. Also the "standard" is based on sea level measurements. This is why your weatherman normally further reduces the complexity by indicating that there are HIGH's and LOW's. All you really have to know is that high pressure normally means good weather and low pressure normally means bad weather.

The question that I like to pose to those who care is, "is it the Barometric pressure that causes different behavior in fish or is it the weather that is associated with these pressure differences.

Many fishermen and at least one study that I have read feel that there are common behavioral patterns associated with pressure changes. Of course based on these behavioral patterns there are suggested fishing tactics that result. My fishing experience has verified this information so I have summarized below.

Pressure Trend	Typical Weather	Fishing Trend	Suggested Tactics
High	Clear Skies	Fish slow down, find cover or go to deeper waters.	Slow down lures and use baits more attractive to fish. Fish in cover and in deeper waters.

Rising	Clearing or improving	Fish tend to become slightly more active	Fish with brither lures and near cover. Also fish at intermediate and deeper depths.
Normal and stable	Fair	Normal fishing	Experiment with your favorite baits and lures.
Falling	Degrading	Most active fishing	Speed up lures. Surface and shallow running lures may work well.
Slightly lower	Usually cloudy	Many fish will head away from cover and seek shallower waters. Some fish will become more aggressive.	Use shallow running lures at a moderate speed.
Low	Rainy and stormy	Fish will tend to become less active the longer this period remains.	As the action subsides, try fishing at deeper depths.

There are also some non-scientific studies that have concluded that the effect of barometric pressure is greater in shallow water than it is in deeper water. I love this study conclusion because it supports my theory that barometric pressure has no effect at all on fish behavior. This theory will shock most experienced fishermen because it goes contrary to what they have used as a guideline for years. If barometric pressure does not cause behavioral changes in fish then what does it do? My answer, when it comes to fish behavior, Nothing.

We do know from experience that there are many factors that do indeed affect the behavior of fish. Factors such as water temperature, depth, light, water clarity, wind surface disturbances, boat traffic, fishing pressure, etc. But, in my opinion, not barometric pressure. Why Not?

Barometric pressure is the weight on everything on the surface of the earth. The standard is at sea level and that is where that kind of pressure stops. The surface of the water, except in very shallow water, is the place where barometric pressure stops having an effect. Below the surface it is the water pressure that takes over and barometric pressure has a negligible effect. If barometric pressure has no effect below the water surface, it can have no effect on fish behavior.

The previous chart however shows that there is an effect so what is the right answer? What is causing these behavioral changes? Simple, it's the weather that is the cause; the pressure is an effect not a cause. Good weather brings out the sun and the bad weather hides the sun. During high-pressure days the sun is shining on the water and during low-pressure days it is not and I believe that the sunlight and its varied effects that really effects fish behavior. That's why there is less effect in the deeper water than in shallow water; the sun simply does not penetrate the deeper areas.

Did you ever take a good look at the eyes of a fish? What have you noticed? First a fish's eyes seem large in proportion to the size of their body. Some small fish have eyes bigger than our human eyes.

The eyes of a fish are well developed and very similar to humans. Fish eyes are proportionally large, in order to see better in the darkness of the depths. If we humans try to see under the water, things look blurred. This is because our lens is a water lens and works because there is air flowing over the outside of our eye. Fish are different; they have a different substance in their lens which is highly curved. Because the outside of our eyes needs to be moistened, we have eyelids which perform that function and also allow us to close our eyes. Fish lack that mechanism but surprisingly they manage to keep debris away from their eye.

One major difference between our eyes and fish eyes is that the lenses in fish eyes are perfectly spherical, which enables them to see underwater since the lens has a greater refractive index to help them focus. Fish focus by moving the lenses in and out instead of stretching them as humans do. The deeper the species of fish lives, the larger their eyes are. Because of the shape of the fish's eyes and the location on the body, their vision is very keen. They can see in almost any direction, which is a characteristic that us humans do not have. We believe however that looking upward and forward is the resting position of a fishes eyes.

Considering all of this, have you ever had the experience of attending a movie matinee and at the end of the movie you rapidly transition from the dark theater to the bright mid day sunlight. The transition is so traumatic that you squint, close your eyes and probably put your sunglasses on or cover your eyes with your hands. Well fish do not have sunglasses, they cannot close their eyes and their fins are rarely long enough to cover their eyes so what does a fish do when the sun is shinning brightly on the water? Despite the refractive characteristic of water, the fish heads for the bottom or hides behind a bush or under a dock where it is shady, in other words the behavior of the fish changes when the sun shines. This change is caused by the weather or the sun and not the barometric pressure.

Now having put that argument to bed we can get back to the issue of finding the fish when the weather conditions change. One thing that fishermen have found, as least those who fish regularly, whatever condition of weather exists, cold, hot, sun or shad, if the condition exist long enough, the fish will again become active or revert to their normal behavior. Why is that? Well it's really quite simple; they get hungry and as we have pointed out several times, fish must eat to survive. Even in sunny weather, fish will do what they have to do to get the food that they need.

Almost every experience fisherman will tell you that there is never a day that is a bad fishing day. Some are better than others but never bad. The challenge is to understand how the elements affect the fish and what you have to do to compensate for the fish's behavior on any day whatever the weather. I have fished and caught fish on hot sunny days where the surface temperature was 100 degrees and I have caught fish when there was ice hanging all over my boat. The difference was in how I fished and where I fished.

All of this dialog about water and air temperature, depth relationships, pressure etc. serve to demonstrate that finding the fish in a given season or on a given day or at a particular time of day can be made difficult by the numerous factors that play on a fish's behavior. Although any one of these subjects may seem very complicated, it is only necessary to understand the basic concepts that we have discussed and to keep them in mind when seeking out the days perfect fishing spot.

Contrary to a popular theory, low and high pressure by themselves have nothing to do with the way fish feel and therefore with their eating habits. What does effect the fish is the cloudy and overcast skies that accompany the pressure changes. This picture illustrates a good fishing condition because the sun is not creating glare off of the water, the water surface is slightly broken and there is plenty of shade. With no glare, fish are more likely to come closer to the surface and to the shoreline to feed without annoyance from the suns rays. This is a low pressure day.

HOW WIND EFFECTS THE FISH
AND THE FISHING

Earlier in my life, before I had the time to think about what I was doing, I would plan a day of fishing and normally because I was excited and didn't get the fishing opportunity every day I would awake long before the alarm went off with little real sleep. I would listen for what was going on outside particularly listening for the rain and the wind. There were days when I would here the wind howling or perhaps blowing in gusts and I remember thinking that I should cancel the fishing that day because the wind was going to spoil the event. Sometimes I cancelled the trip, other times the circumstances didn't permit canceling and I fished as scheduled. What I recall about those times is that it wasn't the effect of the wind on the fish that I was concerned about but more the effect of the wind on me and my comfort and my safety. Even today when I know more about fishing than I did back then, I realize that the real negative factors associated with a windy day relate to my comfort and safety and the effect of the wind on the control of the boat. But today I know that from the point of view of the fish habits or actual fishing conditions, wind can be a positive effect because I understand how wind affects the waters and how the resulting underwater changes affect the behavior of the fish. If I can put the personal discomfort aside and find ways to overcome the boat control factors, I know now that some of the best fishing days are the windy days. I also know that if the wind has been blowing consistently in one direction for several days, I can have a great day of fishing but I may have to work a little harder.

A steady wind will concentrate minute organisms near the shore or along timber or brush lines. Baitfish will therefore feed on these collected organisms attracting the larger fish to feed. There are also seasonal effects. In the spring, warm winds blowing from the same direction for several days can pile up warm water on the down wind shoreline. The warmer water will hold more fish in the spring than the colder water elsewhere in the lake.

Wind causes waves that wash on to the shore. These waves loosen the soil and debris along this shore creating a band of cloudy or muddy water. Fish often hang out along this mud line avoiding the bright sunlight and hiding in wait for passing baitfish in the clearer water. The muddy water gives them the security of hiding and they can dart out into the clear water to snatch a meal. If the wind becomes too strong or a strong wind blows for a long period of time, it can hurt the fishing success in the shallower water. Turbulence that may be caused by continuing winds and heavy waves can spook the fish into the deeper water where they are harder to find. But, if we know these factors, we can adjust our fishing habits accordingly. Heavy boating and surface craft activity on weekends can often create the same conditions and we have to adjust our fishing habits on Mondays to compensate for the conditions.

There is another often overlooked factor associated with the lack of wind. Calm water and calm surface conditions sometimes enable the fish to see objects above the surface of the water. Fishermen and boater can spook the fish as a result of this condition in the shallower waters where the surface is calm. Wave action caused by the wind bends or refracts light rays making it harder for the fish to see movement on or above the surface.

Continuing wind will create a current moving toward windward shoreline. It also causes a secondary effect that the water hits the bank it sinks and comes back on itself causing a small flow in the opposite direction. This is illustrated below.

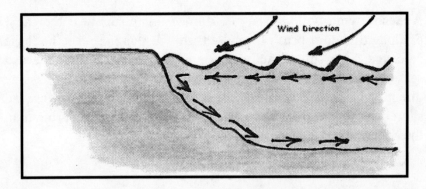

Knowing these current flow conditions will permit us to change our fishing habits. There is an often heard folklore that wind from the east causes fishing the least and wind from the west makes fishing the best. There is some truth to that superstition but it isn't the result of the wind itself. Winds out of the east normally mean a changing weather system is approaching and we have already learned that changing weather conditions cause fish to behave differently. The only time that an east wind would always be bad is if we had a lake that only had a west facing shoreline and that of course is not possible.

This however brings up another flaw in many fishermen's fishing habits. Because of the adverse effect that wind has on boat control and even fishing comfort particularly in the colder months, some fishermen fish the leeward side of islands or shorelines when the wind is blowing. This is the absolutely wrong thing to do unless your intent is to stay warm, ease the boat control problem or take pressure off of your trolling motor battery. There is little or no underwater effect from the wind on the leeward shoreline because as we have demonstrated the real changes are on the windward side. This does not mean that there are no fish on the leeward side and it is possible to catch fish there but the real action is where you have to work harder out in the wind.

On a non river lake, it is important to understand the effect of the wind on water currents. Even on Lake Norman, which is a river lake, wind created currents are important in areas distant from the main water flow such as in channels, creeks and large coves. In general we know that fish when at rest will face in the direction of the upstream water flow. The dynamics of the fish's body, tail and fins along with the floatation devices built into a fish's anatomy make it less stressful for a fish to rest facing upstream. This fact is important not only to understand fish behavior under windy conditions but when we deal with bait presentation we will learn that a fish likes to attack its prey when it is approaching it from the front and dislikes motion approaching from the rear. Like us humans we like to see what is coming at us and we suspect things behind us that we cannot see.

Fish can see to their rear but their resting sight direction is to the front. So if there is a current caused either by normal water flow or wind, we should understand that current flow to help with both fish location and bait presentation.

Wind generated currents are complex and I will not attempt here to provide a course in meteorology or geology but some small amount of knowledge is always useful. Winds generally only create very weak current near the surface that move in the direction of the wind until approaching the shoreline. A strong prevailing wind blowing in the same direction for several days may create a deeper flow. In very large lakes there is an effect on currents caused by the rotation of the earth but we will not even attempt to understand that because most lakes are not that huge to be affected by the phenomenon.

Speed of the currents generated by the winds is about two percent of the speed of the forming wind if the wind speed is substantial say greater than 35 miles per hour. At slowed wind speeds the resulting current is about 1.3 percent of the wind speed. At 10mph wind would therefore create a nearly negligible current but a strong wind of 35 mph would create a current that starts to get meaningful in terms of water flow since it would be nearly 1 mph which I consider an optimum trolling speed. A 35 mph wind speed, depending on its direction, can however create a lake condition that many consider unsafe especially for the inexperienced boater or fisherman using very small boats. Catching fish is never that important to us that we are willing to put safety aside in the interest of fishing. As experienced a fisherman and boater that I am, I have indeed had days when I put myself into situations on windy days that bordered on being unsafe. That is not wise under any circumstances.

There is another seldom seen condition that is caused by continued winds that is nice to know about and that is the "windrows" that are sometimes created. These are long lines of foam that run parallel to the wind direction. Winds stir up the water in a circular motion and windrows sometimes form where there is a down-welling of water created when two adjacent blocks of water are rolling side by side in opposite directions creating a downward current where they meet. Algae and plankton collect along these lines attracting the baitfish and their predators.

Shorelines deflect currents as we pointed out earlier. Underwater humps and narrow passes can accelerate the currents. Wind currents can gain speeds in areas where wind driven water is forced into small gaps or channels. Wind created flow that runs directly into a straight shoreline may be broken up and become multidirectional and therefore causes very unstable swimming conditions for the smaller fish making them vulnerable to their predators. These areas therefore will attract the bigger game fish and can produce good fishing when the winds are relatively constant. But we must keep in mind that even the large fish will stay away from very large wave action.

After the winds calm down, there is still a wind created current that continues due to its momentum for a period of time. Time and consistency are more important to current direction than wind speed. A constant wind blowing in the same direction for several days has the time t create a constant current that is predictable. Therefore a knowledgeable fisherman can use a constant wind to his advantage. But variable winds in speed and direction can confuse even the most experienced fisherman.

I have gone into a little more detail than you may have wished for in this section on the wind. If you are going to put together a successful fishing plan however, you need to know the elements that will alter your success. You know as an example that bait coming down current will be more effective than bait approaching the fish from the rear. But since the movement of subsurface water is not always the same as the surface water, you may have to adjust your fishing technique in the deeper water to compensate for these changes in current. Deep fish facing into the current may be facing a different direction than those at or near the surface or those in the turbulence near the shoreline. As a general rule however we can have success under constant wind conditions if we run down wind and fish the downwind shoreline. Also remember that the mud line can be productive if you move your bait just outside this line or move it in a manner that it goes in and out of the line.

Summary of Facts about the Wind

- The clearer the water is the more important the wind effect. Wind breaks up the surface, diffracting the light and making the fish more aggressive.

- If the wind is not a factor you can fish the deep points, when the wind comes up move to the windy banks with surface baits and lures.

- When you see a wind caused dirty area you can throw a spinner bait into that area and have success. Spinner bait on a windy bank is a good consistent way to catch fish.

- A breeze strong enough to ripple the water will stop the light penetration and bring the fish to the surface. Gentle breeze not disturbing the surface will cause light to enter the water and drive the fish deeper. (Fish deeper on calm days.)

- Waves caused by winds churn the water and loosen minute fodder from the bottom as they break toward the shore. The waves also oxygenate the water, which is very important in the hot summer months.

- The fish make adjustments when the wind starts to blow and you have to make changes if you want to catch them. You can use wind to your advantage just like the fish do. Remember, we may never get smarter than the fish but the closer we get to them with our intelligence, the better chance we have of a good catch.

- The most stable weather patterns generally occur when the wind is blowing from the south, west and southwest. Stable weather encourages predictable fish behavior and a better catch. Winds out of the north, east and northeast normally signify changes in the weather pattern and cause the fish to be neutral or negative in their feeding patterns.

- On windy days keep your pole tip close to the water to reduce the wind effect on the line cast and retrieval.

- Wind can increase or decrease the water temperature quite rapidly. In the spring a southern wind can warm the water by a few degrees which is often enough to significantly change the fish behavior.

- Experience has shown that after a major change in weather and water condition, the bigger older fish are the first ones to go out and explore, therefore you will catch the bigger ones after the change has occurred.

- Wind changes the water flow and when this happens the fish are repositioning themselves into the slack water and near the current breaks. Fish want to reserve as much energy as possible so they will hide behind rocks, stumps, humps and the back side of bridge pilings and from those vantage points they will wait for a meal to swim by.

- Sunlight is less of a factor on windy days since the waves caused by the wind deflects the light and makes the fish feel more secure.

- All of the rules of fishing in the wind are reversed in the winter when the fish are looking for the warmer water. In winter months fishing the leeward shore is more productive and sunny waters may produce more fish in the winter when the fish are looking for the warmer water.

THE EFFECT OF THE SEASONS

I have noted several times in this book that my approach to understanding the best fishing strategy is to simplify every situation as much as possible and put the fishing jargon into language that everyone understands. I have often compared fish behavior to human behavior and I will do that again as we discuss the effects of seasonal changes on your fishing strategies.

Think of your own behavior. In the hot summer months you slow down, become a little lazy, put off some of the heavy projects, go on vacation, etc. As the weather begins to cool in the Fall, you seem to get more energy, everything is crisp and dry, the leaves are changing color, and you go from tee shirts to sweatshirts and your overall activity level increases. After a couple of months of this the jackets come out as the winter approaches, you drain your outside water lines, rake the leaves, start scheduling your inside activities and as the cold weather starts you begin again to get inside more with more time spent in front of the TV. Three months of this is enough and you begin to get cabin fever, you can't wait to get outside again and the first day that the sun heats things up to where you can take the jacket off it seems that all of your pent up energy suddenly explodes again. We can all relate to this and of course it all involves the temperature of our surroundings.

Fish behavior is exactly the same, the only difference being that their surrounding is the water and their moods and behavior are totally controlled by the temperature of the water. As we have already pointed out, there is one difference between us humans and the fish in that our bodies do not adjust to the temperature changes since we are warm blooded and the fish do adjust. But fish behavior is almost totally dictated by the water temperature and it is that water temperature change that we have to understand in order to develop our seasonal fishing strategies.

The illustration below is of the water temperature variations in Lake Norman over a twelve-month period. This data is typical of a southern lake. Consider these numbers as averages and of course they will vary from year to year. I believe we all understand how variable the weather is but in a general sense every lake will have similar temperature variations throughout the year. Also remember that these are surface temperatures and we have discussed elsewhere the temperature depth relationships. Looking at the temperature variations, no matter how accurate they are, will help us understand the seasonal effect. This illustration also includes the idea desired temperature ranges of the various fish that reside in this lake. In general we can see that water temperatures between 50 and 75 degrees are the ideal conditions for the fish and therefore the best temperatures for fishing. It is also clear that the months of the year where those water temperatures exist are the spring months of March, April and May and the fall months of September and October. Hence we see that the best fishing months on the average are in the Spring and in the Fall of the year. Does this mean that you should hang up your rod and reel during the winter and summer? Absolutely not but you will have to adjust your fishing strategy during those months and by examining fish behavior as it relates to temperature and season we hope to make it easier for you to make that adjustment.

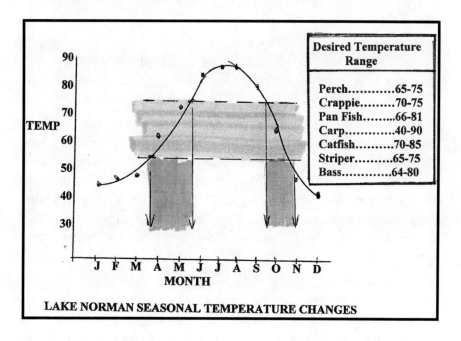

LAKE NORMAN SEASONAL TEMPERATURE CHANGES

Your fishing enjoyment will be influenced most by your understanding of the seasonal effects. How you adjust your fishing habits will of course depend on what type of fish you desire to catch. For purposes of this discussion I will base my conclusions on the behavior of the two game fish that are most sought after in the Lank Norman, the Bass and the Stripers. I think you will find however that the conditions and behaviors of these two species will closely apply to all of the other species in the lake. Where there are differences, these differences will be discussed else ware in the book when we get into the details of the various fish types.

THE SPRING SPAWN

In the early spring we see that everything around us beginning to come to life. The trees are budding, flowers start to pop up and this above water is echoed by what is taking place beneath the surface of the lake. The fish have been in a state of hibernation all winter, they have been in the deeper oxygen rich water and they are smart enough no to have been exerting any more energy than their winter food source has replaced.

As the water warms, the metabolism of the fish starts to increase and they come up from deeper water in search of food, following their normal search routes. The spring "pre spawn" has begun.

Underwater plant growth begins to spring to life providing a new fresh food source and other underwater life becomes active adding to the new food source. This is an exciting time for the fish and the fisherman. Bass are starting to group together in staging areas. Theses staging areas are picked out because they provide the fish access to the best food sources before they head for their shallow spawning beds.

There is no exact time or date when this pre spawn starts. It seems that nature protects the fish by having different fish types start their spawn at different times, different temperatures and different water clarity levels. Generally speaking however, water temperatures of 55 and 65 degrees will create the pre spawn characteristics for Lake Norman fish.

Animals like humans change their habits drastically during the periods when their sexual urges take control of their bodies. They tend to abandon their normal instincts in pursuit of satisfaction of those urges. Fish similarly throw caution to the wind during the pre spawn in pursuit of food, a partner and a spawning site. They are also protective of the site once it has been picked. One professional fisherman has written, "this creates what every angler dreams of, a hungry, horny aggressive fish which reminded him of his college years."

During the pre spawn, bass are normally moving back and forth from shallow to deeper water several times each day. They seek out the energy rich food like crawfish and baitfish that will provide the protein needed for egg production. Your knowledge of the lake bottom conditions during the pre spawn will point you to the areas where 40 ft deep water is adjacent to 10 ft depths. You should also look for sunken trees, pilings, stumps, rock piles and other debris running into the shallow water. Roadbeds make great pre spawn routes for the fish.

During the pre spawn it is advisable that you be aware of the coloring of the natural bait that is available and try to match it as close as possible. Remember however that during the pre spawn, the water is still relatively cold so that the bait should be moved slowly. Fish will hit as a reaction during this period and slow moving worms near the bottom often work well for bass.

Bass will normally start spawning when the water temperature hits 60 degrees and they will look for some kind of cover where they can lay their eggs. Since the eggs are normally laid in the shallow water near cover, polarized sunglasses are always a help since they help penetrate the water making the fish and the cover more visible. Lures used during the spawning period are those that permit the greatest water coverage such as spinner baits do. These baits allow you to cover large areas of water quickly and they draw a reaction strike meaning that the fish hit the bait simply because it was dragged through their zone rather then because it was a good meal.

Female bass will retreat to the deeper mid layers of the water column after they have spawned. They will often stay there for 30 to 60 days and sometimes all summer. Although holding in the deeper water, they will also feed aggressively to regain the strength that they lost during the spawn. Remember when fishing for these fish that the females are stressed fish and they will remain a big lethargic until they gain their strength back. As a result of this, post spawn fish if caught should be handled very carefully especially if you are returning them to the lake as I do. Also to be considered, fish of the sunfish family normally spawn later than the bass. They also are reluctant to leave their spawning beds and are therefore easy prey for the bass and other hungry fish. Not to be forgotten, bass will eat their own, so newly hatched bass fry are a great food source during the post spawn period.

Some of the most exciting fishing is in the early spring months of March, April and May. The fish have had the luxury of several months in the cold water where they have moved throughout the whole lake in both the shallow and deep water. At this time fish can be found at nearly all reasonable depths and they are usually very active. I have had many early spring mornings when I am on the lake before sunrise with a calm surface and I can hear the Carp breaking the surface or I can see the Stripers pushing the baitfish to the surface. I have had days when I watched 3 foot Carp swim along side my boat as I was trolling for Stripers. I'm not a Carp fisherman but I have had the thrill of a 10 pound Carp hitting my line on a troll at 5:45am before the sun has risen and I learned quickly that pound for pound the Carp has to be considered one of the best fighting fish. During their spawn they are on the surface making a racket and they will hit a trolling bait.

During this spring transition if I am after Stripers, I look for the subsurface schools of perch. If I identify a perch school, I will always troll around the perimeter of the school of perch and can depend on a Striper hit. The Stripers will feed off of the same baitfish that the perch are feeding off of and the Stripers also love to eat the small Perch. A good practice at any time of the year but specifically in the spring is to throw out a marker at the edge of where the Perch school is. Throwing the marker into the school can have a bad effect of scattering the school and we do not want that. A good sonar will show the Perch and sometimes a quick jigging with a simple jigging spoon will quickly hook a small Perch and you will then be sure of what you are dealing with. My experience has shown that a sizeable school of perch in the spring in 20 to 30 feet of water is worth spending a few minutes circling. I call this "circling the wagons." Remembering that what you are seeing on your sonar is only a small portion of what is below the surface, extend your trolling circle from where you think the Perch are and more often than not you will find a Striper, if only a stray one feeding off the Perch.

Many Lake Normal fishermen consider the Perch to be a nuisance. I do not subscribe to that feeling for several reasons. First, a 10 or 12 inch Perch is a great fighting fish to catch; Perch schools are great for teaching fishing to your children who have a short attention span and want to catch a lot of fish fast; Perch may take away some of the Striper baitfish food but they also provide a nice diet for the Stripers and even other Bass; Catfish love to eat small Perch and some of the largest Catfish that I have caught were feeding on the Perch schools. If you are so inclined, Perch are very good eating.

In the spring when the Stripers are spawning or just enjoying the cooler shallow water, they can be caught with surface lures or even flies and this is very exciting fishing and a fine technique for spring fishing. Even though Stripers do not multiply in Lake Norman, they do spawn and their behavior during this spawn is similar to all other fish. They are more aggressive and their actions are more predictable.

Generally my ground rule is that when the Gulls leave Lake Norman to return to their regular homes for the summer, the spring fishing is finished and the warm water season has arrived. This is usually in early June.

HOT SUMMER MONTHS

Many fishermen just write off the summer months of July and August when the lake temperature goes near the 90 degree mark and the outside air temperature holds close to 90 degrees for many days at a time. The lake is crowded with boats, personal water craft, skiers and swimmers and caution is required on the water to prevent serious burning of your skin. Most boaters could care less if you have four poles hanging out of your boat as you troll along looking for the fish, as a matter of fact these poles seem often to be magnets to attract the loud fast boats to with feet of your position. I seem to attract the personal water craft people and my boat seems to be the one that attracts the 360 degree spins that they just need to make near me churning up the water and creating havoc with my ability to control my trolling motor.

Well, I love the Summer for fishing and I try to get out on the lake at least four or five times a week during the summer, I just don't do it on Saturday and Sunday afternoons when the sun is shining. Because of my fishing habits, I get a fine deep tan that is the envy of many of my friends who still have to work for a living. I keep the top of my Pontoon boat covered all year so I have an escape from the hot sun in the Summer and from the wind and rain during the Winter. Having the top always in place causes some problems during high wind days but what the heck you can't have everything.

Except for the absence of the large schools of Stripers in the Summer, it is the time of the year when I have caught my biggest fish in every category and I have not had to travel very far to do that. The Summer is the most consistent time of the year for fishing. The fish behavior is consistent because the water temperature is fairly consistent. Baitfish usually school near the same structure during the Summer so from day to day there is some predictability to their location. Bass have schooled up and often show up at the same areas to feed every day. Strong weather fronts occur less often in the Summer, fish are at all levels of the water column so there are a variety of ways to try and catch them. Fish will hang out near vegetation providing them a hiding place and a cool spot and I have found that fishing areas between the vegetation and the shoreline produced a good Summer catch. I find that for the Bass I rarely catch a real big Bass during the hot Summer but I catch more of the smaller ones.

The fish that provide the most fun in the Summer months are the Catfish, Carp, Perch, Bass and Gar. The Gar is normally my early Summer challenge. They are near the surface in the early summer and will hit any bait presented to them. They represent a challenge to get into the boat because they clamp the bait in their bony snout and will fight viciously resisting the retrieve. They will fly out of the water like a Marlin trying to escape the hook when all they have to do is open their mouth and the fight will be over. The Gar will swim sideways to the retrieve. Once they see the boat they seem to instinctively let go so it is very difficult to actually make the catch with a Gar. When you do get them into the boat, you will usually have a 40-inch fish that wants to tear your boat apart but what a great fishing experience. I watched my 12 year old grandson land a 42-inch Gar and neither he nor I will ever forget that experience.

Catfish are the most commonly caught fish in Lake Norman during the Summer. They are relatively easy to catch because they will hit almost anything that will sink below the surface. They are least effected by the warmer water of the summer and they actually seem to gain strength during these months. The biggest Catfish are the Flatheads that live nearer the bottom. The best fighting catfish are the channel cats, and the blues. The Catfish are the biggest and heaviest fish in this lake and it is not unusual to catch several 5 or 6 pound Catfish on any given day. I will talk more about the various foods and methods of catching Catfish in other sections of this book.

White Perch are the new addition to Lake Norman and these fish are nearly everywhere during the summer and other seasons. They are relatively easy to find with even the most inexpensive equipment and they make excellent food for the other larger fish in the lake.

Fishing techniques in the summer are not much different than the other seasons of the year except that you will fish in deeper water, you can fish faster than in the cooler water and you will often want to fish the shady sides of the shore lines.

I LOVE THE FALL

If it possible for a fisherman to fall in love with a season, it is the Fall season for me. This is the time of the year when we can really relate the changes in our behavior to the changes in our surroundings. Just looking around you in the Fall can signal the good fishing days. There is a great debate among fishermen as to whether it is Spring or Fall that produces the best fishing. The thing that is common to both seasons is the great change that is taking place. The air is getting cool and crisp. The summer humidity is gone and the leaves are starting to change their color. On the fishing grounds the summer boaters have disappeared from the lake, the jet skies are gone, the summer homes are being closed p leaving their docks to become quiet hiding places for the fish. These changes above the water surface means changes below the surface. Probably the only real difference between the fishing in the Spring and Fall is that you will probably get more fish in the Fall but fewer and bigger fish in the Spring. I love this dilemma.

As September approaches, the cold fronts start to move in from the north. The Shad move to the mouth of the creeks and later in the Fall they move to the backs of the creeks where the water is shallow. Naturally the predator fish follow the shad. Once the predator fish are in the back of the creeks, they are obviously easier to catch since they are gorging themselves in anticipation of the coming Winter months when their metabolism will slow down and they will not need as much food.

Nearly every fish type will hit at just about anything in the Fall. The cooling water temperature means that the fish are feeding more often than they did in the Summer. The aquatic underwater life will start to die off. When the plants die, they consume more oxygen than they produce making heavy plant areas unsuitable for the fish so don't fish the underwater growth areas in the late Fall. The fish will move to the deeper areas where the plant life is still alive. Deep weeds will stack up the fish during the Fall.

Bass will often start grabbing up the small Blue Gills and other Bream to fatten for the Winter. The fish will often get very aggressive in the afternoon and on cloudy days it should be good fishing. Fall means that you should fish the long tapered points, the rocky shorelines since the shad will get much tighter to these rocks in the Fall. Because some fish are closer to the shore line in the Fall, it is a good time for top water baits and lures.

Fall signaling the approach of Winter affects the instinct of the fish telling them to begin the process of preparing for the Winter which means to prepare for the dormant period. Preparing means eating more and schooling together for easier survival. Fish will therefore grab almost anything that goes by them in the Fall which makes the catch much easier.

The real excitement in the Fall is with the Striper fishing. There is almost no fresh water experience that comes close to a good day of Striper fishing in the Fall. When the water temperature drops into the 70 degree range the Stripers start their change over from their deep summer locations to sites closer to the surface, often even on the surface. As the cold fronts cool the water, the Stripers start their Fall feeding frenzy. The small Stripers start first since they can more easily adjust to the warmer water. As the cooler water is more consistent later in September, the larger Stripers start their surface feeding and there are days when you can truly say, "it doesn't get better than this."

In the Fall the northern Gulls return to Lake Norman where the weather is warmer. These Gulls often become a great assistance to the Striper fisherman signaling when the Stripers are pounding the schools of shad to the surface. The Gulls also have a feeding frenzy.

Striper fishermen have had to adjust their outlook on Striper feeding habits in recent years due to the growing numbers of Blue Back Herring that now live in Lake Norman. Contrasting the Shad that swim in schools near the surface, the Herring like the colder water and the

Herring schools are usually nearer the bottom. Fall and Winter Striper fishing has traditionally been driven by watching the surface activity and the birds to determine where the Striper schools were located. Now however the sonar devices are playing a more important roll when the Stripers are feeding off of the Herring deep below the surface. The results of this feeding will not always drive the baitfish to the surface and there will be no birds to signal the fish.

The mouths of the main channels and creeks are good starting points for Striper fishing at the beginning of the cold weather season. Since the Stripers are normally schooled at this time, finding a school of stripers, whether at the surface or closer to the bottom is an exciting experience unmatched by any other fresh water fish. Striper fishing in early fall is like hours of boring searching coupled by a few minutes of absolute frantic chaos. But the periods of chaos are wonderful times if you are ready for them. I have had several personal experiences where I have been fishing alone with four lines out on a slow troll. Shortly after seeing a school of Stripers on my sonar I got hard hits on all four lines at the same time. Remaining calm, with a pre-designed plan, I have been successful in retrieving all four fish without a snag or tangle. I would have loved to have a video of these occasions since it was a sight to behold and I probably could have won a home video contest with my antics.

If you hit a school of Stripers like this in the Fall, you may get two passes at them because it is rare that the Stripers will remain in the same area for a longer period of time. On the very rare occasions that they do remain, you will end your day far more exhausted than the fish that you caught.

THE COLD OF WINTER

The months from September through June are my best fishing months on Lake Norman. During the late Fall and Winter months, the Stripers dictate the underwater activities. Bass and Perch will follow the Stripers but they will usually head for the deeper waters when it gets real cold.

You have to change your attitude and your fishing strategy in the Winter. You will have to settle for fewer but larger fish in these cold months. Most of the record Bass and Stripers were caught in the Winter months. When the colder water slows down most fish, this can be viewed as shrinking the size of the strike zone. The fish being much slower, they will not strike out as far and as fast. It takes more patience to fish in the Winter since you have to get the bait closer to the fish to get results. The fisherman has to cover more water area in the Winter because of this.

Generally the fish will seek deeper water in the Winter. Steep drop off areas that have vertical growth are good Winter fishing areas. Vertical structures such as pilings and bridge abutments attract the fish because they can move up and down along these structures without using much energy. This makes jigging more popular in the Winter.

It has been theorized that when the water temperature gets real cold, below 45 degrees, many fish like Bass need to feed only once very 10 to 15 days. That doesn't mean that the fish won't eat, it means that they won't go out of their way to get the food and we have to fish for them very slowly and nearer the bottom with the bait or lure moving very slowly.

I have had some of my best days particularly with Stripers when there was ice hanging off of my boat and my deck was slippery with solid ice formations or snow. Personal comfort is certainly not ideal during these periods but fishing is not about comfort to the serious fisherman.

WINTER HOT HOLES

It is necessary to address this subject to complete the Winter fishing story. It is during the very cold months that the warm water discharges of the two Lake Norman power plants are interesting places to fish. It is not unusual on a 40-degree Winter morning to fish the "hot holes" and find dozens of boats doing the same thing. Hot hole water temperatures reach 95 degrees on some days. It does not hold these temperatures constant for long periods but there are tremendous temperature variations, which drive the fish crazy. Normally only the smaller Stripers like this warm water and even the Bass and Perch will be smaller where the water is this warm. But it is an unusual experience to see a school of hundreds of Bass or Perch breaking water for short periods of time in hot water, it excited your fishing emotions. Don't get me wrong, because there are large schools of fish in these warm waters doesn't mean that you will necessarily catch a lot of them, the rapid changes of temperature in the hot holes rapidly changes the behavior of the fish and it is a real challenge to get a large catch.

I have found that the transition areas outside the hot holes where the water temperature starts to cool are better areas to catch bigger fish more consistently. This perimeter area is like an artificially created thermocline and we have learned that fish hang out above and below a thermocline.

I have also found that whatever the time of the year, if you catch a large fish in the hot water, it will tend to be oxygen starved and it will have little stamina. It is therefore necessary to take great care in handling these fish in order to get them returned to the lake in this weakened condition. It is for this same reason that I do not fish for Stripers during the hot summer months. Stripers can be caught in the deep water during these hot months but they will rarely survive the trip to the surface. Rather than kill a good game fish, I will not fish for them.

THE EFFECT OF RAIN

This is another area where people have conjured up all kinds of folklore and superstitions. Most of these beliefs are based on the comfort of fishing rather than the facts about the rain affecting the fish and the fishing. I can never remember a time when I enjoyed a day of fishing in the rain as much as I did a day without rain. But that has to do with my comfort. Fishing in the rain is practically never pleasant even if the fish are biting like crazy. (Although this makes it a little better.)

Rainy weather usually improves the fishing therefore not to go fishing because the fish won't bite is a lame excuse. Rain is almost always accompanied by or created by overcast skies. This means reduced light penetration into the water and the fish are more comfortable in the shallower water. Heavy rain causes runoff flows into the back ends of coves and channels giving the fish cause to go there and feed. The same situation exists in areas that have water run offs, drainage pipes or storm sewers. Look for these areas and know where they are so that you can fish them during light rains.

Rain showers that pelt the water surface help to oxygenate the water, which makes the fish more active. It is known that better hatching conditions for water life exist during rainy seasons that when drought conditions prevail.

Bad storms on the other hand have a negative and often dangerous effect on fishing. I would never recommend being on the lake during a heavy thunderstorm. Lightning can strike miles away from where you think you see it so don't try to be a weatherman. If you are the only boat on the lake, you could be the highest object in the area of a lightning strike and very vulnerable to being struck by lightning. Lightning tends to drive the fish to the deeper water and fishing conditions are not good during these storms.

Fish are normally more active after a storm because the water may contain higher levels of oxygen and the nutrients washed into the water bring the fish closer to shore to feed. Knowing this will help you plan your fishing strategy in the rain or after a storm.

If you find an area where shore material is being washed into the lake after a storm, fish that area even if the water is murky because there will be fish feeding there.

THE BAIT CONTROVERSY

Since the purpose of this book is to improve your knowledge about fishing so that you can enjoy the sport more and hopefully catch more fish, it would not be wise to thrust you into the middle of any great controversy that simply adds confusion and discouragement to your fishing experience. When it comes to bait selection, this is one of those subjects that offers the danger of such an introduction. I really don't know how many experienced fishermen there are in the USA but I do know that whatever the number, that is the number of opinions that exist on the best type of bait to use.

There are of course some legitimate reasons for a difference in opinion. The region of the country, the water being fished and of course the type of fish being sought are all variables that will change the slant on the bait selection argument. Unfortunately the effects of commercial marketing has provided the greatest input to causing confusion on this subject since there are thousands of different artificial lures being marketed all over the country and each one claims to be the best that exists. In fact the question of what kind of bait is best is simply answered by stating that whatever catches the most fish is the best bait.

In gross terms the argument that starts the controversy is whether it is best to use live bait or artificial bait. One professional fisherman once told me that real men use artificial bait and live bait is reserved for the pansy set. Well then I guess that clearly places me in the pansy category since I use live bait about 90% of the time that I fish unless I am fishing the northern regions looking for the real big fish in which case artificial lures seem the best solution.

I will have to repeat a statement here that I have included elsewhere in this book that is very appropriate to this argument. I was listening to a mild debate between a professional bass fisherman (it was a women in this case) and a striper guide at a seminar. The Striper guide countered the artificial lure argument by stating "it is easier to feed a fish than it is to fool it." This struck me as a very appropriate statement.

There are entire industries that have developed with the sole intent of providing a product that will fool the fish better than the last item produced. I mentioned in the very beginning of this book, that one of the important elements of catching fish is to present the fish with food that is more tempting than other choices that are available to the fish. If we keep this in mind, then we have only to ask ourselves, can a lure be produced that looks more like a real live fish than a real fish looks? The answer to me is very simple, no way.

Shad are a very common baitfish that is widely used in many areas of the country. I went on to one website one day and looked for the lures of only one company that were supposed to substitute for live Shad. On one page there were 106 different versions of a Shad lure shown and not one of them came remotely close to resembling a live Shad.

Now every argument has several sides that must be understood. There are some States that forbid the use of certain live fish as bait. Where this is the case, of course, there is no choice but to use artificial lures. Also there are many professional tournaments that also forbid the use of live bait and of course again here, there is no real argument.

But! As a general rule, if live bait is available and legal to use, it is in my opinion, always the best solution and will nearly always provide good results.

It seems like I have jumped right into the water here without first testing its temperature. Let's keep in mind that we are trying to provide knowledge here that is good for all levels of fishermen and fisherwomen. So let's take a step back from the big argument and discuss some of the basic related to types of bait available for the average fisherman.

I don't discuss much about fly fishing in this book because I am not a good fly fisherman. I have fished with flies and have fine equipment, but my circumstances dictate that other types of fishing are my standard. Fly fishermen however can give you a fine lesson in fish baits if you ask them. If an experienced fly fisherman goes to a new fishing area or a new creek to fish, the first thing that he does is sample the living creatures that are in the water to be fished and on the surrounding land masses. He collects these samples and tries to build flies on site that most closely duplicate those that he has sampled. Why? Well he knows that his samples represent what the fish in that area are eating as a regular diet and his chances of catching fish are better if he duplicated that diet.

The same theory can be applied to nearly all other specifies of fish. In any given body of water, there are natural foods that provide the diet for the fish. The fish are accustomed to this diet and prefer it over other food types. In the section of this book describing various species of fish, I have in each case indicated what the diet of the specific species is at its different stages of the life cycle. This is very important information, which points the fisherman to the type of bait that should be used to best temp the fish of the species being sought.

I have had many occasions to fish in strange waters that I have not had an opportunity to study in advance. My childhood fishing experience kicks in, in these circumstances because my bait of choice is always worms. I never fished with anything other than worms as a kid and I always come back to that as the "old reliable" fish bait. And you know what? It almost always works. Using worms may not provide an image of an experience fisherman, but it almost always catches fish. With that result, who cares about image?

Why worms? Have you ever taken a walk after a long rain shower in the summer? What do you see on sidewalks, road pavements, and many other surfaces? Worms all around you. Well these worms are also being washed into the nearby ponds, lakes and streams and they are a food standard for the fish. I don't know of one species of fish that will not eat a worm. Even those fish that normally eat vegetation like Carp, will eat a worm if presented to it under the right circumstances.

For beginning fishermen and particularly the kids, worms are a great starter bait. They are readily available all around us or they can be purchased at nearly all stores that sell bait. I suggest that you take a young person out and try to have the child find his own worms. After a rain, worms and night crawlers come to the surface of lawns. They can be located with a flashlight and picked right off the surface of the grass. This is a great way to have a child get the complete fishing experience.

Another bait commonly available in the summer months is the cricket. These critters are found in almost any nook or cranny that provides a hiding place for them.

Another readily available bait is the grasshopper. They can normally be found around weed streams and in almost any over-grown field from mid spring to late fall.

Caterpillars will also catch fish for you. The best types to use are the ones with a smooth body. Most people consider caterpillars to be somewhat of a nuisance but they make fine bait for the beginner fisherman.

Of the various baits described, I consider the worm to be the bait of preference over the others but there is much to say about the cricket as bait. A cricket will often catch fish when nothing else will especially when fishing for pan fish.

The most common way to fish when using crickets as bait is with a float or bobber. Using a small number 8 or 10 hook, insert the hook right behind the head of the cricket with the barb exiting through the crickets back. Use a small shot for weight, attaching the shot about six inches above the hook. Set the bobber about three feet below the surface. If there is no action in a few minutes, lower the bait deeper until you find the right depth.

Crickets, grasshoppers and caterpillars are good bait for pan fish and a good starter bait for kids but at this level I still prefer worms or night crawlers. When using worms or night crawlers, the hook size depends on the type of fish being sought. The bait will catch nearly any kind of fish so I suggest a circle hook sized for the specific fish. A number one for the larger fish like Bass and Catfish and smaller size for the smaller fish.

Worms should be hooked either in the middle or at the head end depending on how you are fishing. If you are fishing still from the shore or anchored in a boat, hooking in the middle is fine. I prefer hooking near the head end to gain maximum amount of movement of the worm. If you are moving by trolling, drifting the worm should be hooked near the head end. The same procedure applies to night crawlers but in general with these bigger baits, the closer to the head end that the hook is located, the better.

If you are using night crawlers for bait when fishing for pan fish, you may want to cut the bait into several pieces because a large bait cannot be taken in at one time by the smaller mouth of the pan fish and you will find that it is hard to get a hook set as the pan fish nibbles away at the large bait.

Even though we are discussing live bait here, there is another bait that doesn't fall into any category and that is corn. Kernels of canned corn have proven to be fine bait especially for pan fish. It is necessary when using corn to use a fairly small hook since that will permit the corn not to be damaged when being put on the hook.

As we graduate into catching bigger fish or perhaps a larger variety of fish, there are a variety of other live baits that are used regularly and very successfully. These are the small minnows, shiners, shad and herring. Again there are interesting arguments as to which of the various live fish baits are better but it is my opinion that any live fish makes good bait under most circumstances. Some live fish baits are preferred by some sport fish species over other live fish types. In the region of the country that I most often fish, there is an argument whether shad are preferred over shiners or herring. In some states shad are not legal bait while in other areas there are restrictions on certain herring as a baitfish. I will discuss each of these types of bait fish and we will see what each one looks like and it may become quickly obvious that they look very much like each other and we have to ask ourselves, can a hungry fish or even one that has just eaten really tell the difference between the various live fish bait types? It's hard enough to tell the difference when looking at their photos. Perhaps more important than the specific species of baitfish is the care taken to keep them in good health and good condition. Almost any baitfish can be rendered ineffective if it is not healthy, and in good exterior condition. The affectivity of live bait can also be changed by the type of gear it is used with and how the bait is attached to the hook. These factors are sometimes far more important than the actual type of baitfish used.

Proper handling of baitfish is very important and can also reduce bait costs if you buy your bait. Water temperature changes must be gradual from the point of capture, through storage and eventual use. Fall and winter months lessen this problem but the summer months make it more difficult to keep baitfish alive and healthy. It is important to maintain a high oxygen level both in the storage tanks and in your live well, if you use one. Some fish, especially Bass do not want to hit a bait that they feel is not able to run from them so a weak or wounded baitfish will not attract a big bass.

Using improperly balanced tackle will also reduce the effectiveness of your live baitfish. As a guide, if your baitfish are around three inches long, you can use a number three ought or less hook size but if the bait is more than eight inches, you may want to increase the size of the hook.

How the bait is attached to the hook is another determinant of its affectivity. Shiners or shad should be hooked through the front lips from bottom up through a nostril. Use care not to break the neck of the baitfish when attaching it. Hooking a shiner in this manner will make it swim with a downward motion and works best for trolling. Hooking it in the dorsal fin will make the baitfish swim upward and away from the line. This provides more action but will tire the bait sooner and it will die faster. If you want the baitfish to swim down and away from the line it can be hooked near the anal fin and close to the backbone.

If you are casting a baitfish keep in mind that your goal is to get it to the fish in perfect condition. If scales are removed from handling or improperly casting, the missing scales will be noticeable in the water in addition to weakening the baitfish.

If you practice care with the above elements, you will have success no matter which type of baitfish you select.

Usually when I am asked what kind of live bait I use I respond that I fish with minnows. This seems a safe answer because all fish under six inches in size that are not game fish are called minnows. But most minnows are not baby fish; they are in fact species that never grow more than a few inches long. The most common of the baitfish that I put into this category are the Golden Shiner, Shad and Herring.

Golden shiners shown below are a lake species of minnow. They prefer to live in lakes, rivers and streams. The eat plankton, algae and small insects. They grow to from between three and ten inches. They are readily available for purchase from bait stores and are fairly easy to keep alive.

This is my personal favorite baitfish because almost every fish that I seek will eat the Golden Shiner. I vary the lengths that I use depending n the season and the game fish being sought. A two to three inch medium is my favorite year round but I sometimes go to four to six inch large ones for the fall and winter Stripers. This is my all around, all American bait, my favorite.

Shad both Threadfin and Gizzard Shad shown below are also a widely used baitfish. Threadfin shad are the most common the shad baitfish and they will grow from one to six inches in length. The Gizzard Shad is a favorite among many Striper fishermen and they will grow to larger lengths than the Threadfin growing up to 14 inches long. They are harder to find, harder to catch but the favorite for trophy Stripers.

Blueback Herring and Alewives are often confused with each other since it is indeed very hard to tell them apart. If they are available they make excellent baitfish for Stripers and other larger fish. Like shad they travel in large schools and when you find a school of Bluebacks, you will also find other larger game fish around. Shad generally school tightly up from the bottom and their schools are hit from below by Stripers and other large fish. The Bluebacks and Alewives school less tightly nearer the bottom and the larger fish normally hit the outsides of the schools. You rarely see schools of Bluebacks driven to the surface by feeding predators as you often do with Shad.

Alewives are very similar to the Blueback herring. Both are silvery in color but the Alewife has a larger mouth and slightly larger eye than the Blueback. The population of both these baitfish has been observed for many years and there is some disagreement between fishing clubs and conservation officials as to the proper management and stocking of these fish. It is so difficult to tell the two fish apart that they are routinely referred to as river herring.

Another favorite bait especially for Bass is the Crawfish. Nearly every species of fish will eat crawfish. If they are in your waters they will normally be found under structure or rocks in early morning.

Hellgrammites are another often used bait. Like the Crawfish, it usually hides under rocks but makes a good meal for several species of fish.

Are there any creatures that should be avoided as bait? Yes, at all costs avoid using common ground slugs as bait. I don't know of one fish that will eat a slug even if it is the last remaining live creature available.

There are many other small fish that can be used as live bait. Stripers and large Catfish love small Perch and sunfish as a fine meal. Perch are a favorite of large predators like Northern Pike and Muskies. Many states do not permit the use of any game fish as a baitfish so you should always check the local fishing laws before using any strange bait.

In many areas trout are sold as bait for Stripers as are Goldfish. That is the case in my home lake but I have never believed that any fish should be used for bait that is not native to the waters being fished; first it probably will look strange to the sport fish that you are after and not attract his attention. More importantly there is a danger from the release of the fish that you may introduce a species of fish into that water that really does not belong there.

One of my largest trophy fish was caught under strange bait circumstances. I was fishing in Northern Canada for Northern pike. The water that we were fishing contained mostly Pike and Walleye. I wasn't really looking for or fishing for Walleye this particular day and a small ten-inch Walleye grabbed my lure while trolling. Because of the gear that I was using I didn't realize that the Walleye was hooked and I continued to fish with it hanging from the end of the lure. You know the rest of the story. I got this great hit and landed a trophy Northern Pike and still on the line was the Walleye, which had become bait for the Northern Pike.

Of course this stimulated a big argument when the daily pool was to be collected since my buddies felt that a Walleye is not a legal baitfish. I argued that I wasn't using it as bait because it had hooked itself. I check Canadian law and it indicated that Perch are a legal bait and I also found that Walleye are a member of the Perch family. I'm not sure who is right but as the argument persists, the trophy Pike hangs on my wall as a reminder that "feeding big fish is much easier than fooling them."

Regardless of your particular bait choice, even if you fish with artificial bait, you must keep in mind that the presentation of the bait to the fish is the one factor that will most influence the action of the fish to attach it for a meal. Putting aside pan fish for a moment, even a hungry fish will not attack bait that he cannot see or hear or smell or looks so bad that it does not appeal to him. At different times of the year under varying water temperature conditions fish will move more slowly and you bait must be presented to them slower and more accurately. Similarly in the summer when the fish metabolism is high and they are very active, the bait must be presented in a manner where it can be easily seen, smelled or even heard. In other words you have to try and match the mood of the fish and its surroundings with the bait choice and the manner of presentation.

If as an example you are fishing in mid summer, at midday when the sun is high the fish are probably deeper and near the drop offs. You would not choose a surface lure for this situation but probably one that will hold at deeper positions. Under this condition, live bait must be fished deeper so the addition of shot weight will bring the bait to the fish.

An earlier point that I made concerned the placement of the fish's eyes. Most fish have eyes that are on the topside of their head. They see best above them because that is their normal viewing position. Even bottom feeders like carp and some catfish will prefer bait that passes above them. If you can see fish on your sonar, their depth is most important. If you are fishing with artificial bait or have to select one that will dive to a depth slightly above the depth of the fish.

Another aspect of presenting bait is to take care not to slam the bait against the surface of the water. This is mostly a problem when casting artificial lures but can also b e a problem using live bait. With large predator fish like Northern Pike and Muskies, there is sometimes a value in making a small splash thinking that it is a frog or small animal. But in most cases it is safe to assume that you should put the lure or bait in the water as gently as possible.

Most predator fish attack the bait at its head or what looks like its head. Why is that? Well look at a fish and you will immediately see why. Most dorsal fins have sharp spines, which can be folded back. If the baitfish goes through the fish's mouth head first the dorsal fin will automatically fold down and not get stuck on its way down. This means that the part of the bait that the fish sees first is the head that is where he is focusing. A baitfish with big eyes is therefore better than one with small eyes since the eyes are the center of what is seen. I make it a practice to insure that my hook never disturbs the eye and I never use live bait that has a damaged or missing eye. Sounds terrible but it does happen. If you examine a baitfish that has been hit and remains on the hook, it probably has damaged eyes because that is the area of most interest to the predator fish.

Using dead bait is not recommended. It is important to keep you bait as healthy and alive as possible. Only under circumstances where I am running out of bait will I ever use a dead bait. There are of course exceptions. There are some techniques for fishing for Catfish where dead bait is preferred. In those cases the best dead bait is also rotten bait that smells badly. You may want to save your dead bait for those occasions where you are seeking that type of fishing.

Now let me make the counter to that argument. What are artificial lures? Are they not dead? They may look like the bait they were designed to represent but they are dead. So why not use dead bait, it has smell, it looks like real fish and it probably can fool the fish better that the artificial lure. A good argument can be made for the use of dead bait but given that I have sufficient bait to replace the dead ones I will save the dead bait to provide the gulls with a meal when they come around or maybe even drop it over the side when I see a school of larger fish in the area, not really chumming if that practice is not permitted but it has the same effect.

ARTIFICIAL BAITS

This is the point in this book where I ran into a serious dilemma involving the presentation of information about artificial baits. I was looking for natural break points that would keep my discussions confined to information needed for improving the skills of the beginner and intermediate fisherman and woman. It became very obvious very soon after starting to write about artificial baits that I could not deal with that subject properly without using a disproportionate amount of space in the book.

By looking over my material and breaking down the subject matter into the most general categories like Crank baits, Jerk baits, Spoons, spinners, jigs etc. there were easily at least 10 categories of this type. In each of the categories there are at least 20 different design types and for each design type there are perhaps 24 different sizes and shapes. For each shape and size there are about 10 different colors and for each color there are five different weights and for each weight there are two different noise-making techniques. If I stop here and multiply this all out I come up with 480,000 different artificial baits. If I tried to properly describe these baits and lures I would have a book of more than 1000 pages just for the artificial bait section. This exercise however did answer one question as to why the super sporting goods stores have dozens of isles presenting these baits and lures for sale.

I decided that it would be more appropriate for this book to describe only in summary some of the types of artificial lures available to you. In my next book where I go into more advanced fishing techniques, I will include more complex information and photos on each of the artificial lure types.

Crank Baits—are among the most popular lures in use today. This is partially because the concept of a crank bait is simply that you cast the bait out and crank it back in. Crank bait popularity has also grown because this bait type catches a lot of bass and who doesn't want to catch bass. Crank baits come in all sizes, shapes and colors but they all have a few things in common. The first of these is the lip extending from the mouth area. The lip is designed to keep the lure at a specific depth in the water column and the actual depth is a function of the size of the lip, the weight of the lure and the speed of the retrieve. Generally speaking, the larger the lure and lip the deeper it will perform. Some crank baits float and some sink. Some rattle and some do not. Some rise to the surface when you stop cranking and others do not so you have many different options when using this versatile and popular lure.

Jerk Baits—are very popular with the professional tour fishermen because if they are used right they can produce catches of the bigger bass. Jerk bait is slightly less popular among those of use who are less skilled because it requires some degree of skill to use it properly and if it is not used properly it will produce a frustrating day on the water. The opposite of course is also true. If you learn how to use jerk bait and you use it with the properly selected equipment, you may catch fewer but bigger fish.

The key is to develop your jerk bait habits. Remember earlier we discussed that you need to try and make your bait look as much like the real thing as possible. With jerk bait you not only have to select a lure that looks right but you the fisherman has to make it act right in the water. The floating jerk baits have to be made to look like wounded food on the surface. The jerk baits that sink have to be made to move like a wounded fish under the surface.

There are essentially two types of jerk baits, the hard and the soft baits. The soft baits are usually made of plastic or other soft material and are usually made to look like some fish or other live animal. The hard jerk baits are made of hard plastics or other hard material and normally take on the form of a fish. The soft baits typically have one large hook that can be hidden in the soft material. The hard jerk baits normally have treble hooks attached and are not used in weeds or grass. Many jerk baits look like crank baits but the jerk baits normally don't have a large lip to drag them down in the water.

Top Water Lures—provide some of the most exciting fishing because it is visual fishing on top of the water where you can see all of the action. There are two types of surface action, the action of the lure itself that is created by the wrist action of the fisherman and the surface action when the fish hits, which is the only action that counts. Top water lures combine the actions of other types of lures such as crank and jerk baits since both of these categories have top water lures.

One reason why top water fishing has become popular is because it can be used at any time and at any place and during any season and it will produce results with a variety of types of fish, the most popular ones being Stripers, Northern Pike and Muskies. Many fishermen say that 50 degrees is the best temperature for top water lures but I believe that they can be used all year round with good results.

Some of the more popular top water lures are the torpedo types with small propellers for motion and noise, poppers are small and easy to use top water lures, buzz baits and spinner baits are very popular top water lures for bass.

Spinner Bait Lures—come in all sizes and configurations and with this type lure you can even make your own configuration. Most spinner baits are designed to produce a smooth flow through the water while attracting the attention of the fish by the reflections of the spinners and also their vibrations. There are three popular shapes for the spinner blade itself, the Colorado blade, the Indiana blade and the Willowleaf blade. The function of each of these blade types if different and it is not necessary here to get into that detail.

Spoons—happen to be my favorite standby type of lure. There are a million different sizes and shapes of spoon lures. I use spoon lures almost exclusively for catching Northern Pike, Walleye and Muskies, the bigger fish. Generally speaking the bigger the spoon the bigger the fish it will attract. I normally use a spoon in conjunction with a Carolina rig when I use the larger spoons.

Jigs—are the most versatile lures and very poplar because it doesn't take much skill to make a jig work for you. Some jigs like the roadrunners can be trolled but most jigs are made to be jerk and snapped off of the bottom and near where fish are suspected to be feeding. Jigs can catch just about any kind of fish if used properly. For bottom jigs the motion of the jig is supposed to simulate a wounded bait fish trying to surface and continually falling back to the bottom. The jig will almost always be hit on the way down so it is important to always maintain some small amount of tension on the line to keep constant control of the jig.

Plastics—offer the greatest variety and the largest selection options for fishermen. Plastics are also among the most popular lure because they are generally fairly inexpensive. Plastics are designed to look like worms, grubs, leeches, minnows, lizards and many other living creatures. Plastics can be used in a variety of ways and they offer every fisherman the opportunity to develop a favorite type and color and his or her own technique for making the lure come alive.

SELECTING THE RIGHT LURE
FOR THE RIGHT TIME

I have mentioned many times in this book the various factors that affect your fishing success. Nearly all of these same factors will have an effect on your choice of live bait or the right artificial lure to use. One of the largest single factors is the seasonal effect. The water temperature changes presented by the various seasons causes changes in the metabolism of the fish and significantly affects their eating habits. Water temperature is of course affected by the weather, water clarity, sun penetration, and wind direction. The best size, color speed and sound of your choice of lure is also affected by these same factors.

Bait size is a seasonal decision. Fish eat almost any creature that passes before them, plankton, nymphs, shiners, shad, herring, leeches and all types of minnows. In the springtime new batches of fresh bait hatch or are born and become the most vulnerable creatures to a hungry fish. Since these new creatures are in demand during the spring, you want your bait to reflect their smaller size. Size therefore becomes a seasonal bait decision. Smaller baits in the early Spring usually work best; medium baits are more popular as summer approaches. In the fall a large bait presentation will normally get better results.

Sound is also a factor. Sound transmitted through sonic vibrations usually stimulates a positive response from most fish. Fish possess a lateral line on their body that permits them to sense vibrations and attach their prey even when they cannot see it. Noise making lures such as spinner baits, buzz baits, spinner rigs and some crank baits will emit a vibration that will attract the fish and trigger them to strike.

Color is perhaps the most confusing factor because it seems to change its effect from day to day and from one body of water to the next. As a general rule you want your lure to blend in naturally with the color of the water that you are fishing. Natural baitfish colors blended with black, blue and green are well suited for clear waters. As the water gets slightly stained, yellow, gold, chartreuse, green and peach will be good producers. For stained or muddy water the highly visible fluorescents like pink, orange and phosphorescent colors are a great bet. If the sun is bright and the water fairly shallow fluorescent yellow and chartreuse are good colors to select.

Everything can come apart if your presentation speed is not corrected for the season. In cold water the fish are relatively dormant and a slow movement is best. During the warmer months fish become more active and will more aggressively chase the bait so you can move the bait faster in the warmer water. Again in the fall when the water cools you need to slow your bait movement. Water depth also dictates the bait speed. Bait should be moved faster in the shallow water and slowed down, as the water gets deeper.

SOME SIMPLE KNOTS

You've done all of your planning, you have your fishing plan in your head, you get to your planned destination the bait is over the side and no sooner you get the lines in, there is a rattle in one of the poles as it bends nearly into a "u" shape. The hit is so hard that you have real difficulty getting the pole out of the pole holder. The hook is set and as soon as you start to retrieve the draw hums and the battle has begun. You know this is a monster since you had the drags set for a fairly heavy weight. You remember all that you have been taught, the trolling motor is slowed but not too slow to keep control, the net is within reach and you begin the challenge, you and the fish battling for the victory. You are making progress, the retrieve is steady and suddenly the fish breaks the surface 20 yards out and you can see that it is a monster Striper, more than 10 pounds by your estimate. The fish veers sideways and again the drag hums but again you are in control. Now the fish is in sight as you reach for the net but before you can get the net into the water everything stops, no more fighting, suddenly the fish is gone, nothing but a memory and another "fish off" story to tell.

You bring in your line with a tear in your eye and an empty feeling in your stomach. This was the fish that you had waited for all year and it got away. No hook, no leader, no swivel, all gone with the fish. But you notice that the end of the line is all curled up in a small curl. It's obvious, the knot failed you. The line didn't break, the swivel didn't fail, the leader didn't fail, the hook didn't break, the problem was a human problem, you just didn't tie the knot right.

As experience a fisherman as you may be, this happens all too often to every one of us and as we think the situation over after the shock has gone away we can usually remember when we last changed that knot, we were rushed, we didn't think about the match of the line with the knot. Perhaps we used a monofilament type knot for our braided line. Whatever the resultant cause, we probably rushed the tie and we know it and a fine trophy has been lost, what a shame.

It's worth the time to try and reduce the knot tying challenge to the simplest terms possible. You can read entire books that have been written about different types of fishing knots to use in different situations. It is my opinion that most fishermen need only to know only three different knots.

If it were the old days, (and none of us wish that was true) we could probably get away with knowing just one knot to tie, when I was a Boy Scout many, many years ago, it was called the Fisherman's Knot. Today it may have different names. BUT! Progress has been made so we have to keep up. There are many different types of lines and therefore we have to apply different types of knots to these different line situations. Again let's simplify the situation; we'll reduce the issue to two line types, the monofilament line and the braided line. Details about these two line types is discussed elsewhere in this book but each type of line requires a slightly different type of knot to compensate for the stretch ability of the line. It is also my experience that the type of fish being pursued will influence the type of knot used. The smaller fish require a slightly different variation of knot than the large lunkers. Let's see what we need to know about fishing knots.

When you get to be a competition fisherman you may want to learn a variety of knots often used for special occasions but for the first ten or so years of your fishing career I believe that there are only three knots that you want to get familiar with and probably one that you will use more than any others. The most popular knot is what used to be called the fisherman's knot, now called the Cinch knot or the improved Cinch knot. The knot can be used for nearly every occasion with any type of line tying to any type of equipment. The only modification that I suggest for line variations is that for braided or heavy monofilament line you will want to add a couple of extra turns above the five turns recommended. Remember that all lines should be wet when tied to assist the tightening process. Be careful not to hook your lip. The Cinch knot or Fisherman's knot is shown below.

Step 1. Pass the line through the eye, hook, swivel or lure. Double back amd make at least 5 turns around the standing line.

Step 2. Hold the coils in place, thread the and of the line through the first loop above the eye, then through the loop as shown.

Step 3. Hold the tag end and standing line while the coils are pulled up. Make sure that the coils are in a spiral and not overlapping each other. Slide the knot tight against the eye. Clip the tag end.

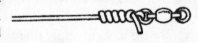

The Trilene knot is a strong reliable knot that will not slip. It is essentially a modified version of the Cinch knot. The Trilene knot is shown below.

Step 1. Run the end of the line through the hook, lure or swivel and double back through a second time.

Step 2. Loop around the standing line 6 times.

Step 3. Thread the tag end back through the double look as shown.

Step 4. Pull tight and trim.

The Polomar knot, shown below, is also a strong knot that is very simple to tie. I like to use this knot if I am getting any evidence of slippage in my other knots or when I am in the middle of a school of Stripers and I don't have time to inspect the tie. It is also good for braided lines.

Step 1. Double about 4 inches of line and feed through the eye.

Step 2. Letting the hook hang free, Make an overhand knot in the doubled Line. Try not to twist the lines.

Step 3. Pull the loop end of the line Over the hook, swivel or lure.

Step 4. Pull tight on both ends and trim.

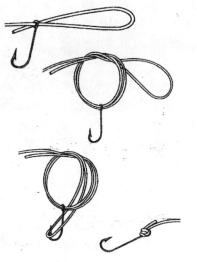

THE ELEMENT OF SURPRISE

When I was a young kid and would go Trout fishing with my Dad, we would sit in that boat all day with hardly a word spoken except in the excitement of a fine catch when the brief celebration took place. If I were to drop my knife on the floor of the boat or my pole slipped out of my hand and hit the floor, I would get that strange scowl from my Dad as if I had just cost us a hour of good fishing. And as a matter of fact, he actually did believe that was the case where the noise that I made was scaring the fish away.

I remember thinking even with my young inexperienced brain that I had to be very very quiet when we were fishing and yet we were trolling with a 10 horsepower Chris Craft Motor with a trolling plate attached and no muffler. "Why: I would think" does the noise of the motor not scare the fish and my dropped knife causes all kinds of havoc?"

Of course as I grew older and had 4 kids of my own I realized that my Dad heard enough of me all week and wanted some peace and quiet when we were fishing.

Back in the beginning of this book I asked you to perform an experiment by going to some clear water and observing the behavior of the fish that you saw. I bet what you learned went something like this. If you threw a rock into the water, it scared the fish and they darted away to another safer place. If you waved your arms up and down, it may have spooked the fish for a short time due to the shadow that you caused them to see. But if you had someone with you and you were both talking in normal volume, nothing happened; the fish went on with their business. If you didn't run those tests, try it and see if that is not exactly what happens.

Fish do have ears or at least sensors that perform the same function as ears so they will be spooked by loud noises but sounds made above the surface of the water are dampened to nearly total silence below the surface. Try going under water in a swimming pool or lake and see if you can hear the noises that are taking place above the surface. Chances are that you won't hear anything but very muffled sounds.

The other side of this story however is that sounds made at or on the surface of the water will transmit through the water so a motor or loud pounding on the bottom of a metal boat will indeed have a negative effect on the fish that are immediately below the boat. If however, I am trolling with my bait 50 to 70 feet behind the boat and 15 feet below the surface, noise that I make in my boat is going to have no effect on the fish that are likely to hit my bait. Noise made while fishing from a shore line will have little effect on the fish underwater.

Shadows on the other hand have a huge effect on fish behavior especially in the shallower water. It is important to understand your position and the position of your boat relative to the sun. You always want to try and keep the sun in front of you when casting or approaching an area where you suspect there are fish so as not to have your body or your boat cast a shadow on the area where the fish are located. This shadow and boat location factor is important to understand when fishing for spawning bass in the Spring, when fishing points or even approaching schools of Stripers.

I'm regularly surprised when Striper fishing in the fall, winter and spring and I see a group of Gulls working a surface area and from out of nowhere along comes a boat with two experienced looking fishermen. They have that tracker and the 200 hp motor that is pushing it at maximum speed right up to the center of the group of feeding Gulls. They stop the boat; feverishly scurry around for their gear and Surprise! Surprise! There are no more fish feeding there. Of course not, they have spooked them and by now the school of Stripers is 100 yards away. There was certainly a noise factor at work here.

Boat positioning with regards to noise and shadows is particularly important in the spring when the fish are in their spawning beds. The fish are skittish at this time and the least noise or shadow will turn away a good bite. Professional Bass fishermen will often shut down their motors 50 yards from areas where they suspect there are spawning Bass. If they use their trolling motors for the final approach, they will take care to run them at the slower speeds to avoid noise and vibration. Many fishermen think that their trolling motor is silent. The only time a trolling motor is quiet is when it is not running. Unless the motor is completely balanced it will have some vibration and fish can sense vibration better than they can hear sound.

Approaching a spawning bed requires a little bit of thought on your part. If it is a cloudy or overcast day, you don't have a shadow factor to deal with because there is no sun. In this case you have only to worry about the noise from the boat. If the sun is shinning however you have to try and have the sun above or in front of you as you approach the bed or your shadow will project itself over the bed spooking the fish. Spawning beds are often located near other structure such as docks, pilings or even grass. Be very careful not to hit these structures or otherwise disturb them or the fish will be gone.

Boat positioning is also an important factor when fishing drop offs and points. A common error made by fishermen around drop offs is to stay out a good distance from the drop off and cast into the structure. Their thought process is that the longer the cast distance, the longer the retrieve and the greater the chance of a strike. Not so!

Most fish will locate themselves in tight to the drop off so when you cast, you want your bait to sink to the fish close in to the structure. If your boat is located far out from the structure, your bait will hit the water and initially sink a bit but as you retrieve it you will be pulling the bait away from the fish. This is illustrated in the sketch below. Your boat should be positioned close to the drop off and your fishing should be parallel to the structures so that when you make a cast, your bait will sink to the fish close in to the structure improving your chances of a strike.

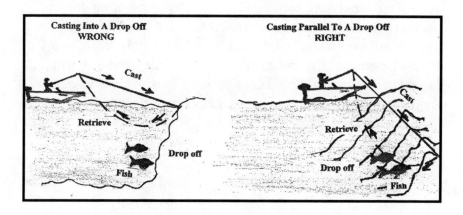

I have discussed points in several other areas of this book. Points are among the best areas to fish. There are many techniques for fishing points and there are several factors that will influence your choice of a technique. In general however when fishing points you have to keep in mind the direction of the water flow caused by either the natural current flow or the wind. Fish at rest will normally be facing into the current or into the wind if the wind is causing the current. Regardless of which side of a point you intend to fish, it makes sense that your boat should be facing into the wind or current so that when you cast out, your retrieve will bring the bait to the fish from the front where you have the best chance of a reaction or feeding strike. If however you are trolling across a point, the exact opposite will occur. Again since you want to pull your bait in front of the fish, you should be trolling with the wind so that the direction of the bait is the same as the retrieve just discussed. Remember however that on sunny days your boat will cast a shadow and you again want to try and insure that the sun does not bring the shadow of the boat directly over the fish. Trolling or casting parallel to the point is also an acceptable technique for dragging your bait in front of the fish even though it will approach the fish from a slightly sideways angle.

There are times when you may have a dilemma as to the direction of the current flow if the wind and the natural current flow are at odds with each other. In river lakes such as Lake Norman there is always a current flow in the main channels from north to south toward the dam. If the wind were blowing from the south as it often does in the warmer months you may get confused as to the real flow of the water. There is however no real confusion since the natural current flow will always be greater than the current caused by the wind. Current flow caused by the wind will be a consideration only in areas where there is no natural flow such as side coves and channels that are off of the main river flow of the lake.

DIFFERENT FISHING TECHNIQUES

To understand my personal fishing preference it is necessary to also understand my background and eating habits. I have a less than aggressive appetite for any fish with the possible exception of Walleye and Flounder. My wife has no desire to eat freshly caught fish. The obvious result of this is that I am a catch and release fisherman. I normally do not care what I catch, my objective is to catch as many fish as possible on any given day and release them alive, occasionally measuring and weighing them to establish my personal best. Fishing to me is the "memory factor." I want to retain the good memories of the day of fishing or the catch itself. Obviously as the stories of the trip or the catch are told over and over, they get better, longer and heavier therefore to establish some credibility; I get the "good looking" size fish mounted. These are not the biggest necessarily but they are the ones that fit on my trophy wall.

My preference on fishing technique is based on my theory about the fish themselves. Fish have a singular purpose in life and that is for the survival of the species. To accomplish this purpose, the life of a fish is based on a relatively simple principal. They have to stay alive, eat and multiply. Fish as all animals are subject to the food chain cycle of life, the smallest ones are eaten by the bigger ones, the bigger ones are eaten by the huge ones and the huge ones are eaten in the restaurants and dining rooms of fishermen. The smallest of the fish are the baitfish that live in the lake. These fish usually form groups or schools that roam the lake feeding on algae and other microorganisms. They're called Plankton and usually grow to about one inch in length. The Plankton are food for the minnows. These are the various forms of Shad, Shiners and other small fish that grow to about two or three inches in length. These are the baitfish that the larger fish of all species thrive on. The usually live in schools for their own protection and are sought after by all of the bigger fish. As a lake matures, there are other forms of natural food that is provided by the lake's plant life that normally exists close to shore in the shallow waters and the bugs and insects that hatch on the bottom of the lake and rise to the surface.

So if you want to develop a strategy to catch fish on any lake you should always remember that nearly all of a fish's life is spent in search of food or eating. The obvious fishing plan would therefore be to have what the fish want on the end of your hook and to have that hook located where the fish are located. Seems simple and it is except that as a fisherman you have to be smart enough to know where to put the bait. On a good sized lake you could spend a considerable amount of time searching for the right spot. But may be you don't have to do that, let's think about that.

Every person that picks up a rod and reel has his or her own fishing style or will soon develop one. Not to over simplify this situation, I have placed all people who fish into four categories, which I will describe in detail.

I will try not to make light of any of the four types even though I have certain preferences. Let's first try to describe the two extremes of the fishing spectrum. We have all seen a cartoon depicting the old man lying on the bank with his hat over his eyes and his fishing line tied to his toe and the caption went something like, "There's nothing like a hard day of fishing."

To the other extreme there are probably people that have their $50,000 boat equipped with every conceivable type of electronic device to assist them, their boat rigged to handle 10 poles at one time with outriggers and automatic line retrievers and maybe even nets over the side awaiting the catch.

These are the two extremes of my list of the four categories of fresh water fishermen and fisherwomen. The categories are:

- The Shore Hugger

- Lazy Boater

- Fish Chaser

- Moving Target

I may use some humor in the descriptions of the four types described above but that is not meant to negate the benefits of any of these types of fishermen or fisherwomen or to suggest that one is better than the other. As I have said many times in many different ways in this book, fishing is an enjoyment sport and you should do it in whatever manner gives you the most enjoyment. There are of course benefits and drawbacks to each of the above types of fishing and I will attempt to point them out. There is also an experience factor associated with each type that needs to be understood to enhance your enjoyment of the fishing experience.

THE SHORE HUGGER

This is the beginner's course for fishing. We all had to learn to crawl before we walked and to walk before we could run. Being a conservative, cost conscious person I will always recommend that you start with this type fishing if you have no experience at all. What the title implies, Shore Huggers are people who want to try fishing without the outlay of a lot of money for a boat and expensive equipment. I was a Shore Hugger for more than ten years as a young man because that was the limit of my capability and it was the only type of fishing available to me. I was part of the "fork stick" crowd that threw in a line and propped my pole on a fork stick that I cut from a nearby bush or if I was lucky, used the stick left by the previous fisherman. I'll bet you that even today, if you were to walk around the shoreline of any fishing hole you will find evidence of the shore hugger having been there and a fork stick still popping up out of the ground.

If you remember anything of what you have read so far in this book you might have concluded that shore hugging is the best way to fish since much of the evidence provided indicates that the fish come into the shallow water to spawn and to feed, usually at night. If the fish come near the shore then why not fish from the shore. Take a look around any large body of water that hosts fishermen, you will see dozens of boats all types and complexities and where are they fishing? Along the shorelines, trolling the banks and shoals. You have to ask yourself therefore, why not just take my gear and bait and my favorite date and beverage throw into the same water to fish from the comfort of a lawn chair. No expense for a boat, you get the same suntan and maybe some of the same fish at far less expense. Seems to make sense doesn't it?

Shore hugging also includes fishing from docks and piers or sometimes sitting on a friend's boat that never leaves the dock. This type of fishing provides great enjoyment and for many, it is all that they ever need to enjoy the sport. The only equipment needed is a modest pole; I recommend a 6-foot pole with a spinning reel and a line test less than 10 pounds. The cost of all of these at most sporting goods stores will be less than $30.

Two techniques are most popular with shore huggers: the most popular is to rig your line with a small hook; small lead shot weight to keep the bait down and a bobber to control the depth of your bait. For certain types of fish like Carp or Catfish you can even eliminate the bobber and fish directly from the bottom.

Your bait can take many forms often depending on what you desire to catch. Despite the many millions of dollars spent each year on fancy baits and lures, the old garden worm or Night Crawler is still my favorite shore hugger bait. They are cheap or even free if you have the time and energy to catch them yourself and the worm seems to be the universal food that every type of fish likes. Worms are kind of like the "Pasta" of the underwater life. Shore hugging fish like Bream, Crappie, Perch and even Bass love worms and if there is one of these fish around, they will hit your worm with a passion. I have found a technique that seems to work well when shore hugging. When I arrive at the spot that I have picked, even if it is a dock, I cut up a couple of worms into pieces about ¼ inch long and throw them around the area that I intend to fish. This pulls in the fish and gives them an appetizer of things to come. I think worms work best if they are held off the bottom with a bobber and this also becomes an alarm for you when the fish are around your bait.

Live bait of all types is also reliable bait. Most shore huggers do not catch their own live bait because it is cheap enough and available at local stores. Live bait used for shore hugging should be hooked behind the dorsal fin, an area that has no vital organs and gives the live bait the longest life. This also allows the bait to swim in a limited manner to attract the other fish. Again keeping the bait off the bottom is a good bet but sometimes the bottom feeders such as Carp or Catfish will find the bait on the bottom. If you choose to let your bait settle to the bottom, make sure you make it move frequently to attract attention.

Since fish feed mostly on water borne life, you can use other forms of live bait such as Crickets, Grasshoppers and any bug that you can get to stay on your hook. If you catch the very small bream, they also make excellent bait for the large fish. Catfish as an example love to snatch a Bream that is having trouble swimming away. Whatever type of bait you use, it is always better to keep the bait alive. Fish will bite on dead bait but far less frequently than they will if the bait is alive and moving.

If you like to fish at night you might consider buying a portable halogen light and placing it close to the water. Bright lights at night attract the Plankton and other small baitfish and when they come close to shore for the light, the bigger fish will follow. Using a halogen light when fishing off of a dock or pier is easy and effective.

One bit of advice for shore huggers. If you are going to use the fork stick approach to hold your pole or if you use pole holders of other types, make sure that your pole is secure. Shore huggers are often distracted and leave their pole unattended. I have personally lost my gear to a large Catfish who decided to hit and run and not stop with my pole still attached to the bait because I didn't have it firmly in place. If I was a betting man I would bet that fish have some special kind of sense that tells them that the fisherman is distracted and that is the exact time that the big one hits. Sounds ridiculous doesn't it but if you fish long enough I know that you will join my club of believers.

Shore hugging is kind of the relaxed type of fishing. The excitement is watching your bobber as a signal of what is going one beneath the surface. The bobber has two functions, it keeps your bait at the desired depth and it is your alarm that a fish is interested. There is absolutely nothing wrong with bobber fishing and with all of my years of fishing I still run into situations where bobbers are my selected preference there are essentially three types of bobbers and dozens of versions of these three types. The first type is the type that you can firmly attach to your line at a specific point to control depth. When the weight takes the bait to the selected depth, it stops and the bobber holds the bait in place. Any fish activity will be reflected by bobber movement. If the bobber goes under and moves steadily, the fish has the bait in its mouth and it is moving. This is the time to set the hook and hopefully retrieve the fish.

The second type of bobber is the one that can permit the line to settle to the bottom as the bobber sits on the surface. This type of bobber is used primarily as a signal of fish activity. The same principal applies however, as the bobber begins to move erratically and goes under, it's time to hook and retrieve.

The third type of bobber isn't really different from the other two except that is contains a light for night fishing. It is used exactly the same way as the other two types but you have a nice bright visual signal to watch and I find it very exciting to see a lit bobber moving through the water as the fish hits the bait. Not to worry, studies show that the light does not bother the fish and to the contrary, there are many stories of fish actually coming up to grab the light. I once had a big Gar come to the surface and actually grab the light and hold on. I was able to bring the fish in but as soon as he saw the dock, he let go of the bobber and swam off into the moonlight.

There are advantages and disadvantages to shore hugging. The big advantage is that you don't have to make a very big investment to start fishing. There is no boat, motor or other complicated equipment involved. You can vary your fishing location and this is a very relaxing way to kick back and enjoy the fishing experience.

The disadvantage of shore hugging is obvious. You are limited to only the area that you can reach from your selected fishing spot. Your fishing area is limited to perhaps a hundred feet and you have to hope that the fish are in that limited area. The second disadvantage is that you are fishing in the shallower water and particularly in the warmer months you will be limited to the smaller fish that live in the warmer water. As the water warms in the summer the larger fish normally head for the deeper cooler water. Don't take this as a firm rule however, I have caught some very large fish from my dock but in most of these cases I was fishing at night when the bigger fish come to shore to feed.

Shore hugging is the best way to introduce young people to fishing. Small fish can be easily caught and with the short attention of most young people, that will keep their interest peeked. For beginners I recommend using a number 1 circle hook or smaller and do not use treble hooks for shore hugging. Circle hooks do not have to be set by jerking on the pole as the "big boys" do on TV. As the fish takes the bait the circle hook sets itself and all that is required is that you start the retrieve steadily without allowing slack line. If you have your pole firmly anchored, using a circle hook, the fish will hook itself and less skill is required except that you should keep your retrieval steady.

Shore hugging is also an effective technique to use for someone who has a fear of the water. You can make it a picnic event with the added attraction of catching a fish. I have found that no matter what their interest, most people get a real thrill from reeling in a good sized fish and that experience can hook them for life on the sport.

My granddaughter was eight years old. She came to my house on the lake many times but never showed any interest in fishing. She would rather do girl things with her grandmother as would be expected. Every once in a while she would get my live bait for me from the bait bucket but that was the limit of her interest. Then one day I gave her the pole to hold for me and just at that instant she hooked a Catfish and managed to get it in by herself. The excitement on her face was priceless. A week later I picked her up to bring her to our house and I suggested that she would want to hang out with her grandmother, she said "can't we go fishing today instead?" "I really like fishing." Well she really like "catching" but that's par for the course with young people but that's how we get them interested.

Where can you fish from the shore? This is a question that I have been asked many times by people that are new to the area and it is a difficult question to answer specifically. You must keep in mind that most waterfront property is privately owned weather or not it is developed. It is always necessary to get permission to fish on private property and you should always leave the area cleaner than you found it. You can however consider the following:

If you have a friend or acquaintance that owns waterfront property, ask them if you can use their dock facilities but make sure it is under their rules. Docks are great for fishing since they provide cover for the fish and easy access to deeper water.

Public launch areas and Parks are also available but these areas are normally busy in the summer months and not the best location for a quiet few hours of fishing. There are many areas within the state operated parks that will provide some quiet fishing areas and make for a nice picnic and fishing outing.

Marinas provide great fishing areas but again these are privately owned and permission should be obtained. Covered boat slips in the marinas are great for Bream and Crappie fishing but again the activity level during the summer months may be restrictive.

Private undeveloped areas are still available but again remember that someone owns this land and it should be respected. If open wooded undeveloped land has access and it is not posted against trespassing, this makes a nice shore fishing area. Never build fires or cut foliage on other peoples private property and again always leave an area cleaner than you found it.

"Shore Huggers" sometimes take advantage of all aspects of the fishing experience. The wind in your hair, the sun baking your body, a coffee at your feet and if you stay awake, two poles to watch for that "Big One". A great way to spend a Sunday morning. (after church of course)

THE LAZY BOATER TECHNIQUE

For simplicity let's call this the LB technique. This fishing style is usually an upgrade form the shore Hugger type since it requires a boat. LB fishing can produce a lot of fish and a very relaxing day but it normally requires more luck than skill to have a good day. LB's are fishermen who take their boat to their favorite area, throw out the anchor, put out a few rods, kickback in a comfortable seat and break open their favorite adult beverage. This setting itself defines a fine day and catching a few fish is simply a bonus. Don't get me wrong, LB fishing is very popular and can produce fine fishing, if you can find the right spot and there are not a few dozen other boaters that decide to use the same area for their enjoyment.

LB fishing does not require a fancy boat, to the contrary the bigger and fancier the boat, the less functional it will probably be for fishing. The best type of boat for this type of fishing is a simple open boat or skiff that is easy to move around in and has a wide enough beam for stability. I always recommend the addition of seats because a four-hour fishing trip can get very uncomfortable without a seat back. Pontoon boats have gained great popularity for LB fishing since they combine a great deal of space to move around and are very stable.

The equipment needed for LB fishing is nearly identical to the Shore Hugger requirements except that the addition of a net is advisable. Because LB fishing takes you out onto the water, you have the advantage of finding deeper water and therefore bigger fish. Catfish are readily caught using the LB technique but the catches are not limited to this species.

The first requirement for LB fishing is to determine the depth of the water. If this style is going to be your fishing technique for a long time, I recommend that you purchase a basic depth finder to assist in this task. It is always wise to understand the bottom area where you are fishing. If the bottom is uneven, has grassy areas, stumps or small brush piles, that is a good area to select. If you don't have any electronic devices to assist you, you can simply determine the depth by dropping a weighted line over the side and measuring the depth in that manner. Why is the depth important? Well you want to put out several lines, at least three or four and they should all be at different depths at least initially. If you start getting action at a specific depth you can adjust the other lines to that depth. Your depth control is achieved by the use of bobbers as previously discussed. The bobber is your control mechanism and also your alarm for monitoring the poles.

If you use multiple poles you will of course require pole holders for each pole. If you are going to fish for any length of time you will require pole holders. I recommend a four pole configuration where one pole is set to permit the bait to rest on or near the bottom. The second pole should hold the bait one to two feet off the bottom. The third pole should be in the middle of the water column (half way between the surface and the bottom) and the fourth pole should be set very close to the surface.

If you start getting bites at a particular depth, then set the remaining poles at that depth. If you have the luxury of a depth finder or fish finder, set the depth of at least one pole just below the depth of the baitfish since most game fish will strike from below. (Specifics of depth finder use is described in detail elsewhere in this book.)

LB equipment is not critical except for the hooks used. I recommend spinning rods. 6 or 7 foot medium rods with 10 pound test line are normally fine for LB fishing. Since the rods will be firmly anchored by the rod holders, a circle hook is recommended for LB fishing. The circle hook with permit the fish to hook itself and this is especially important when you get multiple hits at the same time which will happen frequently. You can land one fish while the other holds firm waiting for your retrieval.

The reason I recommend spinning rods for LB fishing is that they are easy to use and you can get the lines out a considerable distance from the boat to cover more water area increasing your changes for a catch. Any other type of rod is fine if you learn how to use it. Casting rods are fine but they normally require that you get some practice using them or you will spend valuable fishing time undoing line snags and back lashes.

The nice part of LB fishing is that you have the entire lake surface to choose your fishing area from and you don't have to ask any one for permission. Unfortunately, you do have to be concerned about other boats and other water craft and it is common for you to be more concerned about them than they are about you. I find that many people lose all sense of reason and common sense when they take control of a high speed boat or personal watercraft. It's unfortunate but it is a fact that you will have to live with as a LB fisherman.

Depending on the type of boat that you sue, LB fishing can be a fine family activity. Those that do not want to fish can still enjoy a day on the water but we do not recommend swimming off the boat when others are trying to fish or conversely we do not recommend fishing when others are trying to swim. It simply is a function of who is in command of the days activities.

LB fishing permits you to try an assortment of baits and fishing techniques. While your rods are in the water and set in their holders, you can practice your casting technique and try different casting lures and baits. I prefer live bait for LB fishing and you can vary the bait on each pole to again investigate the best bait for that day. Worms are sometimes good on or near the bottom. Minnows or other live bait are good at all depths. If you are in an area where catfish are located you can use almost anything that is eatable and has an odor to catch the cats but be sure that the bait used will stay on the hook. If the fish seem to be near the surface, casting for them with surface bait or lures is preferred by requires a little skill and care especially if others are on the boat with you.

LB fishing if often call "Still Fishing" because you are sitting still in the water. Some fishermen use a variation of this technique by tying their anchor so that it is just off the bottom. This permits the boat to drift slowly covering more water area. This technique is fine but requires that you adjust your pole location to prevent line tangle.

As we have discussed in another area of this book, don't prolong a bad thing. If you have chosen an area where there are no fish, don't stay there for more than 30 to 45 minutes without altering your technique. Try different bait or different depths and if you cannot get any improvement, move to another location. Sometimes moving a few hundred feet to another location will change your results completely.

I have to mention another fishing technique used successfully by some LB fishermen who really use this fishing method to give them a restful day or night of fishing. I have found that on a quiet warm sunny day with little lake activity, it is sometimes hard to keep the eyes open especially if the fishing is slow. There is a night fishing technique that you can add to your daytime LB technique that permits you to hook bells or electric alarms to the end of your poles. Should you kick back too far and fall asleep, the alarms or bells will alert you when a fish has taken your bait. You can check your local fishing supply store for these devices.

There is another recommendation that I like to make to those who select the LB style of fishing and it involves the location that you select. We have discussed locating fishing areas in other areas of this book but if you are going to fix your fishing position, I recommend finding an area where you can anchor about 100 feet from a shoreline that has a brush line, a rocky shoreline or even some form of shore structure. You probably don't want to anchor close to someone's dock but there are many dock structures that may be abandoned. This type of a location will permit you to cast a lure toward the shoreline where fish may be feeding and increase your chances of a catch. It also permits you to practice your casting techniques getting you ready to graduate to the next level and the third type of fishing called "Fish Chasing."

THE FISH CHASER

I have to be a little careful when describing the Fish Chaser so as not to offend the Pro's who make their living fishing. Most professional fisherman would consider themselves Fish Chasers by my definition since they spend a good deal of time traveling around the lake in a competitive pursuit of the big fish. Right up front let me excuse the professional fishermen from falling into this category. They do not. Fishing in competition for the big bucks requires certain techniques that we amateurs cannot and should not criticize.

Putting the pro's aside, the Fish Chaser type fisherman is the guy who has a boat with no less than 150 horsepower on the back. His sleek smooth craft can travel the waters at speeds exceeding 50 mph. In the course of a day he will cover a great portion of the waters that he is fishing, constantly in search of those signs that the big fish are in the area. He will change bait often and use several different poles and lures during a days fishing. His boat has a live well for the fish that he catches and most Fish Chasers keep the fish that they catch to bring home and eat.

The Fish Chasers boat contains a fishing box with no less than 100 different lures, five or six different line types, at least two distinctly different types of poles, a half dozen pole holders bolted to the boat, at least one large net and he is equipped at any given time to fish for any and all types of fish with almost all types of bait and lures.

The Fish Chaser is normally a caster, using either spinning rods or casting rods. He is usually proficient at casting and can cast repeatedly into a 2 ft circle from 50 feet away. On any given day he will try surface lures, jerk bait, plastics, live bait, crank bait and a variety of other lures. He can put his boat into an area hardly large enough for a duck to swim and still have enough space to cast his bait. He looks like he is on a mission and rarely sits still except when he is driving the boat. He usually spends no more than fifteen or twenty minutes in any single spot and if no fish are caught, he moves on at a great neck speed to his next destination.

The Fish Chaser almost always has a top of the line sonar and probably a GPS for his long distance journeys and his GPS map if cluttered with the way point markers that show where he has caught fish in the past. On a given day the Fish Chaser is not content with anything less than his limit of the species that he is after but as most fishermen, he is often disappointed. He carries an anchor but rarely uses it and almost all Fish Chasers can launch or retrieve their boat to its trailer in less than five minutes. Three minutes in the rain.

Fish Chasers have the benefit of being able to try any type of fishing at all times. They will troll, still fish, cast the banks, drift in the wind or tie to a tree limb and fish the bushes along the shore line.

Bass fishermen and Crappie fishermen are almost always Fish Chasers. They have fished areas before and know where they are most likely to catch fish on any given day. They always have a detailed map on board and it is well used since they put many miles on their boat on any given day.

I may have made the Fish Chaser sound like a bad guy but he is certainly not. On most bodies of water the Fish Chaser represents the majority of the fishermen. It is probably safe to say that the Fish Chaser has many years of experience fishing and he probably catches a lot of fish.

There are two negative issues that bother me about the Fish Chaser. First, they hardly ever will tell you where they caught the fish and if they do you probably can't take that information seriously. They have spent a lot of time and gas searching for the good spots and they aren't going to share that valuable information with you. That certainly is their right.

The second negative that I have with the Fish Chaser is that there are a few among them who have little respect for other fishermen. There have been many occasions when I have been slowly pursuing a group of birds working a school of Stripers and a Fish Chaser will come with his 150 Hp full throttle right into the center of the birds and right into the center of the Striper school. Then he gets that disappointed look on his face when the birds suddenly fly away and there are no fish around because he has driven them to the bottom. Although this type is rare among good fishermen, they can ruin your day.

I believe that the majority of lake fishermen are Fish Chasers and most of them are real good fishermen. They have invested a lot of money in their boat and gear and they are serious about the sport of fishing. They take pride in their boat and normally take better care of the boat than they do their car or truck. Their equipment is good and they have respect for the fish in the water and treat them accordingly. Every Fish Chaser owns a real good set of rain gear since they fish in all kinds of weather and most of their boats have no cover to shield them from the elements. Fish Chasers generally know the law and obey it, they know the fish limits and they adhere to them, they know the waters that they fish and they have their favorite spots. They will take only their closets friends fishing with them and they will be on the water ready to fish before sunrise. Fish Chasers have weathered skin from sun and wind, chafed hands from the cold water, cut fingers from the fish they have caught and nearly every fish Chaser has had a hook driven deep into his flesh at least once in his or her life.

To become a professional fisherman, you first have to pass through the Fish Chaser category. To be a good Fish Chaser you have to know how to read the water your in, how to interpret the maps available to you, how to find and fish the good banks and shoals. You have to know when to move on and you need to possess the patience and understanding not to get upset when someone else is fishing your selected areas.

I am not a Fish Chaser although I have fished as one on occasion. My reasoning is as follows: Let's examine the fishing types that we have discussed so far. The Shore Hugger fishes an area of perhaps 500 square feet from one spot. The Lazy Boater fisherman covers maybe 5000 square feet in a few hours. The fish Chaser if he stops to fish 20 times in a day has his bait in the water to cover maybe 20,000 square feet in a day. I am the "Moving Target" or the "Troller" and I have my bait in the water about 90% of the time that I am on the lake. If my average trolling speed is 1 mile per hour and I fish for 6 hours with four poles covering a span of 15 feet, I am covering 475,200 square feet of water with my bait in the water trying to catch fish. Of the four types of fishermen described who has the greatest chance of catching fish? It's simple math to me so let's look at the fourth type of fisherman, the "Moving Target."

THE MOVING TARGET

For sake of simplicity let's call the moving target fisherman the MT type. MT fishermen of course have a boat, maybe two, that they use almost exclusively for fishing. Why the exclusivity? Well if you outfit your boat so that it is efficient for fishing on the move, you will probably ruin the capability of the boat for purely pleasure events. There are of course exceptions and these exceptions occur mostly on pontoon type boats which can be used for both MT fishing and relaxation.

The outfitting of your boat for MT fishing is more important than for other types of fishing because when you are fishing you are always moving, usually by the power of a trolling motor and when you are moving you already are performing one important function, running the boat. During the summer months and during windy conditions, this function becomes your most important function because it often involves safety. The safety and courtesy requirements for piloting your boat can never be relegated to a position less than the most important one on your craft. It's easy to forget this if you are in the middle of a large school of game fish and getting multiple hits and you don't have a fishing partner. The tendency under this condition would be to forget the boat and attend to retrieving the fish. This would be a mistake. If you are the kind of a person that cannot handle multitasking, then you probably should not consider MT fishing.

As we stated at the conclusion of the last section, MT fishing is the method used to cover the most water area in a given time period. It is also the method that keeps your bait in the water for a high percentage of the time that you are on the water. Both of these factors should result in a higher probability of catching fish.

MT fishing normally permits you to troll your favorite area with at least four rods in the water at one time. With the use of a simple device called a "Planner Board" you can increase this to 6 rods in the water at once but this requires some experience and is not recommended for the beginners. We will discuss Planner Board use later in this section.

The way you rig your boat for MT fishing is key to your enjoyment of this method. First and foremost you need to have constant access to your method of control whether it be your main motor or your trolling motor. The best control position will dictate the location of your pole holder mountings because you want to have control of the boat and be able to see all of your poles at the same time. This normally indicates that all of your pole holders will be at the back of the boat. You can use front mounted holders but these are normally limited to situations when you have more than one fisherman aboard.

Normally it is wise to have a spread of at least four feet between the lines. This does not mean that the pole holders need to be mounted four feet apart because you have the length of the poles on the side facing poles to consider. Most boats are wide enough to accommodate two rear facing pole holders and two side facing holders. With pole lengths of about 6 or 7 feet this will provide adequate spacing for the lines. The illustration below shows a typical layout for a 6-pole location set up.

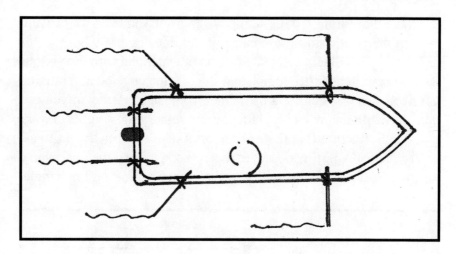

The main consideration for the MT fisherman that makes this technique desirable is the ability to cover very large water areas and fish over the complete extent of the water column. This means having the largest number of poles in the water at one time that you can properly control and have your bait at several different depths at least until you find the depth where the fish seem to be concentrated. Once you determine the proper depth for good fishing, you can adjust the depth of your bait to maximize your catch chances. Keep in mind, the more lines you have at the same depth, the higher your chances of getting a line tangled and those tangles can result in a great deal of time spent doing things other than productive fishing.

Since your boat is going to be moving at some speed and that speed will be constant for all of your poles, the only way to get the bait to different depths is to use weight or weighted line. Weighted lines or leaded lines should be left for the very experienced fisherman and we will not discuss them in depth here.

Using the illustration below consider how you should set your weights to achieve proper depth if you don't know where the fish are. The forward most poles should contain the heaviest weight so they will be the closest to the bottom. As you move the poles further back they should have slightly less weight. The rear facing poles can have very light weights attached or even be used with no weight at all which is called "flat lining." This set up will permit you to move forward or turn the boat with little chance of the lines tangling. Using this technique you will cover a wide section of water and with the various depths you will have the complete water column covered maximizing your chances of catching a fish. Once you catch a few fish you can note the depth that works best for you and re-rig your weights to work that depth. It's rare that there is an exact depth that is the only one where the fish will hit so I never recommend having the exact same weight on all poles because this will almost guarantee a line tangle.

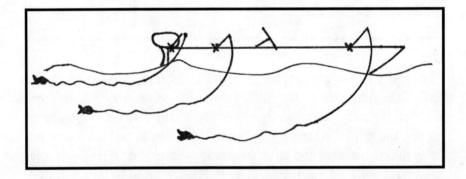

Talk to almost any experienced fisherman and each one will tell you his different method of rigging your lines but there is one fairly common technique that many fishermen use that make the MT type fisherman more effective. This is illustrated below and is often called the Carolina Rig.

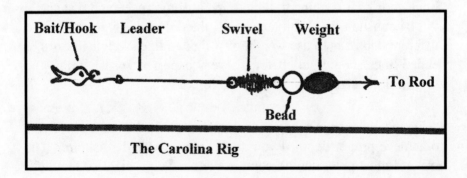

The Carolina Rig

The weight can take many forms depending on your preference. Many fishermen use simple lead shot so that they can easily change it by adding or subtracting additional shot. I prefer the symmetrical lead weights that are strung through the middle. I believe that this permits the smoother flow through the water without creating water disturbance. The bead has a critical function in this set up, it provides a smooth no-friction connection between the weight and the swivel to permit the swivel to work as it was designed to do and also functions to protect the knot. The swivel itself is also an important part of this set up. Some lures that you might use will spin in the water and it is necessary to keep this spinning from twisting the line, this is the function of the swivel. Even with live bait or lures that do not spin, your line will twist as you continue to troll over long period of time.

The leader can be almost any monofilament type line. I prefer the Fluorocarbon type leaders and normally use one of about 10 pound test. The leader should be about three feet long but that length will vary with the preference of different fishermen or will vary with different fish that are being sought. For the hook I generally recommend a circle hook but there are many other choices that are available. The important things with the hook is not to get one that is too big and make sure that the hook is always sharp and properly shaped. I have discussed the hook care in another section of this book.

Some fishermen feel that the color of the bead is also very important. I typically use red beads since I have been told that red is the least visible color under water. I personally do not believe that the bead color has any effect at all on your ability to catch fish.

There is however another important function of this bead and a bright color makes this function more effective. I use the bead to tell me when the fish is nearing the surface in a retrieve. If the water is murky or not clear, the bead will let you know that the fish is about three feet from the top and that is the time to reach for the net. Of course, the weight or the swivel will also tell you this but the bright colored bead is much easier to see.

I will demonstrate later in this book, the importance of using depth finding equipment to locate the fish. Knowing the approximate depth of the fish makes it critical that we know the depth of our rig and also how to vary that depth since we always want to keep the bait slightly above the fish.

I have done considerable testing with my boats and trolling motors to determine which weights will drop to what depths for various speeds and cast distances. The chart below shows some of the results of that testing but keep in mind that these figures will vary some for different lures and different weight live bait. The tests that formed this data were performed without bait attached but weight was used to duplicate the weight of the bait.

	Boat Speed			
Weight	**1 mph**	**.8 mph**	**.6 mph**	**.4 mph**
1/8 oz.	4	6	7	9
1/4 oz.	6	10	12	14
3/8 oz.	10	15	18	20
1/2 oz.	14	16	20	22
5/8 oz.	16	17	22	25
3/4 oz.	17	19	25	27
1 oz.	19	24	30	32
Controlling The Bait Depth				

There are many factors that may change these figures including the accuracy of the speed measuring equipment, bait or lure weight, line type and weight, cast distance etc. This data was collected for a cast distance or the distance that the bait rests from the boat, of 50 feet. The numbers shown in the boxes are depth of the bait in feet and the line used was 15 pound test monofilament.

It is not intended that you use the data presented here as a guide for your fishing, but only to illustrate that there are factors that you must attend to when deciding on your equipment setup. If you have your own boat and trolling equipment, it is worth a couple of hours of your time to develop data such as this which will save you a great deal of time determining how best to bring in the largest catch.

I selected the MT technique for most of my fishing experiences for several reasons. The largest single advantage of this type of fishing is that you spend the greatest amount of time with bait in the water. When your bait is in the water you also increase your chances of a catch by covering the greatest amount of lake area in a given time period. Selecting this technique however is really only important for purposes of your boat setup because once having completed a setup for trolling, you always have the option to use the same boat and equipment for any of the other type of fishing techniques.

Since I have tried to give both sides of every situation I should do the same thing here. There are some down sides of MT fishing. The primary one is that this technique requires constant control of the boat therefore you don't get a lot of rest time when MT fishing, especially when the wind is blowing and boat navigation is your primary concern.

I have mentioned at least once before in this book that fish seem to have a sense that is rarely discussed and that is the ability to know how to hit your line when you are pre-occupied with other duties. In a mild wind of 5 knots or less, I have had my boat to a 90 degree turn in a matter of seconds when I was reaching into my cooler for a drink, or I was attending to a fish hit leaving the motor control to chance. This is the greatest way to have a line catastrophe that could loose you a lot of fishing time and fishing line not to mention one or more nice fish.

On a good fishing day with 4 lines in the water it is not unusual to get what we call double headers or even triple headers meaning that two or three lines are hit at the same time. I have also experienced "quads" where I had four fish on at the same time. After a few panic retrieves I learned a few things about this type of situation. First by using circle hooks as I do almost exclusively, the fish will hook itself when trolling so it is not necessary to have three or four sets of hands to set the hooks. Secondly when a fish hits, I have learned that stopping the trolling motor is a serious mistake, conversely I normally with actually increase the speed when I get multiple hits. This keeps the lines out and gives you a degree of control over the fish. What a fish does when it is hooked is not always predictable so keeping the lines tight by moving straight ahead at a good speed will prevent the fish crossing the liens.

When I have multiple hits at the same time, I always retrieve the outside fish first or the fish that is on the outermost line. This gives me more room for a retrieve since I only have another line on one side of my retrieve. Bass will normally retrieve straight in and they will normally come to the top soon after being hooked. Stripers on the other hand head down and sideways, Perch will come straight in and Catfish will normally head down, come in straight and roll as they are retrieved. In any of these situations, retrieving the outside lines first increases your chances of boating the fish without tangling with the other lines. Subsequent retrieves for multiple hit then simply take the inside line next. If you were to stop the motor when you hook a fish you only send the un-hit lines to the bottom where they will almost certainly get tangled.

The other aspect of a multiple hit is your netting technique. Most of us carry only one net. When I am Striper fishing I carry two because it is not unusual to have multiple hits with Stripers. I do not like to keep the fish out of the water for long periods of time and letting the fish bang around on the floor of the boat while you retrieve another fish creates unnecessary trauma for the fish that it may not be able to survive. Keeping the fish in the net buys some time without causing excess damage to the fish.

Turning when you are retrieving is also dangerous in terms of line tangles. It is sometimes not possible to avoid a turn when retrieving so remember that the line that is on the inside of the turn will settle furthest down into the water because it is moving slowest. If you happen to get a hit on a turn, retrieve the inside fish first to gain the maximum control of the retrieve.

USING PLANER BOARDS

As I have pointed out, one of the advantages of using the MT technique of fishing is that it permits you the opportunity to cover a wide area of water, perhaps 16 feet wide for an average width boat. Some fishermen want more area coverage in order to further increase their chances of a catch. To do this they use "Planer Boards."

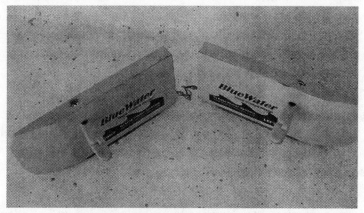

Left and Right Side Planer Boards

Planer boards are devices that permit you to extend the width of your water area coverage by a factor of two or even three in some instances. The Planer Board with its design shape acts as a rudder. When the boat is moving this rudder is biased in one direction for the left Planer and in the opposite direction for the right Planer. The biased shape of the front rudder pulls the Planer out to its designed direction and holds the line there until retrieved. You the fisherman decide how far out you want the Planer to hold and also the depth that you want the bait to achieve. The depth of the bait is determined in the same manner as a standard troll, by the weight attached to your line and how far you permit the line to play out before you attach the Board. Once the board is attached, you simply continue to play out line until the Planer Board reaches the distance out from the boat that you desire. At that point you simply put the pole into its holder and let the Planer Board do the work.

The line is attached to the Planer Board at two points. The rear of the Board contains a clip that simply clips over the line to let it play out freely through the clip. The front of the Board contains a friction clip that holds the line firmly into place at whatever point you choose. You begin by feeding your line out to the point that represents how far you want the bait from the board; this could be 30, 40 feet or more. At this point you stop letting out line and attach the board by the friction clip then you continue to play the line out. When the board is where you want it you stop feeding and set the pole in its holder. When a fish hits the line that is on the Planer Board, the friction clip releases the line, the Board rides back toward the fish and you can make your retrieve without the full pull of the Board.

Planers can be any color. They are usually yellow to give you the best visibility. It is important for you to know where the Planer Board is located and in crowded waters it is more important that other boats can see it so as not to cut your trolling path.

Planer Boards are always marked to indicate the left and right Board. Left means you use that Board on the left side of the boat facing forward. If you use worn boards where the markings are removed, it is possible to determine the correct side.

The Planer Board normally has some weighted element on its bottom side. If you stand the Board on the weighted side with the pointed end facing forward and the clip facing into the boat, the will be the correct side for that board. If for some reason you have two boards that come out telling you that they should both be on the same side, you do not have a set of matched Boards.

I use Planer Boards only when I have a desire to catch a larger number offish. It is also an advantage when I am trolling in deep water and want to have at least one line near the shoreline, the Planer Board will accomplish that for me. Tournament fishermen will often use Planer boards to increase their chances of catching additional fish. Since the Planer Boards come in several sizes, they do place extra stress on the pole. Light spinning rods are not acceptable for Planer Boards and it is advisable to use a stiffer pole than you usually use and a non spinning reel. The drag on your reel is normally set fairly high since the Board itself creates significant drag on the line.

The depth that you want the Board bait to reach is your decision and should be made consistent with where the remaining lines are set. The most common use of Boards is for trolling the "flat lines" or the lines with the least weight but that is not a firm rule.

My personal preference is not to use a Planer Board but that is simply because I normally use the lightest pole that I feel will handle the fish that I am after. I like to feel every bit of the fish and lighter gear permits that. I feel that the presents of the Planer Board ads weight and bulk that takes away from the feel of the fish. Despite my personal feelings Planer Boards are in very wide use among many types of fishermen.

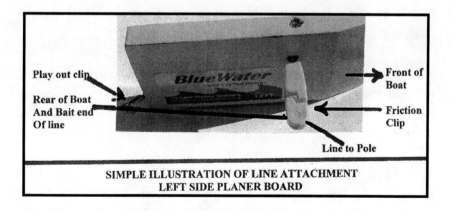

SIMPLE ILLUSTRATION OF LINE ATTACHMENT
LEFT SIDE PLANER BOARD

DON'T PROLONG A BAD TECHNIQUE

Any time that you can spend fishing is very valuable time in your life so it is important that this time not be wasted. I have often been guilty of "stubborn fishing" where I go out determined to use a particular technique and hours later when that technique has not produced I have been hesitant to change it. Well, that's simple foolishness. As we have indicated several places in this book, there are many factors that effect when and how fish are caught and if a particular technique that you are using is not working, you must change it to increase your chances of success. It isn't always a major change that will produce different results. Sometimes simply changing the depth at which you are fishing will change the results. If you are trolling, a slight change in your trolling speed may help. If you are bait casting, a different lure may help. Sometimes it can be a simple change in the way the bait hits the water than will change results or even a simple change is the color of the lure.

I have had days when I just knew that trolling at 15 feet depth would produce results and despite that fact that it didn't, I kept trying for hours. That was when I was young and foolish and I didn't realize that I would never recover those lost hours. Today things are different. After studying fish habits and lake changes and weather effects for many years, I now never spend more than an hour holding to a specific fishing technique. After an hour I change the depth that I am fishing at, that is the easiest thing to vary and it is also the thing that most often changes the result.

My second most popular change is to change my trolling speed, which also usually changes the depth at which I am fishing. Changing the speed effects not only speed but depth and it is very easy to accomplish.

Third in popularity on my changes list is to change the bait that I am using. Most of the time I am using live bait so this is the most difficult thing to change since I don't often carry different types of live bait on the boat. Sometimes just taking off a weak or near dead live bait and putting on a fresh one does the job.

If I am bait casting, I always have a couple of different poles ready with different bait so that I don't waste time re-tying lures. There was a time in my fishing life when I used swivels and clips for quick lure changes but I later realized that lures are designed by people that have given the action of the lure a great deal of thought and by using a swivel and clip I was changing the design action of the lure. Even if I am in a situation where I only have one pole available, I consider it worth the time to re-tie the lure rather than use a quick change technique.

Today with the electronics that are available to most fishermen some of the guess work I taken out of the change game. Sonar and fish finders can tell us the depth of the baitfish and therefore the fish we are after. This takes some but not all of the guess work out of that decision. Since most fish feed upwards, I always try to fish just below where the baitfish are so as to get a better shot at the fish's strike range.

I am also mindful of the fact that my sonar is only seeing a very small area beneath the boat and I could be fooled by that information.

There is another aspect of technique change that is work discussing and that involves fish that are biting but can't seem to be caught. If fish are hitting but not hooking, there has to be a reason. Most often I have found that the wrong hook size, a dull hook, or a bent hook is the cause. Just the other day I was trolling for Stripers and I hooked a large 8-pound fish and after an unusually hard fight I got the Striper into the boat. After releasing the fish I immediately put on another live bait and cast it out. I almost immediately caught a vision of the circle hook that I was using and felt that it was straightened out by the previous catch so I retrieved that cast and examined the hook. The hook had indeed been bent but anxious to get the bait back into the water I grabbed the pliers and re-shaped the hook and recast the line. Several minutes later I got a blast of a hit on the same pole almost taking the rod out of its holder but before I could grab the pole the fish was gone but I knew it was even bigger than the previous fish. When I got the line in, the bait was still attached but very scraped and nearly dead. One look at the hook told me exactly what had happened. I was using a circle hook that when new is precisely designed with a certain twist that digs onto the fish as soon he hits the bait. When I re bent the hook after the previous fish, I bent it at a bad angle and it was impossible for the hook to work so the bait simply slipped out of the Stripers mouth without giving the hook a chance to do its job. The fish never felt the hook. Had I taken the few minutes that was required to change the hook when I realized that it was bent, I would have had a second big Striper and a more successful day. Another lesson learned. It also proves that no matter how long you have been fishing, you can still be tempted to make stupid mistakes.

Examining your hook seems so simple but it's something that we usually don't do as a matter of habit. Hooks get dull from use and they get bent from snags. Whenever you have a bottom snag or you have been using a hook for a long period of time, check it for shape and sharpness and if you have any doubts, put on a new hook, the time will be well spent. When in doubt, throw the old hook away. The cost of a new hook is small relative to the disappointment of losing a nice fish.

YOUR FISHING MOOD

Have you ever been watching your favorite football team play and they start making mistakes? They play just fine until the first mistake is made. Then it seems that more mistakes follow hence the term "mistakes breed more mistakes." The frame of mind that you're in while fishing has a bigger effect than you might think on the results of your fishing day. I have taken people out fishing and they often say that they are the jinx and every time they fish the boat gets skunked. This is often just a subconscious excuse before the fishing starts in case they lose a fish or two. How about the golfer that joins his foursome and reminds the other players immediately that he has not played in a year and hopes that they are patient with him. Again another excuse for potential failure.

I can't remember a time that I went fishing that my attitude was not positive and I was convinced that I was going to catch the first fish and the biggest fish and the highest number of fish. My frame of mind was positive and my reactions followed.

Mood is important because it influences your reactions. If you are not calm, you will not act calm. Your casting will be less accurate, your bait placement will be less accurate, your retrieves will be less considerate of the others in the boat and I'll be that you will have at least one line tangle of great magnitude before the day is over. When your mood is not generally calm, you probably won't finish each retrieve properly or you will try to set the hook before it is time, or you will crank away and not let your pole, reel and drag do its magic. Maybe you won't have patience to wait for the net man to get to you and you'll try to jerk the fish into the boat. All of these actions will cause you to lose fish on a repeated basis. During the colder months, fishing slow is the secret of catching many types of fish. If you are impatient, your fishing will be too fast for a good fish reaction.

When you start your fishing day, were you too impatient to do a quick line pull to insure that the line and swivels and hook or bait is securely fastened? Did you give your hook a quick inspection to make sure that it was still sharp or if it was dull, were you too much in a hurry to take the time to put on new equipment? Or perhaps you were too much in a hurry to check the drag on every real. The drag of the real is vitally important for making a good catch if you have your line strength properly selected for the fish that you are after. I've seen fishermen smash their gear to the boat floor or even throw it overboard when they lost a nice fish. They were not in the right frame of mind to be fishing that day.

So if you have had a bad day, adjust your mood before you get on to the boat. Place yourself in a positive frame of mind and if you make a mistake, which we all have, try to understand what you did wrong so the mistake will not happen again. You'll find fishing much more enjoyable if you do this.

THE RIGHT EQUIPMENT
WITHOUT GOING BROKE

This is not the last section of this book but it was one of the last chapters that I wrote because I knew that it was going to be the most difficult chapter to write. Why you ask would it be so difficult? Well! Do you remember the last time that you were in one of the many sporting Super Stores? If you are anything like I am you were probably amazed and confused at the selections that you had for everything that you wanted to buy. There were hundreds of rods and reels, thousands of different types and colors of baits and lures, scores of different hooks and different hook colors and an entire wall loaded with any kind of fishing line that you could imagine. I would guess that if you had a simple catalog listing of all of the products stocked in one of these stores, you would have a document two or three times larger than this entire book. So I ask, how can I possibly instruct you on which of these thousands of products you should buy?

Like several other subjects in this book I decided to take the simple and easy route through this maze of possibilities. First I decided that I would try not to mention one single brand name while describing a product. This would minimize my legal problems and keep me from pointing you in any specific direction. Secondly, I would try to keep the learning process simple by dealing only with the basics and staying away from attempting to cover every type of fish and every possible situation that you might find yourself in. Thirdly as in other areas of this book, I would lean in the direction of the equipment that I personally have used and favor for the type of fishing that I have done. Lastly I decided that the best way to get into the subject of equipment was to go back and remind the reader of what the objective is here and how it can best be achieved.

Earlier in this book I indicated that the challenge of catching fish is to first find them (which we have discussed in detail) and then present the fish with a food choice that is better than other choices that the fish has. This latter challenge is what equipment selection is all about and if we try to make it more than that, things will get real complicated. When thinking about fishing equipment you have to first understand what type of fish you are after and try to match your equipment to that type of fish.

I have gone through several distinctly different chapters in my personal life that exposed me to very different types of fishing and therefore widely different equipment needs. When I started fishing as a kid, I fished in a small pond stocked mainly with trout, carp and bream. I grew up understanding what I needed to catch these types of fish. Later in life I moved to an area nearly surrounded by ocean and changed my fishing habits to salt water fishing which required that I get all new fishing equipment. This stuff was heavy and stiff and designed to haul big fish up from deep water as quickly as possible.

Then at a later date I moved back inland and again started fresh water lake fishing. All of the heavy stiff equipment was now discarded and a completely new outfit was required. I was back fishing for the fresh water fish some of which I had sought as a kid, BUT the equipment was now completely different. It was made from different materials that were now available and not even discovered many years earlier. Instead on one or two hook types I was faced with hundreds of different hook types. This set me back a bit until I sat back and thought about it a while and I decided to try and understand what had really changed through the years. The water makeup was the same, a combination of Hydrogen and Oxygen. The fish were biologically the same, no change there. Only the technology had changed with new materials available for lighter and stronger equipment and of course, the market had changed. New people had more money to spend on their leisure hobbies like fishing and of course the manufacturers of the new equipment had bundles of money to spend telling us why we needed their new product to catch bigger and better fish.

OK, I said but the basic science is exactly the same, we still have to get some good looking food in front of the fish that will make it want to bit on our bait rather than the next guys. It didn't take me long to realize that the task of fishing equipment is to get the bait to the fish under whatever conditions prevail and to help me hook and retrieve the fish when that process succeeded. Now I had reduced the equipment selection process to its simplest terms. I only have to decide what type of fish I am after and which gear is best suited for that task.

As in all other areas of this book I am excluding fly fishing equipment from this section. Let's start with the first and most basic piece of fishing equipment, the Reel. There may be hundreds of different brands and styles of fishing reels but thee are basically only three types, the spin casting reel, the spinning reel and the bait casting reel.

The spin casting reel shown below is considered the most basic type of fishing reel and is almost always used by the beginner fishermen or woman. There are many fishermen today however who have never graduated beyond this easy to use reel. The spin casting reel has a stationary spool, with the line leaving and returning at one end of that spool. The spool is enclosed so that you cannot see it. The line is released by the use of a thumb button on the back of the reel. The ease of the release using this button is what makes this reel a popular one for starter fishermen.

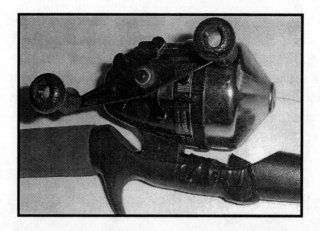

The spinning reel shown below is among the most popular reels because it is relatively easy to get a long cast with a light lure with this reel. This type reel is also relatively inexpensive. To cast with this reel you open the bail and hold the line with your index finger. The line is released as you move the rod forward during the cast.

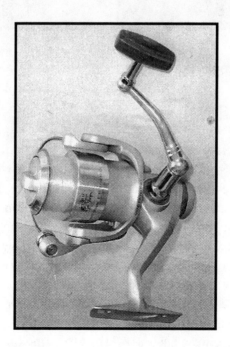

Bait casting reels shown below differ from the other two types because the spool sits crossways to the rod rather than parallel to it.

The spool revolves as the line is cast out. This type of reel requires some practice and is definitely the more difficult of the reels to use for casting. There are many different styles of this reel. The one shown on the left below is a low profile reel that is used when short distance casting and flipping. The reel on the right can also be used for casting but requires more practice. This type reel is most popular for trolling for heavier fish.

Although the proper use of bait casting reels requires practice, once mastered this reel permits very accurate line control when fishing or playing the fish on a retrieve.

If you are a starting fisherman or teaching your child to fish for the first time, you are of course interested in more than the reel and you will not purchase the reel separately but most likely will buy a rod and reel already matched to each other. Only when you become a truly skilled fisherman will you start buying your rods and reels separately and at that time you may find yourself spending big bucks for your equipment. I always recommend that the rod and reel be purchased as a set, already put together by the manufacturer. A rod and spin casting reel for a beginner child or adult can be purchased for less than $20 at almost any fishing supply store and these "package deals" are very adequate for a successful start to a fine fishing experience. My wife, although not a skilled fisherperson, has been fishing for several years and uses only her favorite spin casting rod and reel. For a beginner adult going well into the intermediate stages of fishing, a good spinning reel and rod combination can be purchased for under $40 and I do not recommend that much more than that every be spent for a combination unless you are well into the advanced stages of fishing. A fine casting reel and rod can be purchased for under $50.

I am going to get much deeper into the equipment selection process but at this point I think it is appropriate that I spend a little time talking about my personal opinion about purchasing expensive fishing equipment. My philosophy is very very simple, don't spend a lot of money of expensive equipment unless you are planning to turn professional or you are moving into the advanced fishing stages.

When I bought my first deer hunting rifle more than 50 years ago, I paid a lot of money for it because I knew that I would be using it for many years to come. It has proven to be a good weapon for me and I have never purchased another rifle to replace it. I'm glad I spent the money. Fishing equipment however is different. I have been fishing for more than 60 years. In that time I have broken several rods, had reels rust on me, dropped rod and reel overboard and had big fish pull the rod and reel from my grasp. I have never lamented this king of loss because my purchasing strategy is simple, I never spend more then $40 for a rod and reel combination. I also don't spend a lot of time taking care of my equipment because I would rather spend that time on the water fishing. If I can get one season out of a $40 rod and reel combination, I am satisfied with that and I am willing to throw it away after that one season. So if I lose one set of gear as described above, it doesn't ruin my day, I simply replace it with another inexpensive set of equipment.

Please do not misunderstand me, I own far more than one rod and reel set but you will not find one that exceeds the monetary value that I have stated unless I received it as a gift. Each of my boats is outfitted with at least six or seven rod and reel combinations rigged for different fishing applications and my garage has perhaps two dozen more sets of equipment but not one is overly expensive. It just is not necessary or wise to spend excessively for a rod or reel.

Let's shift now to the subject of fishing rods, after all, other than the fisherman himself, the rod does all the work. The rod simply has two functions, to get the bait to the fish and once hooked to bring the fish to you. Wouldn't it be nice if we could keep the whole discussion of the fishing rods at this simple level? Well let's try.

First let's deal with the cast, the method of getting the bait to the fish. If you are a casting fisherman, or that is the selected method for a particular day, you want to make your cast as accurately as possible in order to lay your bait in front of the position where you think the fish are located in general whether using a casting technique or a spinning technique the longer casts can be produced with the longer rods given the same casting energy from the fisherman. However more accuracy can normally be achieved with shorter rods. So what is the best compromise? There really is no compromise it is simply what is most comfortable to you under the specific fishing conditions that you are experiencing. In general I feel that a 6 ½ foot or 7 foot rod is adequate for catching almost any fresh water fish.

When I was young and learning how to ski, I was told that you should select your ski length by holding the ski upright along side of you and you should be able to hook your fingers over the top of the ski if it was the right size. That was the simple rule that all skiers used back then. Today of course that has all changed for reasons that I don't choose to understand. Selecting a fishing rod length has little or nothing to do with your height but to make the length selection simple let's say that the length of the pole should be taller than your height. With this in mind if you want to get out a long way with your cast then use a longer or 7 foot rod. Otherwise a 6 ½ is fine. Have you ever heard of this standard for selecting a pole, probably not, but how can you go wrong, unless you are a professional basketball player and a rare one at that, you can't go wrong with this suggestion. If you are selecting a rod for trolling or still fishing where you may not be interested in the casting distance, a seven foot rod will satisfy most conditions.

There are several of the larger fish types like Big Carp, Catfish or other heavier lake specimens where much longer rods are used, sometimes as long as twelve feet but as a general rule the lengths discussed above are fine.

Another consideration of course for the rod length to be used is the actual fishing situation. If you are fishing off of a bank or shoreline, you may want the longer rod to clear obstructions. If you are trolling several rods at one time, you will want to vary the length of the rods to permit better pole spacing as we have discussed earlier. If you are still fishing from a boat, there are some types of fish that may require that you get further away from the boat with the bait and again here a longer rod might be wise. Other than these special situations, the 6 ½ and 7-foot pole can be your standard.

How about rod weight? Fishing rods are normally rates by their flexibility and stiffness. An ultralight rod is very short and very flexible and normally used for close in fishing for smaller fish under two pounds in weight. The ultralight rod provides the best "action" since it is very thin and very flexible and you can feel every movement of the fish as you play or retrieve it.

There is some science associated with fishing rods that you need to know to make the proper rod selection. Most of the "action" or bending of the rod takes place on the upper one third of the rod closest to the tip. The further away from the tip you get the less flexible the rod. Ultralights will bend almost 360 degrees. Rods rated "light" have very flexible tips, Medium ratings get slightly stiffer and Heavy rated rods are fairly stiff. If your primary interest is hauling your fish to you or into the boat, with little or no play, then a heavy rod is for you. I prefer a medium rated rod for most fish types up to about 10 pounds in fish weight. This provides the most thrill on the retrieve and the flexibility of the rod moves with the fish as it fights. In my opinion the flexibility of the medium rod increases my catch probability and reduces my loss rate for most fish. You have to keep in mind that most fish don't just come to you when hooked, they want to fight and they should be allowed to "play" as they are retrieved, that is the thrill of fishing. The flexible tip of the rod keeps constant pressure on the fish as it struggles to escape. You want to feel all of this action while decreasing your chances of losing the fish. A medium weight rod gives you all of this. Using a heavy or stiff rod puts all of the tension of the fight on the fish and can often tear out the hook and damage the fish. For the larger fish above 20 pounds, a heavier rod can be used.

At this point it is probably a good place to discuss the drag setting of the rod and reel combination. Even with a properly selected rod and reel, many fish are lost to a drag setting that is too tight. This will also cause a condition where the hook will tear out if the fish puts up a good fight.

Drag is a setting that can be adjusted on almost all fishing reels. If you find a reel that has no drag setting I suggest that you do not buy it. Drag on a reel permits the line to feed out when a big fish is hooked that may exceed the weight capability of the line being used. A common technique used by experienced fishermen is that you retrieve the fish or reel it in only when the fish is not trying to swim away. If the fish is pulling away, it should be allowed to go. When the fish stops running or pulling away you can reel the line in. the drag setting will allow the fish to pull away even as the reel is being retrieved. This permits you to catch a fish that is much heavier than your line rating by tiring the fish. Proper drag settings come with experience but in general you should be able to pull out line with moderate resistance if the drag is set properly. If you are retrieving a fish and the drag never permits you to accomplish a retrieve, you can tighten it slightly to solve the problem. If you have a situation where your fish are breaking off continually there is a fairly good chance that your drag setting is too tight. Drag is also a useful setting if you are trolling and you hook up on a foreign object on the bottom. The drag will permit line to feed out and not cause the line to break.

Rod flexibility is also useful to maintain tension on the line when a fish is hooked. Nature has given fish the capability to sense slack on your line and when they feel slack line they have an instinct to flip off of your hook. If the line is kept tight the fish cannot release the hook. Line tension is largely the responsibility of the fisherman but the pole and sometimes even the type line being used helps keep the tension tight. You may have heard the expression to "keep the tip of the rod up." If the rod tip is kept up, the rod flexibility allows the fish to swim and prevents tearing out the hook. The lower the rod is kept to the water the less flexibility the rod provides and the greater the chances of pulling out the hook.

Manufacturers that couple the rod and reel with normally indicate the ratings of the combination. These ratings will be imprinted on the rod itself. The ratings will normally tell you the weight of the rod, light, medium or heavy, the ideal strength of the line to be used and sometimes the length of line to use. You should try not to greatly exceed these ratings. Most reels are also rated by the manufacturer. Reels are rated by the number of bearings and the gearing ratio. Both of these ratings are important to know. Obviously the more gears, the smoother the handling. The gear ratio tells you how much line is normally retrieved with one complete turn of the handle. This measurement is normally expressed in feet. A ratio of 2:1 means that two feet of line is retrieved with every complete revolution of the handle. This is important information if you may be jigging off of the bottom and you want to keep your bait or lure a certain distance off of the bottom. Letting the jig settle to the bottom and then making two turns will bring your bait four feet off of the bottom. If you are using sonar equipment where you can see where the fish are, this feature is very important to your fishing experience.

Understanding that there is reason for matched rods and reels is important to you in all fishing situation. A rod designed for casting is significantly different from one designed as a spinning pole. As the line comes off of a spinning reel, it casts out the line and unfoils in loops approximately the diameter of the spool. The lower eyes on a spinning rod therefore are very large to permit this and prevent line tangles. Since the line on a casting reel comes off of the reel without this large circular motion, the eyes of a casting rod are much smaller at the base near the reel. Because of the position of the hand when holding a casting rod, there is normally an index finger grip on a casting rod that is not present on a spinning rod. If you try to interchange reels and rods for the two types of situations, the combination will not work effectively.

I remember when I was young and worked on construction with my father he would often joke with me when I missed hitting a nail that I was left handed but using a right handed hammer. For some time I thought that he was right but eventually learned that there really are no left and right handed hammers. Fishing reels are different, it does make a difference whether you are left or right handed. If you are left handed you normally cast with your left hand and retrieve with your right hand. Since your hand wants to retrieve by cranking away from your body, the handle must be on the right side of the reel to accomplish that. Most spinning reels provide the capability of switching the handle to accommodate both left and right handed fishermen. Casting reels however cannot provide that flexibility but can be purchased as either left or right handed versions.

As you progress as an angler there are other factors that may concern you especially if you are experiencing long fishing days and hopefully catching lots of big fish. One of these factors is the balance of the rod and reel combination. If you are fishing with large lures the weight of the lure is also important in the balance of the rod, reel and lure combination. There is no universally accepted method of balancing a rod and reel combination, it kind of becomes a personal thing. The rods and reels that I use on my boat are used by all people that fish on my boat and I have never had anyone complain that the balance was off. If you were to become a tournament fisherman, however, you may start to get interested in your equipment balance.

As a general rule I try to measure the balance of my rod and reel combination by attaching the bait or lure weight that I will be using and holding the rod as I would normally be casting. The point on the rod handle where my index finger rests should be the balance point of the combination or the fulcrum. If I were to let go of all other fingers, the rod and reel should balance around my index finger. If that happens, the combination is perfectly balanced. If it does not happen, then what? There are actually weights that can be added to the back of the rod handle but I have never added any weight. If the combination does not balance, I try to understand why, but there is little that I can do except change the reel to a lighter or heavier one. I have never done this since I believe knowing of the imbalance is the important thing and I can adjust my hand position slightly if I start to feel a problem. If I catch so many fish that the balance of the rod and reel combination gets to be a problem, then I guess that its time to quit for the day. I'll exercise my hand that night to prepare again for an unbalanced combination tomorrow.

LINE SELECTION

Fishing was much simple 60 years ago when I was fishing as a kid that simply could not afford to consider alternative fishing equipment. I had to fish with what I had and that was ok since there were not many choices. I used the same type line for about 10 years before I even knew that there was anything else. My fishing line was a black braided line that was about as thick as my Mom's clothesline rope. How on earth did I ever catch fish with that stuff considering the hundreds of choices that are available to the fisherman today?

Well, technology has certainly moved things ahead in terms of the materials available and the manufacturing techniques that turn the raw materials into useable products. BUT! What has really changed the fishing product marketplace is the marketing and merchandising that takes place to prove to us that one product is superior to all others. With today's wide open communication media capability, if one fisherman wins a major tournament and happens to mention the line that he or she used that day, the next day there will be hundreds of thousands of purchases of that particular line. There is nothing wrong with this if you are concerned about stimulation of the economy, but for the average guy that wants to effectively equip his fishing stock, it presents a very confusing dilemma. So as I have attempted to do in other areas, let's try to simplify this complicated subject.

Let's try to put the subject of fishing line into some perspective by reminding ourselves that one of the crucial elements between the fisherman and the whopper that he just hooked is the fishing line. We certainly would not want to spend hours in search of that whopper and then fail to land it because the line tangled or broke. If a fish is hooked and then lost there are only three reasons for the loss; the hook was not set properly or tore out, the knot holding the hook failed or was improperly ties, the line itself broke. In my experience the first of these causes is the most probable, the second is the next most probable and the line breakage is the least probable. That however does not mean that the line breakage rarity gives us cause to neglect the line importance because it is very likely that the hook set and the knot failure were both a function of the type of line chosen and how it was secured and handled.

It's fairly easy to discuss fishing line without using brand identity and that will greatly simplify the discussion because in general there are only three types of fishing line, monofilament, braided and fluorocarbon. Each of these types of line has distinctly different characteristics that make the choice of the type of line used somewhat simpler. Let's discuss each line type.

Monofilament line or "mono" for short has been standard for fishing line since the early 1940's. It's the "old standby" and it is a safe selection at any time that confusion complicates your selection process. Mono is made of several synthetic components combined into a gel that is then drawn and processed into a slick, relatively strong string like substance. The manufacturing process can be varied to produce different diameter line which has different strength and stretch characteristics. Over the years different companies have developed different production techniques so that there is some difference in the products produced by the different companies, however the basic characteristics of all monofilament lines is nearly the same. Excusing the professional fisherman for this discussion, if your father voted Republican, you probably started voting by voting Republican. Similarly, if your father used a particular brand of monofilament, you probably also started using that same brand and you most likely swear by it.

There are some differences between manufacturers with line diameter, color shape, and stretch but I think that you will find that these differences are minor. Advertising has taken over and caused the battle of the adjectives, "ultra think", mega strength", and ultra low stretch" are a few of the advertised differences especially since other non mono lines have hit the market. Do you even know if stretch is good or bad, probably not unless you recently read an article or attended a seminar in which case you were probably influenced by the author or lecturer. There are situations where stretch is a minor factor. One situation would be if your fish suddenly took a dive near the boat where you pole could not offer any give. The stretch in this situation could give you the fraction of a second required to change your drag or open your bail or spool.

There are some minor advantages with certain types of lures of using mono line. Crankbaits will behave better with some small amount of stretch provided by mono. Topwater fishermen may also prefer mono and situations where you may be fishing in weeds, near wood or rocks may suggest the use of mono line. If you are using spinner baits or shallow crank baits, you may prefer mono line and this is also the general choice for close in fishing and pitching.

The clear other choice, not as popular as mono line is braided line. This type of line was the first place that the "mega advertising" took over the line selection process. Suddenly a few years ago those who used the old standby mono line were somehow secondary type people. The new superbraids had taken over and still create a lot of interest even among the pro's in some situations.

Braided line has literally no stretch and provides excellent sensitivity. If you are fishing in tough situations like heavy weeks or garbage water that may require that you tear out of a tough situation, braided line excels. In general however you would not use braided line near rocks or wood. Braided line tends to cling to soggy brush and it will not part easily if hooked in brush, rather it will dig in deeper. Many fishermen prefer braided line for top water fishing and for spinner baits that you want kept in the middle or upper section of the water column.

There is certainly no doubt that the braided lines are stronger and thinner than most mono lines and where tough fishing is expected, braid rules. Braided lines however, are not really new; they have been around for many years as a matter of fact some braided lines are older than the monofilament types. The "ultra toughness" however is relatively new. It is no surprise that the braided lines are strong since the line itself is made form materials that were originally used for stitching bullet proof vests for law enforcement officers. One of the first braided lines produced actually took on the name of the process used to create the strength. The process was similar to a spider web construction where the individual lines are woven using individual spinnerets that were very tightly braided together. The manufacturing process is complicated which explains why the price of the braided super lines is high than monofilament lines.

There are some specific characteristics other than strength that identify with braided line. First, these lines tend to float which makes them undesirable for top water situations. Secondly, you have to keep a keen eye on the line as it is used since it tends to deteriorate. It is difficult to detect pock marks or unraveling of the strands but they do occur with use. Braided liens should be inspected regularly. A third disadvantage of the braided line is that it can raise havoc with the line guides on your reel and the guides on the rods. If you intend to use braided line continuously, it is recommended that you purchase rods with titanium lined guards. You can help this situation by periodically apply a good quality car wax to your line guides.

I have found that braided lines because of their construction are often hard to cut properly. Line snipers need to be new and sharp to make a good cut in braided line. It is also necessary to use good typing techniques for braided line since they tend to be more slippery. I prefer the Polymer knot for braided line and I also use the improved Cinch Knot but I add a couple of extra turns when using braided line. These knots are described in another section of this book.

The third type line available today is the Fluorocarbon line. Many fishermen think that this is a new type line but indeed it has been used for some time as a popular leader material. Fluorocarbon line has the same light refractive index as water so it is virtually invisible under water.

Fluorocarbon's chemical composition and the techniques used for its extrusion create a very very strong durable line. Most of these lines are manufacturing in such a way that they are closed cellular and therefore they do not absorb water like the nylon monofilament lines do. Fluorocarbon is also not effected by the ultraviolet rays of the sun so they will last significantly longer than the monofilament lines last, some fishermen have indicated that their Fluorocarbon lines last four to five times as long as their monofilament counterparts. Even with the high cost of the fluorocarbon line, the longer life makes it a cost conscious preference.

Fluorocarbon also has far less stretch than the monofilament type lines. Hook sets are usually better with a low stretch line. This offers an advantage when fishing deep or using long casts or when trolling. The stretch factor for the fluorocarbon line is about equivalent to the braided line however the sensitivity for fluorocarbon is much better. Bites are much more detectable with fluorocarbon line.

Another advantage of the fluorocarbon line is that its composition makes it sink faster than the other lines. This makes it preferable for baits that dive or sink such as crank baits and deep diving jerk baits and for jigging.

Knot typing fluorocarbon line is also different and much like the braided line. An improved Cinch knot or Polymer knot is preferable with additional twists for the Cinch. It is also necessary to completely wet the knot before you tighten it for the Fluorocarbon lines. This wetting technique should also be used when typing monofilament lines.

If you are a beginner fisherman, you might not want to start with fluorocarbon line, especially if you are using a spinning reel. This line tends to be stiffer and will often unspool itself from the spinning reel. A good technique to use for new fluorocarbon line on a spinning reel is to load the spool and then hopefully in a boat, let the line slowly out into the water about the distance of your normal cast or troll. With no weight on the end of the line, slowly reel in the line applying some resistance with your forefinger. This will take out the normal curl that exists and lessen the unspooling problem.

Comparing the three types of fishing line can make your selection easier however your particular situation should dictate which type to use. The three lines are rated below as they compare to each other on a few of the important factors.

	Cost	Stretch	Life	Visibility	Strength
Monofilament	least	most	shortest	fair	fair
Braided	high	none	longest	poor	best
Fluorocarbon	highest	little	very long	excellent	good
Common Fishing Line Ratings					

Overall, if you are a starter or intermediate fisherman who does not fish regularly, I would recommend that you stay with monofilament line. Even in this case however it is always good practice to check you line regularly with a pull test and examine the hook end for nicks or other damage. At the start of every fishing trip, cut off about eight to ten feel and re-tier your hook or bait.

Spooling your line is not difficult but as in any situation there are right and wrong ways to do it. In the case of line there are two distinct ways to spool, one for spinning reels and the second for bait casting reels.

For bait casting reels run the line through the rod guides and the level wind device on the reel. Attach the line to the reel spool. Hang the line spool on a nail or other object or put a pencil through the center hole and have someone hold the pencil and spool with a slight amount of tension as you reel the line onto the reel. You can add tension by using your forefinger and thumb as you wind the line onto the reel. The reel should be filled to within about 1/8th inch of the lip of the spool. It is also possible to drop the spool of line into a pail of water. It will probably float and the spool will turn as you spool the line onto the reel, but this technique will not provide tension to the line as it is spooled.

For spinning or spincast reels, the spool does not rotate so the line spool should also not rotate. Lay the line spool on the floor with the label side facing upward. Uncoil line from the line spool and run it through the line guides and tie the end to the reel spool. For a spinning reel make sure that the line is run properly through the bale guide. Add tension to the line with your thumb and forefinger as you spool it. After about 15 turns, stop turning and lower the rod tip to permit line slack. If the line lays in relatively neat coils, continue spooling. If the line twists or knots turn the line spool over and continue to spool on to the reel. Fill the reel to about 1/8th inch of the tip of the spool.

Some Tips for Good Line Care

- Store your line spools in a dark place with normal room temperatures.

- Do not expose your lines to chemicals such as gasoline.

- Frequently check the line for nicks or abrasions by running ten feet of line through your fingers.

- If you are not fishing for long periods, cut off a couple of feet of line regularly and re-tie your lure or hook, do a pull test on your knot.

- Do not operate with knots in your line. Cut them off and re-tie.

- Re spool your reels once every month if you fish regularly, less often if you only fish occasionally but always do a pull test on the action end before every fishing day.

- Use line strength appropriate for the fish that you are after and the water conditions.

- Since water almost always has a green tint, use line with a green color as a general rule.

- However many turns you normally use on your knots, use at least ten turns for braid line, and two more than your usual for fluorocarbon line.

Tips for Better Fishing

- Remember that luck happened when preparation meets opportunity.

- Take every opportunity when on the water to have a line in the water. You can think and plan but a line in the water creates a better opportunity.

- If you fish from the shore, good areas to look for are inlets, shoreline drop offs, bridges, docks, weed beds and boat landings.

- During cold fronts go to the smallest reasonable line and lure size.

- If the water is stained, fish the shallower water.

- Move your bait faster in shallow water and slower in the deeper water.

- Start you fishing in shallow water and move progressively to the deeper water

- If there is a current caused by either water flow or wind, try to fish into the current for best results.

- If the water is clear and the summer heat makes day time fishing uncomfortable, try night fishing for better results on both you and the fish.

- If you are fishing over weeds or grass, hook your stinger hook to the top side of the bait to avoid hang ups.

- Weed beds are almost always good places to fish since they provide cover and usually have a good oxygen supply.

- If you are going to weigh your fish, have all of the equipment readily available so as not to keep the fish out of the water for long periods of time. Also keep your camera handy for a permanent record.

- Always preset and test the drag on your reels before you start fishing.

- Plan your fishing day and have all of your equipment ready and in good working condition.

- If your casts seem to be short, check your line spool, it may not have enough line on it.

- When moving your boat to a new fishing area and there are other fishermen nearby, use your trolling motor or a very low speed on your main motor.

- Always treat other fishermen as you want to be treated.

- In the summer months, night fishing is a good way to avoid the daytime crowds.

- Use the lightest weight rod that is appropriate for the type of fish being sought. The rod is an extension of your arm and the shorter, lighter rods will help your cast.

- Try to determine the size of the bait fish in the area that you are fishing and use lures that are the same size as the bait fish.

- Remember that the creeks and channels are the fish highways and a likely place to find a good sized fish.

- If you are using a bobber, use one that is just large enough to keep the bait where you want it.

- If you are using a bobber and keeping the bait more than 8 feet from the surface, use a slip bobber, it will ease your casting problems.

- Non stretching line requires a drag set that is looser than normal.

You don't have to use expensive equipment or fancy bait if you are persistent. Susan Mims of Mooresville North Carolina caught this nice Largemouth with a spin casting reel and 6 foot rod using a red plastic worm.

FISH HOOK SCIENCE

I titled this section as I did because the hook is one of the smallest and least complicated pieces of fishing equipment that you will be equipped with. If it is so simple then why are there rows of different hooks in the fishing super stores? Again it is the growth of marketing and merchandising that has complicated this rather simple equipment.

Since the earliest known humans, fish have been a valuable source of food on this planet and as such the existence of the fish hook goes back thousands of years. The earliest known fish hooks were carved out of stone and bone and were very primitive as most things were in those early times. Over the thousands of years that have passed, many other techniques have been examined for catching this valuable food source and the fish hook has been the lone long-term survivor. It remains today the preferred tool for making a nice catch.

There is however some standardization to fish hooks. The first is the nomenclature associated with the fish hook. The standard fish hook is illustrated below.

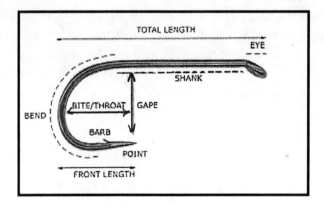

Hook measurements have never been standardized and there is no universally accepted method of hook measurement today. There have been attempts to standardize hook measurement by fractions of an inch, this system fails because it only defines the length of the hook which is two-dimensional and the hook Gape can vary greatly from one hook pattern to another. Here are the common individual definitions:

- Gape: the distance between the point of the hook and its shank.

- Bite/Throat: the distance from the apex of the bend to its intersection with the gape.

- The Bend: the section of the hook that bends around.

- The Shank: the length of the section that extends back from the eye to the point where the bend begins.

- The Eye is the loop at the end of the hook. This is considered the front of the hook.

- The Point is the business end of the hook that grabs the fish.

- The Barb is the spline pointing backwards that keeps the hook from coming out of the mouth of the fish.

So how are hooks sized? Well they are sized by simple numbers that really mean nothing relative to the hook descriptions that I have just given you. The smallest hook made is a number 32 and the largest is a 20/0. If you follow the numbers backward from 32, the hook size will increase. Once you reach size 1, the hook size again increases until you reach 20/0. Some typical actual hook sizes are shown below with bend diameters shown in inches.

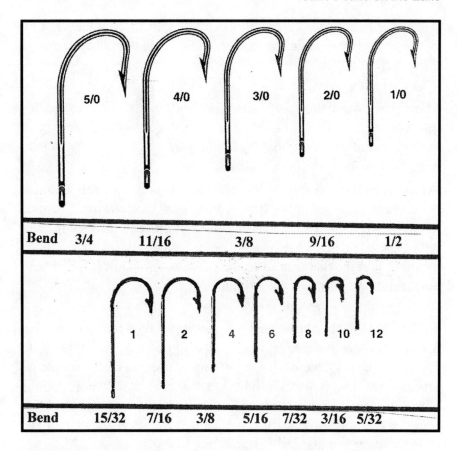

The above science is great to know but I had to ask myself, "in the 60 years of fishing did I ever have to know hook terminology to catch a fish?" The answer is NO! I have had many occasions to identify with hook sizes but even then it was to ask a store clerk for a particular hook size when there were none on the shelf.

The only real thing that is important to know and it isn't really science is that the gape of the hook should not be larger than the relaxed open mouth of the fish being sought. That information I can see with my eyes.

There is also an element of common sense that has to be applied. The hook size should be somewhat matched to the line weight which should also reflect the type and weight of the fish being sought after.

If you are fishing for 15 pound fish with a 15 to 20 pound line, it would be foolish to use a number 6 hook because it will bend straight if the fish is caught.

There are however some different types and shapes of hooks and this information is often important to know in order to match your hook to the fish and method of fishing being used.

WORM HOOK: the title described the function of this hook; it is normally used for either liver worms or plastic worms. This is a strong sharp hook that is probably most often used for fishing Bass with plastic worms. Most Worm hooks are defined as wide gapped meaning that the distance from the point to the shank is larger than normal hooks shown on the previous page.

TREBLE HOOK: the treble hook is essentially a normal hook but manufactured with three separate points forged together at the top to create one eye. Treble hooks are normally used as replacements on artificial lures such as crank baits but there are several applications where this hook is also used for live bait such as for Northern Pike, Muskies and sometimes Stripers. Although trebles are made in many sizes the most popular treble sizes are 1 to 2/0.

BAITHOLDER HOOKS: these hooks are designed specifically for holding live bait such as worms, crawfish or minnows. This hook has a longer shaft than normal and has extra barbs to help hold the bait on the hook for long periods of time. These types of hooks are often sold with a premolded monofilament leader attached. A 2/0 or 3/0 Baitholder hook would be ideal for good sized Largemouth Bass.

CIRCLE HOOKS: circle hooks have gained significantly in popularity in recent years. The Circle hook happens to be my personal favorite for Bass, stripers, Perch and Catfish. One reason for the favoritism to this hook is that I am a catch and release fisherman. The design of the Circle hook lets the live bait be swallowed by the fish and it is pulled out of the gut to become hooked on the side of the mouth as the fish fights by diving or swimming sideways.

JIGHEAD HOOKS: these hooks are seen most often with a leadhead molded on during the manufacturing process. These hooks have longer than normal shanks to hold the live bait that is attached below the lead head.

There really is some science to the manufacture of fish hooks but I begin to wonder where the gimmicks stop and reality starts. There are at least ten different types of hook point styles from the knife edge type to the curved in type to the needle point type. There are several types of barbless hooks since many fishing preserves and private fishing establishments in addition to some state controlled waters that will allow nothing but barbless hooks. The theory of this hook is that it gives the fish a better chance of escape, requires a more skilled fisherman and is less likely to harm the fish when being removed from its mouth.

There are also different eye manufacturing techniques for different applications and we are now finding more and more colored hooks with the most popular ones being black and red. There seems to b ea theory that red is not visible underwater however over many years of alternating between red and black hooks, I have found no difference. Hooks are normally manufactured with a bronze or nickel plating or they are galvanized and as such are normally bronze, silver or gray in color.

There are some important ethics associated with the fish hook especially for the catch and release fisherman. No matter how careful you are with your hook selection, your retrieval technique or your hook setting habits, there are inevitably situations where the fish takes the bait and hook down deep in its throat. I have seen fisherman yank the hook out with brute force just to save the hook. If this is one and the fish is returned to the water it will simply roll over and die.

If you run into a situation where the hook is lodged too far down in the throat to get it out, simply cut the line off as close to the hook as possible and return the fish to the water. In time the normal chemical reaction inside the fish will rest and erode the hook and the fish will not be permanently damaged. If you can see the shank of the hook and have wire cutter, cut the hook as far down the shank as possible. With normal movement of the fish it may eventually dislodge itself.

Even though I have described the fish hook as the simplest of all fishing gear at the beginning of this section, it is also at times one of the worst weapons for the careless fisherman. I have dealt with hook removal from human flesh elsewhere in this book but it warrants a reminder again here that if you fish long enough, you will eventually get a hook caught in your hand, finger or elsewhere on your body. The best hooks are the sharpest hooks so handle all hooks with CAUTION.

OTHER HOOK CONSIDERATIONS

Now that you have become expert on the science of fish hooks we can talk a little about other factors that you should keep in mind. One important factor is the sharpness of the hook. When you purchase a good quality hook either individually or in packages, you will note that the point is very sharp, almost sharp enough to penetrate your skin with very little pressure. (Don't try it, take my word.) I know you think that the hook will stay that way forever, well it won't. With use you will scrape rocks, get snagged on wood brush and yes, you will wear it down by catching fish with it. Hooks don't stay sharp forever and a dull hook will cause you many missed fish. Whatever brand of hook you buy, check the initial sharpness and try to remember whatever gauge you use. Usually touching the tip with your finger tip will suffice as an indicator.

If you have been fishing a while and caught a few fish, check the hook every hour or two to insure that it has maintained its sharpness. Remember the sharper the hook, the easier it is to dull it. If you are catching fish that are big fighters, like Stripers or big Bass, check the hook sharpness every hour or so. If you are catching fish with teeth like Northern Pike, check your hooks after every catch. Tips can easily get dulled and hooks are often bent due to a hard fight or when you are trying to take the hook out, especially with big fish where you may be using pliers.

There are tools that can be purchased to sharpen hooks but the price of hooks today dictates to me that a hook is a throw away item. When it is dulled or bent, replace it and throw the old hook away. Never try to straighten a circle hook, it has been factory shaped and you will never duplicate the factor condition.

I have been asked if there is any easy way to determine the size of the hook that should be used. This of course is determined by the size of the fish that you expect to catch, more specifically the size of the mouth of the fish. I have developed an experience factor that I use to size my hooks. If I am fishing for smaller species like Crappie, Bream or Perch, I use a hook that will fit around the tip of my little finger. If I am after medium sized fish in the two to four pound range, I select a hook that will fit around my index finger. For large fish in the ten pound range I select a hook that will fit around my thumb. Since you are not always sure what size fish you will catch, it might be wise to start with a number one circle hook and resize if the fish are not hooking up.

There is another factor when using circle hooks that needs to be mentioned. Most of us who were raised using the standard old fish hook are also accustomed to a hard jerk when setting the hook. With a circle hook this habit must be abandoned and it is harder to accomplish that it may at first seem. With a circle hook you simply apply pressure to the rod tip and start reeling in the fish, the hook will do the rest. If you jerk set the hook it will simply pull out of the mouth of the fish without hooking the jaw.

Most fish will attack their prey from the head. If you look at a small fish you will immediately see that the shape of the fins flow back toward the rear of the fish making it easy to swallow it if it is taken head first. That is why in most cases you hook the bait through the mouth from the bottom up through the upper lip. (For live bait). Shown below.

There are some fish, not many, that will attack your live bait from the rear on occasion. Perch will sometimes do this. When this happens you will notice that you are getting hard hits but not bringing in the fish. There is a solution, the Stinger hook. Shown below.

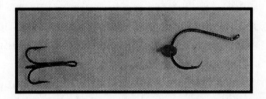

Stinger hooks are usually treble hooks, much smaller than the main hook that you are using. The stinger hook is made with a monofilament line about two inches in length and an eye that is closed with a silicone rubber. The main hook is pushed through the silicone eye after the bait is attached as shown below. One of the three treble hooks is hooked behind the dorsal fin where there are no crucial body parts. This permits the bait to swim (with some difficulty) and the rear mounted treble will raise havoc with the fish that attack from the rear. Stinger hook and live bait is shown below.

I believe that the catch rate with stinger hooks is increased by more than 50%. You have to keep in mind however that the addition of the stinger is impeding the motion of the baitfish and the life span of the bait is also significantly reduced.

Since we have described a few hooking methods here, this is as good a place as any to also show another method of hooking bait that I often use when still fishing, bottom fishing or fishing with a bobber. With this hooking method the bait fish is hooked through the upper body just behind the dorsal fin. (Shown below). This method permits the bait fish to swim around to the limits of the line attached and since there are no vital organs in this area the bait will live until taken by a big fish.

This photo shows a medium Golden Shiner hooked with a number 1 circle hook. This would be a typical hook up for fishing for medium size (3 pound) Catfish. This method is also good for Crappie fishing but of course the bait and the hook would be much smaller for the smaller fish.

Tips About Hooks

- A wide hook gap increases the chances of setting the hook in the fish's mouth.

- A long shank hook will give you a better hook set.

- Your fishing box should contain a stone to insure that your hooks are always sharp.

- A good way to check for hook sharpness is to drag the hook across your fingernail; if it sticks or scratches your nail it is sharp enough.

- Check your hook after every hang up.

- Check your hook after every large fish that you catch.

- Even new hooks are sometimes not as sharp as required, even new hooks should be checked for sharpness.

- If you are hooking the fish outside its mouth, you have to change the action of your bait. Proper hooking is inside the mouth.

- If you are using large night crawlers, use a multiple hook harness.

- If you are fishing with worms and you are feeling multiple taps on the bait, set the hook on the first tap. The second one is when the fish is spitting out the worm.

- Weighted hooks are fine to use for fishing a plastic worm, they help you control the cast.

- Make sure you are completely familiar with the procedures for removing a hook from your hand or finger. There is no time for reading after the stick happens.

- Always treat your hook and your lure as if it is a weapon. Be aware where the other fishermen are in relationship to your casting area.

ABOUT THE MANY DIFFERENT TYPES OF FISH

Most of the information presented in this book can be useful in almost any fresh water lake in the United States. Learning a little information about the fish that you may be after must take on some boundaries. There seem to be an unending number of types and variations of fish species that swim somewhere in this country and I cannot deal with all of them here. There are some species of game fish however that have certain characteristics that make them most interesting to examine. I have tried to select those fish that have common elements such as:

1. They inhabit a large number of fresh water lakes

2. They are popular as a game fish for a wide range of fishermen

3. Most fishermen have heard of the species

4. They are fun to catch

The types of fish located in different waters will be defined mostly by the year round temperatures that exist in these waters. Northern lakes that extend well up into Canada where the winters are severe will contain mostly the fish that survive well in cold water like the Musky,

Northern Pike, Walleye and Bass representing the most popular ones. The southern lakes that witness less severe winters and have a more temperate climate and therefore less variable water temperature will contain Large and Smallmouth Bass, Crappie, Carp, Stripers, Catfish, Perch and a variety of Bream to mention only a few.

In order to develop your preferred fishing technique, you have to have some knowledge of the species that you are after and the habits of that species in your area of the country. I am going to attempt only to summarize the most popular of the game fish and give you some insight into how these species may be fished and caught. As I have repeated many times in this book, there is no sure thing when it comes to catching fish but I feel that if you put the various bits of information together with some knowledge of the habits of the fish, your fishing experience will be a better one.

UNDERSTANDING FISH ANATOMY

Before I got serious about fishing many years ago I never thought that it was very important to understand the technical or biological aspects of the prey that I was seeking. As I grew older I realized that in any sport, but today's standards, it is vitally important to gain knowledge and understanding of all aspects of the competition and after all fishing is man competing with the fish.

In almost all sports, the management gathers every statistic about his opposing players and uses that information to formulate a game plan. A prizefighter reviews tapes of his opponents to understand his moves and motion and habits. Successful athletes understand their opponent's strengths and weaknesses and they lay out their game plan around those characteristics. So why not with fishing?

You could probably become a fairly good fisherman without understanding the details of the section. I feel however that you will become a better sportsman if you grasp the basic of the anatomy of a fish. It may give you a better understanding of why the fish acts as it does, how it moves as it does, and how you can better handle your catches to reduce their trauma if you intend to release them.

We will examine the external characteristics of a fish in addition to the internal anatomy and this information may prove useful to you in your fishing plan. If nothing else it will provide you with some information that you did not know.

The illustration below shows the significant features of the external anatomy of a common game fish.

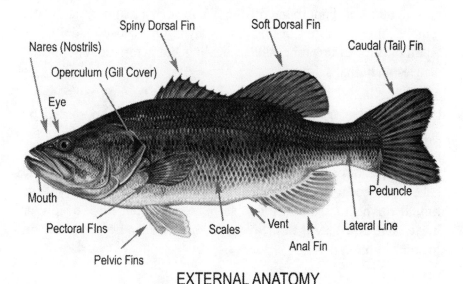

EXTERNAL ANATOMY

For purposes of illustration, I have used the Largemouth Bass to illustrate these features. In the simplest form fish are cold blooded animals that have fins and a backbone. Most fish have scales and breathe with gills. Most fish, like the Largemouth shown have a torpedo shaped body.

The fins of the fish are the appendages used by the fish to maintain its position, move, steer and stop. The fins are either single fins along the centerline of the fish or they are paired fins which are on either side of the fish's body.

The fins are the primary tools for achieving motion for the fish. The Caudal or tail fin is the mechanism for achieving forward propulsion. The dorsal and anal fins control the roll of the fish. The pectoral fins act mostly as rudders to control yaw and pitch, in other words the up and down steering and the side to side movement. The pelvic fins mostly control pitch and assist with steering, stopping and hovering.

Most freshwater fish have scales and there are two types of scales, the smooth scales and the jagged scales. Most fish have a very important mucus layer that covers their body. This layer provides the function of preventing infection to the fish's body. Catch and release fishermen have to be careful not to handle the fish in such a manner that would remove large quantities of this mucus layer. I have also read articles that indicate that this mucus has a healing characteristic for cuts and bruises on humans.

In many of the freshwater fish species, the fins are supported by spines that are very rigid and may be very sharp and therefore they play a roll in the defense of the fish against predators. Catfish as an example have pectoral fins that are very hard and sharp and fishermen need to take caution with Catfish not to be pierced by these fins. If the pectoral fin of a catfish penetrated your flesh deeply or hits a bone or artery it can leave a residue that can be very harmful to some humans.

The gills of the fish are mechanism for their breathing. The gills are covered and protected by the gill cover which is a flexible cover that protects the sensitive gills. The gills contain a high concentration of blood vessels and therefore they are bright red in color. Water is inhaled through the fish's mouth, passes over the gills and is exhaled from beneath the gill cover.

A fish sees through its eyes and they can see color. The eyes are rounder in fish than they are in mammals because the refractive index of water, focus is achieved by moving the eye lens in and out, not distorting the lens as is the case with mammals.

Paired nostrils in a fish are used to detect odor in the water. These nostrils can be very sensitive. Some fish such as Catfish have a very well developed sense of smell.

The mouth shape and size is a very telling part of the fish's anatomy because it tells a lot about the fish's eating habits. A large mouth is designed to take in big prey. Fish have a sense of taste and often are known to taste the prey before swallowing it. Some fish have teeth and others do not.

Perhaps the least known external feature of the fish is the lateral line. This is a sensory organ consisting of fluid filled sacs with hair like sensory apparatus that are open to the water through a series of pores that create a long line along the side of the fish. The lateral lines main function is to sense water currents, pressure and the movement of the water.

The vent is the external opening to the digestive urinary and reproductive systems. In most fish it is immediately in front of the anal fin.

As we review the many species of fresh water fish later in this chapter, the differences in the appearance of the fish will be defined by using the external anatomy that we have just reviewed.

COMMON MEASUREMENT TERMINOLOGY

Most fishermen may never have the occasion to take a critical measurement of a fish but some; particularly those who go on to competitive fishing may find it useful to know exact terminology when it comes to measuring fish. If you catch a trophy fish and want to purchase a replica of that fish, you will need to know the measurement criteria. The illustration below is self explanatory.

Common Measurements

In Freshwater Rules only Total Length is used. The measurement is taken flat, not along the curve of the fish.

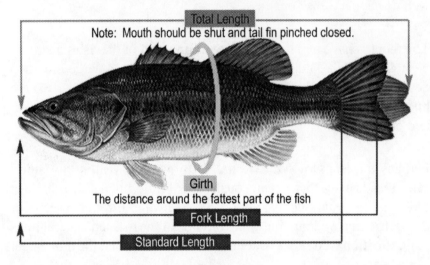

Note:
The source of this illustration showing both external anatomy and common measurement terminology were furnished by the Florida Fish and Wildlife Conservation Commission. (www.myFWC.com). John Cimbaro modified the sketches by Duane Raver.

LARGEMOUTH BASS

The Largemouth Bass is perhaps the most popular American freshwater sport fish among competitive anglers. Fishermen of all ages strive to conquer this species and there are thousands of different types of lures and baits that have been specifically designed to snare this popular fish. Professional fishermen seek the millions of dollars in prize money that is offered annually all over the world in tournaments specially designed to test the skills of man against this species of fish.

The color of the Largemouth Bass will vary slightly depending on the clarity of the water. In murky water its color is somewhat faded while its colors are brighter in clear water. Its primary color will vary from deep green to olive; Its belly is white or yellow. Its mouth extends back beyond its eye when closed which is a distinguishing feature from other bass types. It has a central black or gray line on each side and may have some blotches on the top of the body.

So popular is the Largemouth Bass that all by itself it has influenced a separate segment of the economy, inspiring boat builders and motor manufacturers around the world to design and build special boat and motor designs tailored to catching this fish. Yet the Largemouth Bass is so common that it can be caught with the simplest pole, a common hook and a worm. Ponds all over the country have been stocked with this fish and it exists in nearly every fresh water body that has decent water conditions. The Largemouth Bass can tolerate a wide range of water temperatures from nearly freezing to more than 85 degrees F.

Because of its popularity and its ability to survive a wide range of conditions, the Largemouth bass has been transplanted to many countries throughout the world and continues to grow in popularity.

The Largemouth Bass is a vicious predator of other water life. It will eat almost anything that is alive and has been known to eat others of its own species including its own young. This fish prefers clear water with little or no current. They stay near the bottom of the lake during the cold months but they stay active throughout the year. The Largemouth hides behind structure, weeds, grass and other growth that will shield it from its prey as it attacks passing food. They eat minnows, small carp, Sunfish, crawfish and any other water life that comes along. It has been said that anything that is small enough to fit into its mouth and wiggles will be a meal for a Largemouth Bass. Its peak feeding times are early in the morning and early in the evening.

The Largemouth Bass spawns in the early spring and its spawning time is dictated by the water temperature normally beginning when the water warms to about 60 degrees. The male Largemouth clears a nest for the eggs by fanning the bottom gravel with its tail in depths of from 1 foot to as deep as 5 feet. These nests are usually located in backwaters, shallow bays and other areas that are normally shielded from the wind. When the nest is ready and he temperature right, the male entices the female into the nest. They maneuver along side each other with their vents close together. The male rubs and bumps the female to stimulate her deposit of eggs and his deposit of milt. The fish do not eat while nesting and the eggs will hatch in about two days if the water temperature is higher than 70 degrees. If the water temperature drops below 50 degrees the eggs will not hatch. A female may lay eggs in the nests of several males.

The female will lay about 5000 eggs for every pound of her weight so a 3 pound female may lay as many as 15,000 eggs. About 2000 of these eggs will hatch and only a very few of these, perhaps less than 20 will survive and the young will remain in the nest for about 10 days.

Bass in the northern climate will live about 15 years and in the south about 10 years. Their rate of growth will depend on their diet. Southern Largemouth bass will grow to an average of about 18 inches in length and northern fish will grow to about 12 inches. Largemouth grow quickly in water ranging between 75 and 80 degrees. Their average weight varies from one to seven pounds but some have been recorded as large as 22 pounds and 31.5 inches in length.

The Largemouth will sometimes school at weights of 1 to 3 pounds but beyond 3 pounds it is a solitary fish which normally lives alone constantly on the search for food. The largemouth eats instinctively and unlike some other fish will eat even when it is not hungry.

The techniques that can be used for fishing this fish will vary with every fisherman. Since they hang near structures such as docks, they can be caught without a boat when fishing from a dock or from the shore. They can be caught while trolling and the depth will of course depend on the time of year and the water temperature. The most popular method of fishing for Largemouth is with a boat, usually one that can come in close to the docks and other structures. Light casting or spinning gear is common with either live bait of more normally artificial lures. During colder months lures colored like shad or crawfish work best and in cold water lures that can remain suspended work well. Trolling for Largemouth is common using live bait of any kind the most common being shiners, Shad or Herring.

There is a never ending discussion between fishermen about live vs. artificial lures for Largemouth. Professional fishermen are not permitted to use live bait for competitive Largemouth fishing and they will almost always discourage live bait use. Still the use of live bait is common and very successful for catching largemouth bass. One of my friends has an interesting input to this argument and he states that is always easier to feed a bass than it is to fool it so why not use the easiest method.

Professional fishermen usually wait until the water temperature reaches 50 degrees to start their hunt for the Largemouth. The early pre spawn starts at temperatures from 50 to 55 degrees. At this water temperature the fish will usually be at about 20 to 25 feet of water. At water temperatures of 55 to 60 degrees the pre spawn starts and the fish move in to water depths of 10 to 15 feet. At 60 degrees the bass get very active. Crank bait and jerk bait works well in colder water with suspended lures meaning that if you stop pulling the lure it will remain submerged and sit still. Since the Bass move slower in colder water this technique will work well.

Plastic worms always work well for Bass with the most popular colors being red, green or purple. In murky water use a shad color or crawfish color lure or worm. Crawdads work well in the spring because that is when the normal crawdad birth takes place and the bass know that. Spinner baits work well with the most popular colors being white and chartreuse. Shadraps are a common lure that will almost always catch bass and other fish and also a flat sided lure that has a slight wiggle to it will work fine.

There are many books that have been written about catching Largemouth Bass and thousands of papers and articles are also available. There are different techniques for different waters and different fishermen. Almost any technique that is comfortable for you is a technique that will catch the Largemouth, the above information should help.

Bass Fishing Tips

- Try to determine the size and color of the bait fish that the Bass are feeding off of and duplicate that size and color as closely as possible with the lure that you choose.

- A large live golden shiner that is permitted to swim freely around vegetation will often bring you a nice Bass.

- In thick vegetation use a single weedless hook for fewer hang ups.

- Try to target your Bass carefully since they position themselves differently at different times of the day. In early morning they may be at the bottom and as the sun warms the water they will rise nearer the warmer water at the top. When

Bass are near the surface, back away further for your cast so as not to spook the fish.

- Creek channels are movement routs for Bass. Fish these areas to increase your chances of a good catch.

- During summer periods Bass often group in one area and you can cast into the same area repeatedly and continue to catch fish.

- Bass tend to group together near points or ledges when the water is falling and will scatter in rising water toward the shallows.

- After you catch a Bass, always cast back to the same area a couple more times to get the other one that is likely in the same area.

- When fishing a tree top in shallow water, always fish the very outside first then work your way toward the center of the tree. This prevents inside fish from being spooked when outside fish are caught.

- In a river lake when the water warms in the summer, go further upstream toward the river for cooler water.

- Points are nearly always productive and are normal holding areas for fish.

- When fishing near bridges, try several different lures and depths to determine where the fish are grouped.

- If you know Bass are in the area but they are not feeding, try dragging a lure past them at a very high rate of speed.

- Use topwater lures to find the Bass during the hot summer months.

- Changing weather conditions will cause the Bass to move. If conditions change look for the behavior of the fish to also change.

THE SMALLMOUTH BASS

The popularity of the Smallmouth Bass has grown significantly over the years because it has the reputation of being one of the most exciting small fish to catch. Pound for pound many fishermen feel that the Smallmouth puts up the greatest fight in a retrieve and it leap out of the water adds excitement to the fishing experience.

The Smallmouth and Largemouth Bass have many similar features. The Smallmouth has a robust, laterally compressed body, a large, long head with dark bars which radiate back from the eyes. It has a long blunt snout with a slightly longer lower jaw. Its two joined dorsal fins appear as one. The back and top of the head are brown, golden brown through olive to green. The sides are lighter than the back. The underside is cream to milk white. The pectoral fins are clear and the others are opaque dark to amber. The body color can vary with the size of the fish and its living conditions. In clear water the colors are more pronounced and contrasting and in turbit water they are lighter with vague markings.

The Largemouth and Smallmouth Bass are often confused because they look somewhat alike at first glance but the Smallmouth has vertical bars on its sides, dark bars radiating from the eyes and its mouth reaches only as far back as the middle of its eye.

The Smallmouth Bass was originally found only in East Central North America but over the years it has been transported to nearly every state and Canada and many other countries. Today perhaps the only state not to have Smallmouth Bass is Florida.

Smallmouth Bass exist in many lakes and rivers provided that there is not a swift current flow. They like water bodies that are moderately deep and devoid of vegetation. They will not live in a lake that is less than 25 feet deep. They love to live near large rocks and tangled roots. The Smallmouth has a huge appetite. It feeds during the Spring, Summer and fall when the water temperature is above 50 degrees. Almost no feeding occurs during the Winter when the temperature of the water drops far below 50 degrees. The adult fish eat insects, crawfish and other small fish. Their growth is moderate reaching 4 to 6 inches the first year of life, 8 to 13 inches in the next three years. The largest recorded catch was 11 pounds 15 ounces.

The spawning habits of the Smallmouth are quite similar to the Largemouth. They spawn in late spring and early summer, usually around May or June when the water temperature reaches 60 degrees. The male moves into the spawning area and the nests are built near the shoreline and downstream from boulders or other obstructions to protect the eggs from any current that exists. The males may spawn with several females on a single nest. The average number of eggs on a single nest is about 2000 up to 10,000. the eggs hatch in about 10 days if the water temperature remains around the mid 50's and can hatch in 5 days if the temperature goes up to about 70 degrees.

The male guards the nest until the fry begin to disperse, a period of about a month. The smaller fry will eat plankton, switching to insect larvae and finally to small fish and crayfish as they grow. The most popular food for the Smallmouth Bass is the Crayfish. There are however states where it is not legal to use live Crayfish as bait.

There have been reported cases where Smallmouth Bass were stocked into a water body and the results were a decrease in the population of the other native fish because they could not compete with the Smallmouth in eating the normal food fish.

Some of the best Smallmouth fishing occurs in lakes in June right after the spawning season and in early fall. Natural food like hellgrammites, dragon fly larvae and crayfish are very effective in the early morning and late evening hours. The best artificial lures are those that work near or on the surface. Light casting or spinning gear is best. You must fish quietly, casting toward the shore, rocks and logs keeping the rod tip up and the line taut. Almost any lure will work but the Smallmouth prefer the smaller sizes. Jigs, crank baits, spinners, streamer flies, minnows and even night crawlers are all effective baits to use for Smallmouth Bass.

Smallmouth Bass Fishing Tips

- Crank baits are great for catching Smallmouth especially when there is movement in the water.

- Smallmouth Bass are among the strongest freshwater fish. They are extremely maneuverable and can turn on a dime making them one of the best fighting fish pound for pound.

- Crawfish are the favorite food of the Smallmouth bass.

- A tough 8 to 10 pound test monofilament line is idea for this fish.

- Smallmouth bass like colder water. When the water warms to 60 degrees this fish is more cautious and the schools will break up and fish will become more individual.

- Early morning and evening provide the best warm water fishing.

- Water clarity affects the depth that carry the Smallmouth. In murky water they hang at between 2 and 8 feet. As the water becomes moderately clear the depth increases to 4 to 10 feet. In clear water the fish will be around 6 to 12 feet deep.

- Cover will attract the fish. Weed beds, transition bottoms, logs, boulders are good places to look.

- In shallow water Smallmouth tend to gather near cover like boulders and brush and in small dips in the bottom.

- Smallmouth Bass are the first fish to move into the shallow water in the spring to spawn when the water temperature reaches 60 degrees.

- On large river lakes the Smallmouth Bass like the lower end of the lake which is normally deeper and has larger submerged structure.

- Rock ledges are a favorite holding spot for this fish. They will sit on stair step ledges at depths of 15 to 20 feet.

- An area that has a transition from small to larger rocks will always be a hiding spot for the Smallmouth.

- On warm days if there is any current in the water, Smallmouth will gravitate toward this moving water.

- Dull colored bait simulating the color of crawfish will work for Smallmouth Bass.

THE SPOTTED BASS

The Spotted Bass sometimes called the Kentucky Spotted Bass seems to have characteristics between the Largemouth and the Smallmouth. For many years the Spotted Bass was actually considered a hybrid of the Smallmouth Bass and it has often been overlooked by fishermen as a good sport fish. In recent years however it has been realized that the Spotted Bass actually possesses the best sport fishing characteristics of both the Smallmouth with its aggressive fighting ability and the Largemouth with its appetite size and habitat.

The Spotted Bass is often mistaken for a Largemouth. Like the Largemouth it is normally greenish in color with a wide strip of broken blotches and a white underside. There are dark blotches above the stripe. Unlike the Largemouth the Spotter has scales on the base of the second dorsal fin (a feature rarely noticed). Its first and second dorsal fin are connected (also hard to notice) but the mouth of the Spotter does not extend back beyond its eye. This is the characteristic that is most easily noticed.

Spotted Bass habitat rivers and lakes in the southern zone of the USA with the largest concentrations in the mid southern regions and Southeast. It prefers water temperature in the range of 73 to 77 degrees but will live nicely in water temperatures of 70 to 89 degrees.

The habits of the Spotted Bass are quite similar to the Smallmouth Bass except that they are more secretive in nature. Spotted Bass spawn mainly in river tributaries and along rocky shorelines at the edges of lakes. They prefer to build their nests in rocky areas. Their nests are much smaller than the other bass, about one third the size. Spawning temperatures are the same as the Smallmouth. Their fry leave the nest in about 8 or 9 days and during their time in the nest the male is very protective of them.

The growth rate of the Spotted Bass is quite similar to the Largemouth Bass during the first year of life but after that the rate of growth is slower. Spotters reach about 4 inches in the first year, 7 inches by the end of the second year, 10 inches in the third year and 12 inches in the fourth year. The world record Spotted Bass is 10 pounds,

4 ounces. The eating habits of the Spotted Bass are similar to the Largemouth Bass except that the Spotters seem to eat less fish than the Largemouth. It has been noted that about 56% of the diet of the Spotted Bass is fish.

Fishing for the Spotted Bass is much like the Largemouth Bass. They do not like blackish water and will gravitate to clear water. The Spring patterns for fishing Spotters are like the Largemouth, the pre spawn period offers the hot bite as the fish mill along the edges of flats sloping from about 2 feet to 6 feet of waters.

Plastic worms 3 to 5 inches work well as do Carolina rigged jigs and crawfish colored lures. In the summer deep diving crank baits work well. In late summer the Spotters move deeper, out of the range of most crank baits and jerk baits. During the summer months, I have had great success trolling with shiners and shad and catch the Spotters much the same way as I do Largemouth Bass. During the summer the spotters love to mill around brush piles and bluff walls and they will also feed off of the bottom in the summer.

Spotted Bass respond to sound so using rattle baits and worms with beads will produce success. If the Spotters are holding along steep banks, you can cast parallel to the bank with each cast going progressively deeper.

Night fishing will also produce Spotters in the summer. They will roam from cover at night and feed along the shallower water.

Tips For Fishing Spotted Bass

- Spotted bass and Largemouth Bass look very much alike and are fished similarly.

- This fish eats about half as much as the largemouth but is a fierce fighter.

- Tackle should be light and bait can be jigs, small worms, crank baits or spinners.

- Many fishermen feel that spotted bass provide the same fishing benefit as smallmouth and largemouth bass.

- Spring is the most active time for spotted bass along sloping banks and in waters between 2 and 10 feet deep.

- Natural brush shorelines, man made brush piles and rocky or gravel bottom areas are also good fishing areas.

- Drop shot rigs work well in deeper water.

- Carolina rig is popular for spotted bass.

- Compact but heavy jigs tipped with small crawfish are excellent all year round.

- Like other bass, summer days bring the fish to the docks, pilings and underwater structure.

- Deep diving crank baits work well when fish are in 10 to 15 feet of water.

- Spotted bass respond to noise so rattling crank baits will work well.

- In the spring and summer spotted bass feed off of the bottom and often suspend near brush or structure.

- Night fishing in the summer provides a consistent pattern of feeding for this fish and its activities are more predictable at night.

- Spotted bass do not like cold extremes so they will go deep in the fall and winter.

- Deep suspended spotted bass can be caught with jigging spoons the same size as the local bait fish.

- The preferred water temperature for spotted bass is 65 degrees.

STRIPED BASS

For many years the Striped Bass (Striper) was considered a salt water game fish found abundantly in coastal waters. It was a popular fish known for its large size and weight and also for its fighting features when hooked. Salt water Stripers normally migrated into the fresh water rivers to spawn so they were capable of living in fresh water as well as salt water. Because they were very popular as a fighting game fish, many game management organizations in states that had temperate weather conditions began to transport Stripers to fresh water lakes and streams so much so that today the Striper has become one of the most sought after game fish in the country.

The Striper is the largest of the temperate Bass family. Its body color is olive green to blue gray on the back with silvery and brassy sides and a white belly. It is easy to recognize because of the seven or eight black horizontal stripes along its sides. The two dorsal fins are separated by a gap. The Caudal or tail fin is clearly forked. When Stripers are young and less than six inches in length the stripes are not visible.

The Striper is related and very similar to the White Bass which rarely grows to more than three pounds except that it has a long and sleeker body than the White Bass. In recent years a hybrid breed of Striper has been created by using the eggs from a Striper and the sperm of a

White Bass to create the hybrid Striper. This hybrid is also called the Palmetto Bass. Even more recently the situation has been reversed by using the eggs from the White Bass and the perm of the Striper. This hybrid has been called the Sunshine Bass. The hybrids have become a favorite stocking fish for fresh water bodies that contain large quantities of gizzard and threadfin shad which is the favorite food of the Hybrid Striper.

The Hybrid Striper and the Stripped Bass look very much alike except that the hybrid has a more compressed body which would normally be hard to recognize and the hybrid has broken horizontal stripes in the area behind the pectoral fins and below the lateral line. This break is more easily recognized and is often the only noticeable way to distinguish a Hybrid Striper.

Stocked Striper, have done well in slow moving streams, large reservoirs, lakes and ponds. They are seldom found in extremely shallow bodies of water and rarely in waters that have large concentrations of aquatic weeds. Stripers normally gravitate to open waters. Herring, alewives and shad are the main diet of the fresh water Striper. Stripers normally do not feed on other game fish so they are often found living cooperatively with other game fish breeds. Stripers prefer water temperatures in the range of 65 to 70 degrees.

The Striper normally spawns in March, April or May when the water temperature reaches 60 to 68 degrees. Stripers traditionally spawn in waters that have a good current and once deposited, the eggs get no protection from either the male or the female. During spawning, several males (seven or eight) will surround a single female and bump her to waters with swifter currents and keep her at the surface. The ripe eggs are discharged and scattered in the water as the male sperm is released. Fertilized eggs must be carried by river currents until hatched (about 48 hours) to avoid suffocation. The hatched fry spend most of their time in lower rivers and estuaries. Because Striped Bass eggs remain suspended in a current until hatched, water bodies that do not have a continuous swift current are not suitable to hatch Striper eggs. In these cases fresh water populations have to be maintained by continual re stocking of fingerlings.

Stripers have very large appetites and will generally consume any type of small fish but prefer the types mentioned above. Younger stripers prefer plankton as their main food and like the other temperate bass they move in schools and all members of the school feed at the same time. Striper feed mostly in the early morning and in the evening but they will feed during the day sporadically, especially when the skies are cloudy or overcast. Striper feeding slows when the water temperature drops below 50 degrees but it does not stop completely.

Stripers are fast growing fish and they live a relatively long life. Sexual maturity occurs at about two years of age for the male Stripers and 4 years of age for the females. Stripers can grow to 10 to 12 inches in the first year. Weight and age of course will vary based on the food supply and water conditions but the following chart depicts the relationship between Striper weight and length on the average.

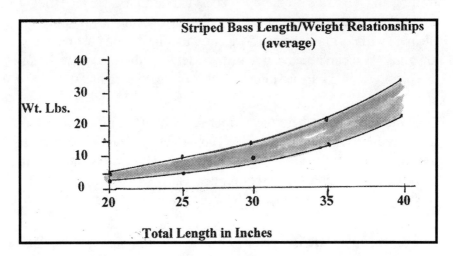

Freshwater Stripers have been found to be very sensitive to water temperature variations, more so than other sport fish species. If the waters warm more than expected, the Stripers will sacrifice feeding to get to cooler waters. Stripers larger than 10 pounds will suffer thermal stress when forced to live in waters that are excessively warm. They will become lethargic; develop poor feeding habits, exhibit weight loss, bacterial and fungal infections and even death. 68 degrees is considered the preferred temperature for Stripers.

There are as many different techniques for fishing Stripers as there are different fishermen. Stripers can be caught year round but the best fishing months are in the fall and March, April & May. The most popular method of catching Stripers is to suspend a live bait fish such as a shad or shiner in an area where fish are congregating, usually around schools of bait fish which can be detected with most fish finding devices discussed elsewhere in this book. Trolling the live bait fish in areas where bait has gathered is also very effective. As mentioned, Stripers usually travel in schools and feed that way although the larger Stripers will often travel alone. Because of the habits of feeding in schools, many fishermen define Striper fishing as "hours of boredom followed by a few minutes of sheer terror." It may take you some time to find the fish but when you do it is not unusual to have multiple hits called double or even triple headers. If you are trolling and have this problem, it is best to maintain a steady straight troll to keep the lines from becoming tangled. Using circle hooks for Stripers will normally keep a Striper on the line as long as the line is kept taut. You can retrieve one fish and let the other one wait. If you are fishing with a partner of course this problem is reduced.

If you find an area where the Striper school is feeding aggressively and driving the bait to the surface you can use artificial bait such as a Rapala or a Redfin, casting the lure into the area where the fish are working. If you find this situation get ready for an interesting few minutes of exciting fishing and hold on to the pole tightly.

Another popular lure is a yellow or white bucktail jig. Spoons, deep running crank baits and spinner baits are also good for schooling fish. Jigging over a school of Stripers can also be exciting using any small green or white jigging spoon and jigging at the depth where the fish appear to be schooled. Stripers will normally hit a jig on the way down so you have to keep control of the lure in all directions.

In the summer months when pleasure boating traffic can be a problem, some fishermen prefer to fish the Stripers at night which can bring success.

I prefer to fish for fresh water Stripers with a medium weight 6 ½ or 7 foot spinning rod and reel with 10 pound test. When trolling I always use a Caroline rig which has proven the best combination for me. I like the battle between the fish and myself with little between us so that combination provides that for me. Normal freshwater Stripers will range from 4 to 6 pounds and this set up if fine for that. If you are in an area where the stripers are much larger you will have to go to stronger gear.

A Striper hit is one of the most recognizable hits that you will witness. When trolling and hit by an average sized Striper, your pole will bend nearly all the way over. The bend will continue and the tip will continue to bounce. The Striper will head for the bottom when hooked and it will also swim sideways when it realizes that it cannot go down. This makes a multiple pole troll more difficult with the sideways motion of the fish. Drag should always be set fairly light so as not to break the line with one of these hard hits. The fish should be allowed to run when it wants to and you should retrieve when the Striper stops running. Continue this process until you see the fish and are able to get it in the boat with a net. Try not to handle the Striper around the body. The fish has no teeth and can be held by the lower jaw as the hook is removed. Stripers will normally have the hook set in the side of its lower or upper jaw and it is rare that you will gut hook a Striper. If you do and you are not intending to keep the fish, cut the line off and leave the hook in.

A Striper that has fought hard as they normally do will be very stressed when boated. If you are releasing the fish, get it back into the water as soon as possible. If the fight has been hard, hold the fish by the jaw or tail while lowering it into the water. Try to keep it upright with some movement to start the water flow over the gills. When the fish seems to be recovering, let it go. If you follow these procedures you will not only be a good fisherman but you will be a fine conservationist.

THE HYBRID STRIPED BASS

The Hybrid was described in the previous section on the Striped Bass. In some lakes most Stripers caught are indeed hybrids and the average fisherman does not know and probably does not care to know the difference. The details of the hybrid have been described earlier but to assist in its recognition, the Hybrid is shown below.

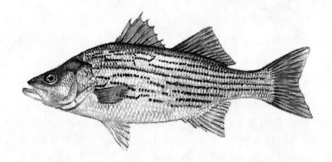

The most recognizable difference between the Striper and the Hybrid Striper is the fact that the horizontal lines along the body are broken and irregular on the Hybrid. This characteristic is quite visible to the fisherman. Although you may not care about the difference, the next time you land a Striper make note of what it really is, there is a good possibility that what you just caught is a Hybrid Striper. They feed the same, they bite the same, they fight the same and they taste the same so who really cares.

Striper Fishing Tips

- When stripers are hungry they will eat almost anything but their favorite food is gizzard shad, herring and golden shiners.

- Down lines with a Carolina rig is a popular trolling method.

- Flat lining near the surface with only a hook and bait is also popular when the stripers are near the surface.

- When fishing deep water more than 50 feet deep expect the stripers to be suspended around 35 feet.

- In the late summer and early fall the stripers will be most active in the early morning and late afternoon.

- Stripers can be caught in most lakes where they live all winter as long as the lake surface does not freeze.

- Many fishermen feel that low light conditions are the best for this fish.

- Stripers normally will not feed on other game fish.

- Do not expect stripers more than 10 pounds in weight to be in lakes where the water warms to high temperatures.

- The ideal water temperature for stripers is 68 degrees.

- 3 to 5 inch bait fish are ideal for the average size striper. Large artificial plugs are also effective at sunrise and sun set.

- Trolling or drifting is a popular fishing method.

- Slow trolling with a large spoon at speeds less than 1 mph has been effective.

- Most stripers are fished from boats rather than from shore because they tend to cover a lot of water in their travels for food.

- September through May makes great striper fishing if the lake does not freeze.

- On overcast days, surface feeding action can explode at any time.

- Striper behavioral patterns are most predictable during the month of October.

- Shallow water can be fished in the early morning. As the sun rises the stripers are likely to be near the points and turns in the creeks.

- On very hot summer days look around bottom humps and bottom structure.

- Trolling is the best fishing method during the summer.

- At any time of the year when you find large schools of bait, start fishing by jigging a white or silver jig slightly off of the bottom.

- Circling a large school of bait when trolling or jigging when stopped will produce stripers.

- If you don't intend to keep the fish during the hot summer months, don't try to catch stripers, they rarely survive a hard fight when in deep water in the summer.

This 20 pound Striper provided the author plenty to talk about when he returned from a day on the Cumberlin River in Tennessee. "Sometimes the 5 and 6 pound Stripers give you a great fight but a couple of these monsters and you know you have had a good day".

WHITE BASS

In the discussions on the Striper and Hybrid Striper, the White Bass is frequently mentioned. It is related to the Striped Bass and the source of the hybrid breeding. It seems appropriate therefore to present some information on the species since it exists widely in the same waters as the Striper and Hybrid.

In the following section I will discuss the White Perch since it is commonly mistake for a White Bass. The White Bass shown above resembles some aspects of the sunfish family. The dorsal fin on the White Bass is completely divided and the rear dorsal is higher than it is on the sunfish family.

The two dorsal fins as mentioned are separated with the higher front dorsal fin containing spines and the rear dorsal being soft. The front dorsal fin has nine spines. Horizontal bars are visible along the side of the body.

White Bass prefer to live in clear water. They usually are found in large lakes and streams that are connected to a major river with moderate current. They like a water temperature range of 65 to 75 degrees. They are normally located within 20 feet from the surface where they school and feed. Most of their feeding occurs in the early morning and late evening. It is not unusual to spot schools of White Bass feeding near the surface on the smaller prey which they drive to the surface. When this happens the small bait fish can be seen breaking the water to escape their predators. The White Bass moves in large schools and regularly breaks off into smaller groups divided by sex especially prior to spawning. Their spawning is random in the spring, usually in April or May. The groups of males will migrate to gravel shoals or a hard bottom and will be followed shortly by the females. The female indicates readiness by rising to the surface. Several males then rush in and crowd around her and the eggs drop to the bottom. A large female may lay as many as half a million eggs that will stick to the rocks or the bottom. If there is no current available, White Bass have been known to spawn on sandy beaches. After spawning the eggs are abandoned and they provide no parental care. The fry hatch in about two or three days and feed on insect larvae and small fish. As they grow they depend on a fish diet solely. Their favorite food is a small yellow perch if it is available.

Most White Bass become sexually mature at the age of three years when they are about 10 to 11 inches long. The average adult weight is about ¾ to 1 ½ pounds. They will live an average of about 10 years. Females grow faster and live longer than the males.

White Bass are hard hitting fish and they are fierce fighters. Their aggressive nature combined with their schooling tendency makes them quite easy to catch. The presents of birds working the surface is usually a clue that the White Bass is in the area. They can be caught on a variety of worms, minnows or spinner baits, small plugs or flies. A light rod and reed is preferred and can produce a lot of excitement if you can find a school of fish.

The White Bass is often confused with the white perch which will be discussed next.

Tips for Fishing White Bass

- White bass are best fished in the spring time before and after the spawn.

- Like stripers, white bass go after the schools of bait fish.

- When around a school of bait, jigging can produce results with this fish.

- Diving gulls are often a sign that white bass are feeding off of a school of bait fish.

- Best baits are worms, spinners and minnows.

- White bass can be caught trolling, drifting or still fishing and can sometimes be caught from shore.

- If you find a school of these fish the fishing will be fast and furious.

- White bass populations are shrinking in many lakes.

- Light gear provides the most fun for this fish.

WHITE PERCH

White Perch were originally found principally along the east coast. In many cases they have been accidentally transported to many lakes and streams from Georgia north to Canada. In some areas they are considered a problem because they feed on the same prey as the more popular game fish such as Stripers and Walleye and have been known to reduce the quantities of those game fish in waters where they have become over abundant.

The White Perch is regularly confused with the white bass. The White Perch are a silvery green on the sides and they have no lines or stripes on their sides, the spiny and soft dorsal fin on the White Perch are connected and they are not connected on the white bass. There are differences on the anal fins but those differences are very hard to spot.

The White Perch is a predator feeding mostly on small fish. When alarmed the White Perch will raise its spiny dorsal fin as a defense, so when handling a White Perch, you must be aware of these spines. They can be painful if they penetrate your skin although they are not known to be harmful to your health.

The White Perch usually spawns between April and June. The females will release from 50,000 to 150,000 eggs over a period of 10 to 21 days. Several males will hover over the female as she releases her eggs to fertilize the eggs. Eggs hatch within 1 to 6 days after being fertilized. White Perch can live up to 10 years feeding on small fish and bottom dwelling aquatic life. A mature White Perch can grow to a length of 19 inches but are more commonly found to be about 7 to 10 inches.

White Perch can be caught any time of the year from the shore line, from a boat or through the ice in the winter. The early Spring is considered the best time to catch them since they are schooled and feeding actively.

The best way to catch a lot of White Perch is to locate a school which is usually at depths of about 15 to 25 feet. Bait can be minnows or worms if live bait is desired or spinners and minnow imitations and jigs if lures are desired.

Most conservation organizations are not fond of White Perch and would prefer that they disappear. White Perch will regularly inbreed with other species and they have devastated Walleye populations in some lakes because they eat the Walleye eggs. The population of White Perch in most water bodies grows rapidly and they eat the same food as the more popular game fish therefore reducing the population of the better fish.

It is illegal to take any fish and transport it to another body of water. Please adhere to this law.

For the younger population White Perch can be fun to catch and therefore there is a mixed view on their presence in leisure waters. In general however it is recommended that a caught White Perch should not be released back into the water where it was caught. This is a fine tasting game fish and can be eaten. It is recommended that the fish either be eaten or disposed of properly.

Tips for Fishing White Perch

- Many fishermen do not consider this fish a game fish but consider it a nuisance fish that should be destroyed when caught.

- The white perch feeds off of the same type food as other game fish.

- This is a schooling fish that is easy to catch and a good starter fish for teaching young children how to fish.

- This fish seldom goes into shallow water.

- This fish can be caught year round.

- Can easily be fished from the shoreline with medium length casts.

- Springtime is the best time for catching white perch.

- They are normally located in about 15 to 20 feet of water and the schools can be very thick with fish.

- White perch sometimes attract bigger predators fish like stripers that will feed off of the smaller perch.

- Bait can be worms, minnows or small jigs or spinners.

- Jigging over a school of these fish can produce large numbers of fish in a short time.

- A white or silver two inch jig is ideal around a school of perch.

CRAPPIE

Many experience fishermen started their fishing experiences as young men and women fishing with simple gear form the shore or from a dock. Their most common early fishing attempts probably involved fishing for sunfish and bream. One day they brought up a fish that looked remarkably like the sunfish that they were catching but it didn't have any color and it was a little bigger than the rest. This was probably a Crappie. Crappie are members of the sunfish family and have body shapes similar to sunfish. There are two types of Crappie, the black and the White Crappie. The Black Crappie is shown below.

There is no need to describe in any detail the two types of Crappie since they have quite similar characteristics. The black Crappie is the darker of the two. It has seven or either dorsal spines and spotted sides. The black Crappie prefer slightly deeper water than the white Crappie and the blacks are normally found in the northern most lakes preferring water temperatures of between 66 and 76 degrees.

The white Crappie which ahs a very light body and six dorsal spines has eight or nine barely visible bands on its sides. It prefers water temperatures from 64 to 80 degrees and is normally found in southern lakes with quiet and sometimes cloudy water.

Both types of Crappie can grow to over five pounds but a weight of ¾ pound to one pound is most common. Both types like brush trees or docks for cover and both will begin their spawn when the water reaches about 58 degrees. Spawning usually takes place from mid March to mid April depending on location. Crappie are nest builders and will build their nests in water depths of 1 to 5 feet. The nests are normally in a protected area, near merged vegetation or overhanging banks. They usually nest in groups and once females may spawn more than once.

When the fry hatch they normally spread out fast and move to deeper water within a few days. Bass love the Crappie fry and Crappie will also eat their own fry so if there are a large concentration of bass in the area, large schools of small Crappie will not propagate.

Young Crappie feed on plankton and as they grow their food is mainly small shad and insect larvae. May flies are a preferred food for the young Crappie.

For the Crappie population to flourish in a given lake, it is preferred that there not be a large quantity of bass present, however where this is the case the population of Crappie grows so large that they become stunted in size due to the limited feeding capability of the particular body of water. For Crappie to reach large sizes, it is preferred that they have a high mortality rate either by natural causes or through fishing harvest. This is why most states have a daily catch limit which is quite large compared to other types of fish.

Crappie are school fish and are usually fairly easy to catch using any of the more popular fishing techniques. They can be caught from the shore while still fishing, casting or trolling from your boat. The spring is the best time to catch a lot of Crappie when they are involved in their spawning habits but they can be fished year round. At dawn they are usually near the surface, as the run rises they will drop to depths of 5 to 10 feet depending on the clarity of the water. As the sun rises in the sky they will go to depths of 20 feet or more and as the sun begins to set they will move back to the shallower water to finish the day at the surface then as darkness begins they will return to deeper water. It is not normal for Crappie to feed during darkness.

It is probably an over simplification to say that Crappie are easy to catch, but indeed they are. It is not necessary to use complicated or expensive equipment to catch them and most Crappie fishermen develop their own technique for catching which is best for them and their fishing conditions.

Equipment needs are very basic and Crappie can be caught with most any kind of tackle. I recommend an ultralight rod and very light spinning reel. Catching Crappie with a fly rod is exciting. Line strength should be about four pounds since there is often bass lingering in the areas where you are fishing for Crappie.

Preferred bait for Crappie are small to medium minnows ranging from 2 to 2 ½ inches in length. These minnows can be hooked up through the mouth and upper lip. It is best to try to maintain a slight movement of the minnow.

Artificial lures are also good but they must be small and light in weight, less than 1/8 ounce. Some of the larger Crappie will take a crank bait, spinner or plastic worm.

Crappie usually move in groups so when you catch one you will usually catch more than one. Sometimes it is necessary to experiment with your bait at different depths using a bobber to locate the right depth. Once you locate it you should stay at that depth. Fish close to structure or brush and keep the bait moving very slowly. If you are not successful within fifteen minutes in one area, move to another area or another depth until you find the spot where they are congregated.

Where you fish will vary depending on the time of the year. Spring has already been mentioned as the best time to catch Crappie but they can be caught year round. As the water warms in the summer they will move to deeper water and they will probably congregate near and just above the thermocline. Night fishing can be productive during the summer months but it is usually wise to hang a light over the side of your boat near the mouth of a cove or creek. Fish near the bottom raising and lowering the bait slowly.

In the fall the Crappie move back to shallower water but will not usually go to less than a depth of ten feet. During the winter Crappie will gather in schools and suspend themselves in water at about 20 feet deep or even slightly deeper, near some kind of structure. At this time Crappie are hard to locate and will only bite at certain times. Winter fishing for Crappie is best near lighted docks, piers or other lighted structures.

Crappie Fishing Tips

- Crappie change locations as the seasons change. During the springtime they congregate on flats and around logs and brush. During the summer they use shade as cover around bridge pilings and around docks. In the fall they are around tree tops, docks and pilings.

- Even In the deeper water the Crappie may be suspended near the surface.

- Jigs can be flavored with shad flavoring which helps attract the crappie.

- Crappies are line shy so use the smallest line strength appropriate for the waters being fished. Less than 4 pound test is ideal.

- Lively healthy minnows are critical for a good Crappie catch. Lake water is normally warmer than the water in the bait wells of the store. You should take care to make a slow adjustment to the warmer water by adding lake water to the bait bucket water slowly.

- 1 ½ inch minnows are a good size for Crappie.

- Minnows should be hooked through the lips coming up through the lower lip first. This lets the minnow swim fairly freely and does not damage any vital organs.

- Crappie are often most active at dusk and after dark.

- Crappie like to settle around the deeper holes at the ends of docks.

- Using a float to suspend the minnow is a good technique. Cast the bait out, let it settle a few seconds then give the line a twitch to get the bait moving, let it rest for a few seconds and if no response takes place, cast to another spot.

- Use a soft cast to reduce stress on he minnow.

- Long limber rods allow you a good feel of the fish action.

- A surface or submerged light is an effect fish attractor at night. Lights attract the insect and small fish which will in turn attract the Crappie.

- Minnows are the best bait after dark.

- If you find a school of Crappie, try casting tandem lures at the same time one white and the other chartreuse.

- There are length and bag limits in most states, be aware of the rules.

- The winter months will find the fish near the deeper water.

- The larger crappie like crank baits, large spinners and even plastic worms.

- From February to May the crappie are normally in less than 15 feet of water.

- During the summer months the fish will be at or above the thermocline.

- If fishing crappie at night try the mouth of the coves or creeks with a light over the side of the boat.

- Sun has a great effect on this fish. The deeper the sun penetrates the water the deeper the crappie will be.

BREAM

It was late in my life before I heard of the term Bream used to describe a general class of fish that contains many specific different types of fish. I would be doing the fishing community a disfavor if I neglected to include information on this family of fish.

As sportsmen and women we all have a desire and perhaps an obligation to bring new talent to the fish community. This is usually done by introducing young children to the sport and we normally introduce them by teaching them how to catch Bream. There isn't really much teaching required because most fish in the bream group are very easy to catch. When you take a child fishing for the first few times it is important that they get action rather quickly since their attention span is usually quite short. If you find a location that contains bream, that problem will take care of itself.

Bream which is pronounced (Brim) is a name that has been given to a group of small fish including a variety of sunfish. The list of fish contained in the bream group will vary depending on the fisherman describing the group and the area of the country that you are in. most of the fish in this group are widely found in ponds and lakes throughout the country. I will identify and describe a few of the most common categories of bream.

BLUEGILL

The Bluegill is one of the most widely known Bream. The Bluegill can be distinguished from the other sunfish by the dark spot at the base of its dorsal fin and a solid black gill flap. The Bluegill also has 6 or 8 vertical bars on its sides. Its mouth is quite small. The front dorsal fin contains 10 spines and is connected the rear soft dorsal. The anal fin also has three spines. These spines, particularly the dorsal ones create cause for caution when attempting to take a hook out of the mouth, once the fish is caught. Because of its small mouth the food enjoyed by the Bluegill is limited in size to include small insects, plankton, small crawfish and fish eggs. Bluegills enjoy warm shallow water with growing vegetation. During the day they seek shade from overhanging trees and branches. Bluegills can grow to about 12 inches but 8 inches is more common. They normally live about 5 years.

The Green Sunfish is not quite as deep in body structure as the other bream fish. It has black gill flap like the bluegill but this area has a red tip. The mouth is relatively large, more like a bass with the upper jaw extending back to the middle of the eye. The pectoral fin is short and rounded and there are three spines on the anal fin. The general color of the body is a greenish blue with a yellow tint. The Green Sunfish can tolerate turbulent water unlike most other Bream.

Their food is mostly small fish, aquatic insects, minnow and small crawfish. They grow to about seven inches and will average a little less than a pound.

The mouth of the Warmouth is like the Green Sunfish with the jaw extending back to the middle of the eye. Its color is dark olive brown with irregular bars running vertically on the sides. It has three spines on its anal fin. Its diet includes mall crawfish, insects and shrimp if available. The Warmouth prefers weeds in its habitat and is usually hiding in the shade of these weeds or other growth. The fish grows to about eight inches and will average slightly less than one pound in weight.

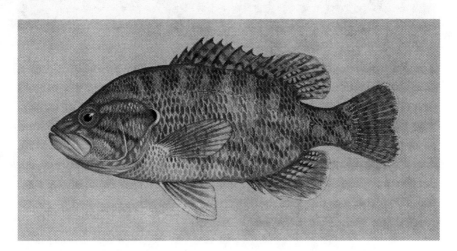

Rock Bass are thick heavy bodied fish with grayish green color with a copper tone. It has red eyes and the jaw extends back to the center of the eye. It has six anal fin spines. The Rock Bass has rows of spots that form lateral lines in its sides. This fish prefers clear water and small lakes with a small water flow. They prefer a boulder covered or gravel bottom or a bed rock bottom with drop offs. It eats aquatic insects and the older fish will eat small minnows and small fish and crawfish. The Rock Bass can grow to ten inches and achieve a weight of two pounds.

The Pumpkinseed is a popular sunfish that is very colorful. It has a deep body with a small mouth. The breasts and the belly are organs or yellow with lighter colored sides containing a variety of colors. The gill flap is black with an orange spot on the border. Their food is normally small aquatic insects, plankton and very small fish. The Pumpkinseed loves worms. This fish is normally found in the northern regions of the country. It enjoys cool clear water and spring fed lakes and ponds. The average size of the pumpkinseed is seven inches and weighs less than one pound.

Fishing for nearly all of the fish in the Bream category is the same. They spawn in water when it reaches 65 degrees so their spawn is later than most other fish. They enjoy water temperatures of 64 to 70 degrees and will live in water higher than 80 degrees. The most common bait for fishing Bream are small crickets or earth worms cut into small pieces. Bream can be caught on small lures such as tiny crank bait or jig heads.

The best equipment to use is an ultralight rod with a line of about 2 pounds test. The line must be light enough to detect a very small bite which is sometimes the case. Your hook should be small, usually a number 6 or 8 wire hook. Most Bream will hit the bait as it reaches the bottom and often will feed off of the bottom. On light gear they are fun to catch and many say very good eating.

Panfish Fishing Tips

- Panfish normally cruise the edges of the weed beds.

- Panfish gather in the cuts, holes and pockets.

215

- A small spinner rig slowly trolled along a weed line will quickly find fish.

- For Bluegills, tip a single small hook with the half of a worm or a small leech.

- Perch as well as Crappie often prefer a small minnow or leech as bait hooked through the lip.

- When you find panfish, cast small light jigs using 2 to 3 pound test line.

- Try crickets or grasshoppers on a bare hook, they work well for panfish.

- When using crawlers, inject the nose with a small amount of air to help the worm float.

- Your nose can help detect Bream in the springtime. In areas where the water is still and the bream are spawning, you can smell the odor of urine around the spawning area. Both mal and female bream urinate heavily to adjust the water ph for best fertilization of the eggs. You will quickly detect he smell.

- Bream near the beds will bite several times in one day so you can rotate you fishing areas returning several times in one day.

- Bream fishing is the best way to introduce a young child to the fishing experience. Their attention span is short and they will likely get excited with the large number of bites from hungry bream.

CATFISH

Some fish are beautiful and others are considered ugly, the Catfish is perhaps the one fish that has the advantage of combining both of these qualities. It is an ugly fish at times and also a beautiful fish at times, it kind of depends on the circumstances. There are about 2200 different kinds of catfish found throughout the world. The only place that has not reported the existence of Catfish is Antarctica.

What makes this family of fish so interesting is the wide variety of unusual types that exist around the world. One of the ugliest is the Sheatfish found in the rivers of Eurasia that can grow to weights in excess of 600 pounds and has been known to eat birds and dogs that swim on the surface. The South American cats are among the most beautiful of the cats. The African electric catfish grows to more than 50 pounds and can develop an electric charge in excess of 250 volts. The Upside Down Catfish also of Africa swims with its back facing downward. The Asian Glass Catfish is transparent under certain conditions. The Candirus Catfish of South America is the smallest species known but can penetrate the human body and has been known to be lethal.

Why the name? Simple, the Catfish have whiskers much like your house cat. These whiskers are called barbells and they serve very specific functions of taste and smell. Most North American Catfish have four sets of barbell around their mouth. These barbells are covered with taste buds and assist the fish with finding food. These barbells are very soft and cannot sting.

Catfish do not have any scales. Some are smooth skinned and others have rows of spiny plates that overlap but none have scales.

Catfish have sharp spines in their pectoral and dorsal fins and these can cause a very painful wound if you manage to get stuck by one while handling a catfish. There are venom cells covering these spines and it is this venom reaches your blood stream it can cause serious problems. It is not lethal but can be very uncomfortable and painful.

There have been published studies that suggest that the mucus covering the body of the catfish has healing properties for human skin. Some fishermen try to rub their hands with this mucus to heal small cuts and scratches.

I can't verify the healing effect of the skin covering but I can attest to the harmful effect of the spine venom. I was stuck by a pectoral fin spine last year and the spine penetrated a vein and went into a bone and broke off. The pain that I felt was excruciating when I finally pulled the broken segment out with pliers and the bleeding would not stop. I passed out minutes later and was taken to a medical emergency facility. The doctor was unaware of any harmful effects of a "fish sting". But did give me a tetanus shot.

From a fisherman's point of interest it is necessary to discuss the senses of a catfish. One author described the catfish as being "supercharged". This fish has sensing devices all over its body. The nostrils are located in front of the eyes and close to a small barbell on top of the nose area. The barbells as mentioned are covered with taste buds. The back of the eyes are coated with a layer of crystals that reflect light. The lateral line across the body detects vibrations in the water. Electroreceptive pores cover the head region and the lateral line.

Why all of these sensors? Well the most important purpose is to detect food sources. The catfish has a keen sense of smell that can locate food at relatively long distances. Taste is assisted by the more than one half million taste buds along the skin. Most fish taste with their mouth; the catfish also does but has the assistance of these external taste buds. Hearing is provided by the sensing of sound through the skin of the catfish. The catfish is unique in that it can detect both high frequency and low frequency noise.

You might ask yourself, with all of this sensing equipment, how in the world is it possible to out smart a catfish and catch one while fishing? Well that's fairly simple, the catfish really does not use all of these sensing devices to detect fishermen but almost always to find food, they are therefore much more likely to detect your bait and strike for it than most any other fish.

Well that's enough about the science of the catfish and its world wide population. Let's now concentrate on the three species of Catfish that predominate North American, the Channel Catfish, the Blue Catfish and the Flat Head Catfish.

CHANNEL CATFISH

Since we are only dealing with the three most common Catfish found in this country, it would probably be best if I described the Channel Catfish last since it is the best looking of the three species to be discussed. Maybe because of this I felt that if I put it first in order you would realize that everything following would only be down hill from this description.

The Channel Catfish is found in nearly every part of the United States with the exception of the very easterly most coast and only spotty existence west of the Rocky Mountains but in general it is the most populous catfish in this country found almost everywhere. Of the three species being discussed the channel has a much sleeker and more attractive body than the others. Most are a silvery gray to almost a brown color with a white belly. The young channels have spots on their bodies but these disappear as they age. The channel has a deep forked tail and its upper jaw extends beyond its lower jaw.

The Channel Catfish prefers water temperatures of 75 to 85 degrees but is often found in water that is even warmer than that. Its size is kind of in the middle of the three species with average weights falling in the 1 to 5 pound range. 6 to 10 pound channels are becoming rather common and a 20 pound channel is a trophy fish. The growth rate of the channel is slower than the blue or the flathead. Its life expectancy is about 10 years but some have been known to live 20 years and longer. Both the growth rate and life expectancy are functions of the living conditions, much like humans. Where food is more abundant, weather is consistent and water temperatures are ideal, the age and growth rate will increase beyond the averages.

For years we thought that Channel Catfish likes murky and muddy water but this is not true. The Channel Catfish prefers clean, warm and well oxygenated water with a mild current flow and a lot of cover such as logs, stumps, big rocks and debris. They like deep water with a sandy or gravel bottom.

In the late spring or early summer when the water temperature reached about 75 degrees the male channel builds a nest in the underwater holes, logs or submerged rocks. The female deposits a large mound of yellow eggs in this nest and leaves. The male stays to guard the eggs and to fan the next to oxygenate the area and keep it clean. In 5 to 10 days the eggs hatch and the fry grow rather rapidly. Young channel cats eat mostly insects, crawfish and other small fish. The small channels are also a preferred meal for many other larger fish.

Channel Catfish are certainly not fussy eaters. They love live worms, salamanders, insects, frogs and all types of small fish. Most fishermen feel that the smellier and more rotten the food, the better it is preferred by the Channel Catfish. Aged or rotten shrimp, fish guts, cut bait Bream, chicken livers and other of those types of food will provide a great meal for the Channel Catfish. Of course you must keep in mind that you also have to put it on the hook. A friend of mine catches bream, cut them up, put the pieces in a canning jar and buries the jar in the sun for two weeks. After that he feels that the bait is ready for the Channel Catfish.

One of the reasons that the Channel Catfish is so popular is that it is very adaptable to changes in water conditions so it is a popular stocking fish for private ponds and commercial pay fishing areas where you take your grandson for his first fish. They are feisty and fight hard so they are fun to catch even when they are small.

Channel Catfish feed both day and night. During the day time they move into the deeper water to hide among the logs and rocks. At late afternoon they begin to move to shallower water also to feed. They take most of their food off of the bottom or near the bottom but at times they have been known to top feed. Channels are best fished from late afternoon through early evening.

It is wise to use a heavier gear when fishing for Channel Catfish. A popular technique is to drift fish from your boat with a heavy rod and line of greater than 10 pounds test. I prefer a 1/0 circle hook and your line should be weighted to get it to the bottom. You could also anchor your boat if you find an area that you feel houses catfish and put out more lines, either resting on the bottom or using a bobber properly measure to get close to the bottom. A slip bobber is ideal for fishing Channel Catfish.

I do mostly trolling and I have found during the summer months during the day time, trolling a live minnow is an effective way to catch Channel Catfish. Channels can also be caught while fishing from shore or from a dock or pier and fishing from these areas is best in late afternoon and early evening when the fish come close to shore to feed. During these hours you might just also catch a nice largemouth bass if they live in your fishing waters.

BLUE CATFISH

Of the three catfish types that I am describing here, the Blue Catfish is one of my favorites for three reasons: first, although not the largest of the species, Blues grow to a fine fishing size and it is not unusual to land an 8 to 10 pound fish; second, the Blue is the toughest fighter of the three species and lastly, when I want a great catfish meal, the Blue has the best taste.

The Blue Catfish is similar to the Channel cat in many ways, both having a forked tail and depending on the conditions, their coloring can be very close to each other. The Blue however normally has a blue-gray color on its body fading to a white belly. If it is really important to you to distinguish the two, there is a very specific difference in the anal fin of the two types of fish. If you want to take the time to count, the Channel Cat has between 24 and 29 rays on its anal fin and the Blue Catfish has 30 or more rays. The anal fin of the Blue is fairly straight where it is rounded on the Channel. Usually the color is the real items of distinctions between the two with the normal color of the Blue being just that, light blue. If the Blue Catfish spends most of its life in muddy water, its color becomes very light and at times it has been named the "white catfish." Normally the upper jaw of the Blue is even with the lower jaw but on occasion the upper jaw will protrude out beyond the lower jaw. Larger Blue Cats often develop a hump back with a bump on the top of its head.

A healthy Blue Catfish in human terminology would be defined as obese and often have huge pot bellies. They prefer water between 70 and 82 degrees and are normally found only in very large lakes and prefer a strong flowing river with clear water and a sandy or gravel bottom. Geographically the Blue Catfish is found in the southerly states and south into Mexico. Few of the top tier northern states have Blue Catfish.

When the water temperature reaches about 70 to 75 degrees their spawning starts. This normally happens in June or July. The males and females work together to build their nest, normally in a deep hole or area behind logs or debris. Once the eggs are deposited in the next, both male and female will guard the nest, unlike most other types of fish. The eggs will hatch in about one week and shortly after this the fry will go their own way. At the end of the first year the Blue Catfish will grow to between 2 and 4 inches. The smaller fish prefer crawfish and other small fish but as they grow, they prefer anything that they can put into their stomach.

Fishing for Blue Catfish is fun because they basically eat anything that is or once was alive. If it smells bad they like it more. Since the Blue is a large fish it likes large pieces of bait for food. When the Blues and Stripers are both located in the same body of water, the Blue will often be found with the stripers feeding off of the remains that fall to the bottom.

Blue Catfish will also respond to live bait of any kind but herring and shad are their preference. A Blue Catfish will rarely respond to an artificial lure but even that is not impossible if the lure takes on a very good likeness to a live fish. Cut bait and almost any type of bream or sunfish will make a fine bait, either cut or whole.

Blues can be caught year round but if the water temperature drops below 40 degrees, a Blue will be hard to come by. An average size Blue will be about 6 to 10 pounds and a 60 pounder would be a trophy.

Heavy tackle, strong rods and reels and heavy line is best when fishing for Blue Catfish. Many fishermen even use salt water gear if they have it to insure boating the big ones. Blues can be caught trolling or still fishing and should be fished close to the bottom. Like the other catfish they feed deep during the day time and move toward shore at night.

Blue Catfish are so preferred for eating that they have become a commercial commodity and in some areas are so heavily fished that their populations have decreased significantly. Stocking is sometimes used to offset this problem.

FLATHEAD CATFISH

For a long time the Flathead was neglected as a game fish that was sought after by seasoned fishermen. In many areas of the country it is the largest of the catfish available to fishermen. Today the Flathead is a popular game fish and many professional guides take their clients only after this big fish.

There are some fish that I will often define as beautiful. The Flathead catfish is certainly not one of those. Of the three catfish species that I have chosen to describe, the Flathead is the ugliest. Although its body is streamlined and muscular, there is little beauty here unless you measure beautiful by the size of the fish caught, then the use of the word beautiful is accepted for the Flathead.

Its back and sides are brownish to yellowish. The belly is light yellow to creamy white. Its head is broad and flattened (the reason for its name) the tail of the Flathead is different from the other two types in that it is square. Its lower jaw protrudes out beyond the upper jaw.

Flatheads are found in the south central and central states and down into Mexico. Because of their growing popularity, they have been introduced into many lakes west of the Rocky Mountains. In most areas of the United States, the only fresh water fish that grows bigger than the Flathead is the blue catfish, white sturgeon and Alligator Gar. 10 and 20 pound Flatheads are fairly common but to get to trophy status the size must exceed 50 pounds.

Flatheads are normally found in large rivers and large lakes and are rarely found in streams, creeks, ponds and small lakes. The adults live in deep, sluggish pools near large logs or structures. They are also found in undercut banks and near brush and debris. They prefer a hard sandy or gravel bottom and rare rarely found in areas that have a soft bottom.

The Flathead is not a school fish. They are very solitary and normally travel and live alone. If you catch one large Flathead, you will rarely catch more than one or maybe two in a given area. They feed primarily on other fish and use their sense of smell and their ability to detect vibrations to locate their prey. At night they will normally feed in the shallower areas. They are normally caught using live bait or night crawlers and do not prefer dead or stink bait as the Blue and Channel cats do.

The Flathead prefers water in the range of 75 to 85 degrees. In the summer when the water temperature reaches 72 to 75 degrees, the Flathead starts its spawn. Like the Channel, the male builds a nest in cavities such as a hollow log but in quiet water. Immediately after the eggs are dropped into the nest, the male drives the female from the nest, sometimes violently. The male guards the nest and fans the water over the eggs until the eggs hatch and the male will attend to the young until they choose to leave the nest. Although the Flathead will tolerate turbidity and will live in water in the 90's it does require a good water flow and well oxygenated water.

Flathead are rarely caught in the winter months. During this period the Flathead finds deep water where big rocks or other debris will protect it from the current. It will remain there through the winter and lay so still that it often gets covered with a fine dusting of silt until the water warms and it decides to move.

Flatheads are not as easy to catch as the other species of catfish but when caught they put up a tremendous fight. Since they travel alone the catch frequency is less than the other cats. Because of the Flathead has little to do with other fish, they will resort to cannibalization eating their own kind if the occasion presents itself.

Heavy gear and line tests about 20 pounds is wise when fishing for Flatheads. I prefer the 1/0 or larger circle hook as I do for each of the other species of catfish.

The Flathead is a very tasty fish. Its flesh is firm white and flaky and when it is properly prepared it is a delicious meal.

Many experienced fishermen say that one you catch a good sized Flathead you become a Flathead fisherman forever.

Tips for Fishing Catfish

- Drifting cut bait across contour changes on the lake bottom is a traditional method of catching big catfish.

- A medium bait casting rod is big enough for most catfish.

- Cut bait the size of a man's thumb is the ideal size for dragging the bottom for cats.

- Cut small filets from the sides of bream or white perch eliminating the backbone is a good method of preparing cut baits.

- Some fishermen prefer bream heads for the big cats.

- Drift fishing with several rods out or slow trolling is the standard for fishing catfish.

- Catfish are opportunity fish, they have to take the bait when it comes by or let it go, they don't attach moving bait normally.

- The appetite of catfish changes and they will not eat anything as is a popular belief. You have to try different baits on different days.

- If you can find bottom humps at 20 or more feet of depth you should find catfish feeding there.

- In summer months you need to drift or troll as slowly as possible and still control the boat.

- If you hit a fish in one area, drift or troll back over that same area again and again until you stop getting hits.

- If you can find the edges of weed beds, drift or troll these edges, catfish will hang there.

- Most very large catfish are caught during the spring and fall.

- Live bait will work year round for catfish with the best being shad or herring.

- During the hotter days the catfish will move into shallow water at night to feed. During the daytime hours they will seek deeper water.

- Catfish don't like to work hard for their food so wounded or dead bait is attractive to them. Flatheads will take dead bait and rarely hit a lure. Channel cats prefer live bait and will occasionally hit a lure.

- Night fishing has always been considered effective for catching big catfish.

- The more a bait smells the better the catfish will like it.

- Many species of catfish have glands at the base of their pectoral fins that produce a toxin that can produce a very painful sting.

- Catfish slime contains sixty different proteins that are considered good for healing wounds.

THREE COMMON CATFISH RIGS

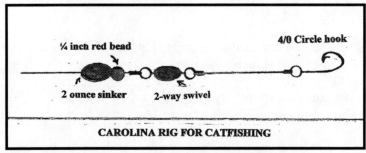

CAROLINA RIG FOR CATFISHING

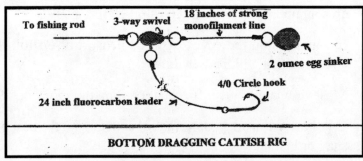

BOTTOM DRAGGING CATFISH RIG

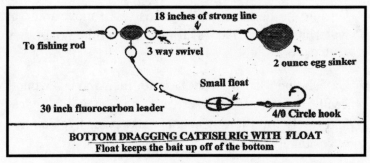

BOTTOM DRAGGING CATFISH RIG WITH FLOAT
Float keeps the bait up off of the bottom

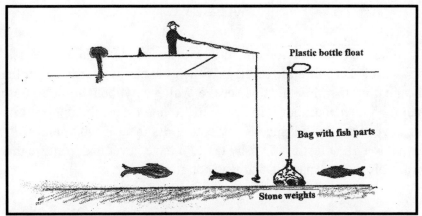

Plastic bottle float

Bag with fish parts

Stone weights

Creating A Honey Hole

Make a point to keep several of your garbage fish. Filet them or chop them up and place all pieces in a burlap bag or net bag and put in the freezer. When you are ready to use, take out of freezer and let thaw slightly. Go to your selected fishing spot and submerge to bottom but secure with a bloat. Let the bag sit for an hour or two before you start fishing this area. When you return there should be catfish and other fish in the area.

Flat Head Catfish can sure be ugly but to the authors grandson Jordan Lyle this 31 inch 12 pounder will remain a beauty in his mind for a long time. Keeping kids interested in fishing means helping them feel this kind of excitement.

WALLEYE

If someone asked me to name my favorite fish, I would have to ask, favorite for catching or eating? If the question was directed to the best eating fish, I would answer the Walleye, without a doubt. I am not a big fish eater but I do my share. When I have the opportunity however I prefer this species for eating. Its meat is white and flaky and has a great taste. No "fishy taste." I have never had Walleye that was cooked in a manner that was not good eating.

The Walleye is the largest member of the Perch family but is not always found where other perch are located. It is found in rivers, lakes and other waters where the water temperature is cool and fairly clear. The preferred temperature is between 55 and 68 degrees and is rarely found in water deeper than 50 feet. Its preferred depth is 25 feet or less.

The Walleye has a variation of colors from olive brown, golden brown and yellow on its back, its sides are paler than the back and the belly is normally yellowish white. It has two dorsal fins, the front most fin containing spines and the rear most fin becoming soft with rays. Both the anal and caudal fins have white tips. The eye of the Walleye is cloudy and quickly turns white when the fish dies. It has sharp teeth.

The Walleye is not the greatest fish to catch and it is often a difficult one to find. The advantage of Walleye fishing is that this fish feeds all year round so winter Walleye fishing is quite good. The Walleye prefers darker waters and tends to shy away from light. It usually travels in schools and will often rest near the bottom of the water body hovering near submerged objects. The best time to fish Walleye is in the very early morning and dusk to dark, both times when the light level is low. During the mid summer months they will often stay near the bottom, even at night. Cloudy days make good fishing and a slight chop on the surface to break up the suns rays helps the Walleye fisherman.

In the early spring months, usually around April or May they look for rocky shoals for their spawning. A normal size female will lay as many as 400,000 eggs and neither the male nor the female protects the eggs. Like many other fish species, the fry eat plankton and small insects but as they grow, their food is primarily other small fish. As the Walleye grows it becomes a greedy predator feeding on small bass, trout, pike, perch and sunfish. The average Walleye caught is about three years old and weighs from one to three pounds. The average length of this aged fish is 14 to 16 inches.

There are many ways to fish for Walleye. If you keep in mind that an adult wants to eat other fish, most lures used for Walleye will take on the look or shape of a small fish. This being the case, minnows are considered the best bait for the Walleye. Even the lead head jigs that many fishermen use are normally designed to look and behave like a fish darting through the water.

Walleye are normally fished near the bottom by using about any technique. You can cast, troll, drift, jig or still fish near the bottom using a bobber but you should keep the bait moving to represent a live fish. If using minnows as bait you have a choice of hooking the bait up through the nose or hooking it behind the dorsal fin. The later technique is preferred by many fishermen because it seems to have the greater catch rate.

If you know that there is structure near the bottom, this would be a preferred area to fish. You may lose some jigs but you will also catch fish. Since Walleyes often travel in schools, if you catch one Walleye you will probably catch more in the same area but you may have to wait a little while as things settle from the last catch.

The Walleye has a very unique method of eating that needs to be remembered when trying for repeated catches. Normally they will approach their prey, open their mouth and take in a large amount of water as they also take in the prey. They then close their mouth and eat the prey. It is at this point that you need to set your hook. This means that the bite is not a hard bite and it takes some getting use to in order to repeat a catch. Patience is the key here and a good sense of feel.

Just about any medium weight rod will work well and your line test should be appropriate for the average Walleye size. 50 to 10 pound test should be fine but you have to keep in mind that in some more northern locations, Walleye are in the same waters as Pike and other larger fish and you must be prepared for a larger catch where this is the case.

Walleye Fishing Tips

- Light 1/16 or 1/32 ounce jigs are best for getting the suspended Walleyes.

- The colors that Walleyes can see best are chartreuse, lime and dark green.

- Jigging spoons are not a popular lure for Walleye but some pros feel they are very effective.

- In the fall months Walleyes are looking for a larger presentation and jigging spoons are very effective.

- Walleye have a very bony mouth, especially at the roof of the mouth. If you find that many of your walleyes are getting off as they are being retrieved, you may have a dull hook, sharpen it or change it for better results.

- You can often have success getting Walleyes on crankbaits. These lures provide flash, vibration, profile and snag resistance and you can control the running depth.

- A "Lindy Rig" is popular for walleye fishing. This rig uses a slip sinker to bring the bait to the bottom and a small float to raise the bait off of the bottom. A bead is used to control where the float rests relative to the hook and bait.

- Walleye fishing is best during low light periods such as early morning, evening or nights and cloudy or windy days.

- On dark days or in dark dingy water the Walleye will be in about 8 feet or less of water.

- When Walleyes are in shallow water they are easily spooked so they should be fished in front of the boat if moving. This requires casting rather then trolling.

- Fall Walleyes are the larger ones during the year, In September spoons the size of perch or shad work well. In October when the water cools use larger spoons and in November the retrieve should be slowed significantly and use large noisy lures but fewer spoons.

- During the summer months the Walleye hang out near the schools of bait and because they are feeding off the bait fish they are often reluctant to chase your lure. During these times use a spinner lure coupled with live bait, this seems to work well as a Walleye attracter.

- Spinner baits provide vibrations that lure the Walleyes.

- Good trolling speeds for Walleyes are 1 ½ to 2 miles per hour.

- Bottom bouncers also work well during the summer months.

- If there are perch in the waters being fished, Walleye are attracted to the perch as a fine meal.

- The heaviest concentrations of Walleye will be near rocky breaks and hard bottom. Some will collect near patches of gravel or near rock piles.

- At night Walleye will be attracted by weed lines, during the day move to deeper drop offs.

- In natural lakes Walleye gather near the natural water in flow areas, rocky shore lines or rock humps or points.

- Walleye schools often move with no notice but when they move they will be moving to another area where the baitfish schools are gathered.

- Be sure that you know and understand the number and size limits where you are Walleye fishing. Many lakes have gap sizes that cannot be kept and must be released.

This 27 inch Walleye provided a reproduction trophy for John Bussolini, the authors son. Taken from Granite Lake in Ontario Canada, the fish was handled carefully, photographed and quickly returned to the water to bite again another day.

NORTHERN PIKE

The second half of the question earlier asked about my favorite fish involves the northern Pike or "Northern." There is a very close race for my favorite fish to catch between the Striper and the Northern Pike. As for overall fight and excitement I have to stick with the Striper but for overall enjoyment of all aspects of the fishing experience from the variety of techniques used to fight presented, to the variety of baits, the Northern Pike stands above all other fish. There have been days when I returned from a full day of fishing Northerns and my arms and shoulders were actually painful from all of the action. I don't consider the Northern to be a great eating fish but it is certainly a great sport fishing experience.

The Northern is exciting because it is not bashful to strike, and strike it does at just about anything that is passed before it. Believe it or not when I am in an area that has a lot of Northerns, I am actually reluctant to jiggle my bare hand in the water to clean it after a catch for feat that I may be near another hungry fish that would just as soon take my finger as it would another fish.

235

Northern Pike are native to North America located from Labrador west to Alaska and as far south as Pennsylvania and Missouri. They have also been introduced and are flourishing in Europe. They are found in almost any type of fresh water because they are very adaptable to different types of water. They have a broad tolerance for a wide range of water temperatures, water clarity and oxygen content. They are considered one of the most adaptable fresh water fish.

The Northern averages about 18 to 22 inches in length. It can be identified by a long slender body, a single dorsal fin and light colored spots against a dark colored body. The body color is normally a dark green to olive green to even brown. It has seven to nine rows of bean shaped yellowish spots on its sides. The belly is white to cream colored.

The Northern is considered a random spawner meaning that is odes not build a nest. It spawns in shallow water when the water temperature reaches 40 to 45 degrees. In some regions it has been known to start its spawn at water temperatures as cold as 35 degrees. The female spawns for 5 to 10 days after which she leaves the spawning area and the male remains in the area. The eggs are adhesive and stick to submerged vegetation. The male will remain in the spawning area for several weeks but it does not protect the eggs and being in shallower water the eggs are very vulnerable to other predators. The eggs that survive and hatch will do so in about two weeks. Because they have exceptional appetites, the young grow rapidly in both weight and length.

Northerns are not a school fish. They are solitary fish that travel alone and they are very aggressive. They are lurkers who hide in an "s" shaped position always ready to strike out at their prey. Their eyes are highly movable and are able to see in almost any direction as they track their prey. The Northern is a carnivorous fish that has very sharp teeth and a complex jaw and skull structure. They are predators of other fish, frogs, small mammals and birds. Northerns are built for fast acceleration and they attack their prey from cover and eat other fish with their needle like teeth. Because of the energy they expend in the attack, they do not want to waste it on small amounts of food so they concentrate on larger prey. It is not unusual for a Northern to feed on fish one third its size. Their normal diet is perch, suckers, minnows and other smaller Northern Pike.

The small Northern Pike live in shallow weedy water much of the year. The larger ones move deeper as the summer months pass seeking well oxygenated water 65 degrees or cooler. The ideal water temperature for the Northern is 60 to 70 degrees. The large fish become rather lethargic in warm water and they often stop eating and lose great amounts of weight. For this reason the warmer summer months are not considered good Northern fishing months.

Northern Pike have a rather long life if conditions are right. In the Northern most regions they have been known to live for 25 years. The females grow faster than the males and normally live longer than the males. A 25-year old Northern can grow to 45 inches and weight more then 24 pounds.

Northerns can be fished in several ways but your selected technique has to keep in mind how they live. You generally have to be outside the weed beds where they lurk. Casting almost any type of lure toward the bed will produce fish. Trolling is also very productive although not quite as exciting. Trolling along weed beds has the same effect as long as the bait is visible. Trolling can be done with live bait or lures. My favorite lure is the Mepps Cyclops. This lure comes in many colors and has a movement that seems to attract the nice sized fish.

Casting into the weed beds is the most exciting way to fish for Northerns. It produces more fish in quantity but smaller fish than can be caught trolling. Northerns will often follow the lure to the boat and hit it just as it is coming out of the water. This lends to the excitement since the retrieve is never over until the lure is out of the water. Many fishermen use a "figure eight" movement making the lure move in that pattern just before they remove it from the water.

If the fish is following the lure to the boat, this gives them more time to strike it.

Quite often the Northern will come out of the water after it hits your lure. This is because it is attacking so fast that it cannot stop at the surface. The fish will also often stand on its tail attempting to shake the lure. This also lends to the excitement of fishing this monster.

Some care needs to be taken when fishing Northern Pike. They are very large fish with a strong body and very sharp teeth. They exert a lot of energy fighting the retrieve and it is therefore wise to try to get them back into the water as fast as possible to avoid trauma to the fish. The only real method of grabbing a Northern is behind the head. You cannot grab them by the mouth. It is wise to have jaw spreaders with you to spread the jaws while you unhook the lure. Unhook the fish, take your pictures and return the fish to strike again another day and do it as fast as possible. If this process takes a longer than desired time, introduce the fish back into the water slowly, holding it by the tail and creating a movement to assist it in reestablishing its balance and bearing.

Equipment requirements for Northern Pike depend on the fishing method used. Trolling can be done with a salt water type pole, casting rod or other heavy rod with a non spinning type real. Casting is most exciting with a medium heavy spinning rod and heavy duty spinning reel. Line test should be greater than 15 to 20 pounds. In any case a short metal leader is required at the lure end to avoid the teeth tearing the line. Even using steel leaders, it is good practice to check the leader at periodic times to insure that it has not been frayed or damaged by the sharp teeth of a previous catch.

Northern Pike Fishing Tips

- On the smaller more shallow lakes, early summer Pike movement starts when 80 degree weather last at least one week. Pike will gather as the water warms to deeper levels.

- The early summer bite last only a few weeks in the shallow lakes less than 40 feet deep. The deeper lakes will produce good fishing all summer.

- The best technique to use when the weather warms is to troll for the Pike.

- Warm water creates more aggressive Pike and they will normally hit a faster moving target during warm weather.

- Casting for Pike in warm water will often result in nips and shallow hits because the lure is moving too slow.

- When casting in warm water move the lure rapidly and keep it at the same depth rather than letting it move up and down in the water column.

- Hard plastics trolled at depths of 10 to 20 feet may be effective in warm water.

- Spoon plugs with a fast wiggle are very effective for triggering a Pike strike.

- Really big Pike of 20 pounds or more are considered among the most evasive fish to catch.

- In most natural lakes during the summer, the outer edge of weed beds at depths of 15 to 20 feet is the place to look for nice Pike.

- Back trolling with a small minnow attached to a lure is an effective way to lure a big fish.

- Trolling or dragging a jig for Pike is best in water more than 15 feet deep.

- Don't let a Pike run when hooked but make a steady retrieve.

- Pike will often follow a lure right to the boat and hit just before it comes out of the water. If you see a Pike following the lure, make a figure eight with the rod tip in the water just before bring the lure out of the water.

- A six foot medium heavy spinning rod with a low stretch 15 pound test line is a good combination for Pike.

- A flexible wire leader is necessary to prevent the Pike from biting off the line.

- Big pike prefer a larger bait over a smaller one; they get more growth nourishment from eating big fish.

This 43 inch Northern Pike provided John Bussolini the thrill of a lifetime when he landed it on Granite Lake in Ontario Canada. John got this big fish on the same day that he caught the big Walleye shown elsewhere in this book.

HANDLING THE FISH

Years ago most fishermen and women caught fish for their own consumption. They enjoyed the sport of the catch but they also enjoyed the taste of a hearty fish meal.

In recent years the trend of fresh water fishermen has been more toward the excitement of the catch rather than the enjoyment or the need for the meal. As a result the issue of handling and releasing game fish has become more important.

Most of today's modern sport fishermen have also become more aware of the environmental issues effecting their sport and they have grown more attentive to maintaining the biological health of the waters that they fish in and the ability of their catch to be properly handled and released back into the water to be caught another day. Protection and growth of many species of game fish has become a major objective of all good sport fishermen. An important aspect of this responsibility is the proper handling and release of fish that are not being caught for consumption.

The problem was a little simpler when most of us used simple hooks that were fairly easy to remove. As hooks and lures became more complex, it also became more difficult to remove the hook or lure

241

from the mouth or body of the fish and fishermen became more alert to the proper methods of handling their catch so as not to cause unnecessary trauma or physical damage to the fish and in some cases to prevent damage to the fisherman.

There are many opinions on the best way to handle fish but the singly most important rule is to keep the fish out of the water for as short a time as possible and when out of the water to handle them with the greatest of care. There are many fishermen, particularly bass fishermen, who choose not to remove the fish from the water but to remove the hook while the fish is still in the water. This of course is always the best course of action but most of us, if we make a large catch, want to at least take a quick look or even a quick picture.

If you have occasion to handle your fish, do it in a manner than touches as little of the body of the fish as possible. Try not to wrap your hand around the fish either for lure removal or for picture taking. If you have to hold your fish up for a picture, try to hold it by the mouth and the tail. Your hand temperature is around 98 degrees and the body temperature of the fish could be as low as 40 degrees in the winter. The drastic body temperature changes that would result from prolonged handling can cause trauma to most fish. Most fish have a protective coating covering their bodies and prolonged handling will remove this coating and hurt the fish.

Another aspect of handling that you should consider relates to your methods of releasing the fish. Large fish normally are also fierce fighters and they use a great deal of energy fighting your retrieve. Most big fish are retrieved by wearing them down during the fight rather than horsing them quickly into the boat. During this fight they have used up most of their energy and they need oxygen to recover. Depriving them of this oxygen will cause lasting damage. With the bigger fish the release is very important. If possible put the fish gently back into the water holding its tail. Move the fish slowly side to side and forward and backwards. This slow action permits the fish to regain its balance and to begin the process of generating its own oxygen through its gill system. When the fish has regained its strength it will decide its time to be released and you have only to release it and watch it swim away. I have had many occasions where the release procedure was as exciting as the catch.

I will provide a brief discussion on the handling of several of the more popular game fish but you can break all fish into two groups, one group that has teeth and the other that does not. Most fish without sharp teeth can be held by the lower jaw and most fish with sharp teeth need to be held by some other preferably bony area of their body. The spiny dorsal fins on some species also dictate the handling technique because these spines can be very painful if they penetrate your skin. Let's look at some of the more common fish handling techniques.

White perch, shown in the two photos below, have a smaller mouth than many other species but a good sized perch can be held by the lower jaw as shown in the photo on the left. This technique avoids the spiny dorsal fin. In some cases where the hook in through the lower lip it will be necessary to hold the perch around the bony gill cover as shown on the right photo. This method uses primarily the thumb and for finger and prevents wrapping your hand around the body of the fish. Most panfish can be handled in this same manner.

Crappie also have a fairly large mouth so they can be handled by holding the lower jaw as shown in the photo below. Here again if the lower jaw cannot be held due to hook location, the gill cover can be held as was the case with the perch.

Stripers and Hybrids are relatively easy to handle due to their large mouth. The one characteristic that make handling a little more difficult here is that they refuse to admit that they have been caught and it might take a few grabs to get hold of the lower jaw as shown below. If you expect a large catch if stripers it is recommended that you put adhesive tape around the thumb that you will use to handle the striper. They do not have sharp teeth but they have a raspy jaw that will wear through your skin after handling a lot of fish. It is particularly important in the summer to get the striper back into the water as soon as possible to avoid damaging the fish.

Largemouth and spotted bass are perhaps the easiest to handle because they have a very large mouth and strong lower jaw. Care however needs to be taken not to hold a large bass in the horizontal position by the lower jaw for a long period since this can dislocate their lower jaw which will cause eventual death for the fish. Most of the time a bass will hook itself by the side of the lower jaw so it can be handled as shown below.

If you catch a bass that has not yet released its eggs like the one shown below, take care not to rough handle the fish or grab any part of its middle body. If you happen to be wearing gloves, remove them before handling the fish.

Fish with teeth such as the Northern Pike and Walleye shown below cannot, of course, be held by the lowed jaw. In these cases he fish should be held with the thumb and fore finger from the top of the head and around the gill cover. In the case of the Walleye, care must be taken to tuck the spiny dorsal fin back so as not to cause damage to your hand. In some cases with Northern Pike it will be necessary to use jaw spreaders to assist you in releasing the lure particularly if the hooks are deeper into the mouth area. The use of a jaw spreader is also shown below on the lower photo.

Catfish are one of the most commonly caught fish and in many cases one of the most feared concerning hook removal and handling. Catfish have a thick protective coating over their body which is important to their health. There is some proof that this coating is useful to humans to help quickly heel cuts and bruises. When catfish are caught they will often role over on the retrieve and leave large amounts of this coating on your line. I use three methods of handling catfish, particularly those that are small enough to actually handle which means most fish up to about 20 pounds. Each of my handling techniques are based on avoiding the sharp pectoral fin that can cause problems if it penetrates your skin.

The preferred technique is to grab the lower jaw as shown in the left photo below. Most catfish will initially resist this method and it may take a little coaxing to get the mouth open. This is the safest handling method. The second method is shown on the lower photo below and requires that you hold the fish at the rear of the large skull bone just above the pectoral fin. This technique can be used if the hook is in the lower jaw preventing holding it there.

The third technique is shown below and involves grabbing the fish behind the head insuring that the pectoral finds are held tightly above your hand and fingers so that they cannot act as daggers. Catfish are hard to hurt but they need to be respected to prevent damage to the fisherman.

No matter what species you are handling, remember that you want the fish to return to its waters to live undamaged so as to feed and grow and multiply and to be caught another day.

FISHING ETIQUETTE, ETHICS & SAFETY

Over the years I have learned to tolerate many unpleasant aspects of sport fishing. I have weathered many storms, fished in glaring sunlight, overcome boat engine failures, run out of bait while the fish were hot. BUT one aspect that I cannot accept or gain tolerance for is a fisherman or boater who has no knowledge of the rules, written or unwritten, and can totally ruin a fine fishing experience.

Most of us, who take sport fishing seriously, have a desire to keep our sport alive by introducing new young people to the sport. Perhaps as important as the excitement that we show them is the need for new fishermen to understand the etiquette, ethics and safety issues associated with fishing.

For the most part the etiquette and ethics part is in the conscience of the experienced fisherman. We take our sport seriously and we understand, whether written or unwritten, we have certain rules that we must follow to preserve the waters that we use to fish, the living creatures that we seek and the relationships with others that seek the same fishing enjoyment.

Out etiquette demands that we; protect the environment around the fish; treat all fish with a degree of respect as living creatures;

participate in the management of our fish; respect the rights of others; respect the environment that we live in.

If we consider ourselves ethical anglers WE:

- Do not spill gasoline or other pollutants on land or in the water;
- Never leave trash behind including bait, line or hooks;
- Leave our fishing site cleaner than we found it;
- Report significant environmental damage to the proper authorities;
- Take care to avoid damaging sensitive areas when boating;
- Do our best to prevent the spread of exotic and unwanted plants and animals;
- Never use live bait that does not normally reside in the waters that we are fishing;
- Know all of the local fishing regulations;
- Use only legal tackle, attend to our gear and value our catch;
- Keep no more fish than we intend to consume or are legally allowed;
- Limit our take rather than taking our limit;
- Practice conservation and use the proper release methods for fish not retained;
- Target more than one fish species so that pressured fish will get needed rest;
- Use tackle that will minimize catching unwanted fish;
- Report any illegal fishing activities to the proper authorities;
- Don't keep fish caught out of season;

- Don't keep egg bearing females;

- Treat other anglers, boaters, and people who we meet, with respect;

- Obtain permission from landowners and never trespass on private lands;

- Respect the space of other anglers and give way to anglers who are playing fish;

- Observe all operator and safety regulations;

- Watch our speed and wake and keep a safe distance from other anglers and boats;

- Educate fellow anglers about fishing ethics;

- Promote ethical behavior through our example;

- Preserve the sport fishing tradition.

Fishing safety is also normally left to the conscience of the individual. If we are boaters we must of course observe the established safety rules for boating and I always advise that a boater take a locally provided boating course to become familiar with the national and local boating laws. There are however a few safety tips that are useful for making your fishing experience a pleasant and memorable one. These tips include:

- When selecting a waterside fishing location, make sure that the area is free from underwater hazards, is clean and large enough to accommodate your fishing plans;

- Inspect your area waterfronts regularly the natural environment is subject to change on a regular basis;

- When choosing a site for fishing, always consider the various safety factors;

- Weather is always a factor. Make sure you get a reliable weather forecast and prepare for the worst of the expected conditions, if possible carry a radio that provides local weather conditions;

- Always wear foot gear that is appropriate for the expected conditions;

- Stay dry, warm and protected from the elements. Wear waterproof sunscreen, layers of clothing with water protective clothing as the outer layer;

- Use appropriate insect protection;

- Keep fishing knives sharp and cover the blade when not in use;

- Handle the fish carefully; be aware of those fish that have sharp spines;

- Be particularly careful and aware of others when casting;

- Practice hook safety and make sure that others in your party understand hook safety principles;

- Always have the appropriate type and number of life preservers in your boat;

- When boating, always know where you are and the fastest rout of return in case of an emergency;

- Make sure that all parties on your boat know your boating rules;

- Always have at least a basic first aid kit with you;

- Don't boat beyond your capability to handle any situation that may arise

- If possible, especially when casting, have all people in your boat wear safety glasses.

FISHING WOUNDS

Most "normal" techniques of fishing provide little opportunity for wounds to the fisherman or those accompanying the fisherman in his quest for a catch. In my more than 60 years of fishing, I have had only one occasion where a wound required me to stop fishing and that situation was very unique and is described elsewhere in this book. Accidents however do happen and they usually take place as a result of carelessness on the part of the fisherman. Whatever the cause, it is important that we understand what actions should be taken when a fishing wound occurs.

First and foremost it is critical to understand that any wound to the eye or the surrounding eye tissue is cause to stop fishing and see the appropriate doctor as soon as possible. There is no safe action that can be taken on the fishing site for an eye injury. Prevention is of course the best solution so it is always advisable to understand where your fishing partners are located and everyone should be aware of the techniques being used and the potential dangers. When casting on a continuous basis, it is advisable that glasses be worn. This will significantly reduce the possibility of any eye injury particularly from another fisherman.

I also consider it advisable for all parties to wear a hat when fishing. In addition to protecting you from long term sun exposure, a hat will be the first item to be caught if a casted hook or lure passes too close to your head.

One good safety practice that is almost always overlooked is to have every member of your fishing party aware of all of the hook types that are being used. Most fishing accidents involve hooks and it can be very important to know what type of hook is being used especially if a hook requires removal as a result of an accident.

The importance of knowing the hook type should be obvious since they each may require a different technique for removal should an accident happen. Let me state here that proper medical attention is always recommended for any wound that deeply penetrates the flesh. Circumstances often dictate the on-site removal of a hook and if that is necessary you should be knowledgeable of the recommended methods of removal.

Again a reminder or safeguard that should be considered, if you intend to do a lot of fishing, make sure that your tetanus shots are up to date. I also consider it good practice to insure that your hooks are always sharp and clean from rust or residue. Rusty, dirty or dull hooks will increase your loss rate and they become more dangerous if you have an accident. Hooks attached to lures are not always convenient to change but they should be inspected prior to use and their condition noted.

There are several methods of hook removal that are practiced but only the three most common methods will be discussed here. The first is the "retrograde" method. The retrograde removal method is the simplest and most commonly used method of hook removal. Simply illustrated in the sketch below, this method will work best for barbless hooks and hooks that are only superficially embedded.

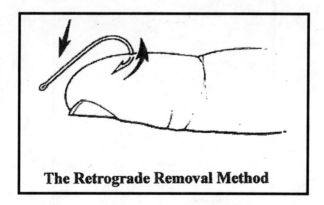

The Retrograde Removal Method

Downward pressure is applied to the shank of the hook. This pressure actually rotates the hook slightly deeper but disengages the barb from the tissue. The hook can now be backed out along the path of its entry.

The "String and Yank" method is a modification of the retrograde method and perhaps the most popular method used by experienced fisherman. It may take slightly more time but it creates no new wounds and provides the least amount of trauma. This method can be used on almost any type of hook but normally works best for the smaller sizes.

For the String and Yank method the hook must be in a fixed part of the body, not an area like an ear lobe. The technique is simply illustrated below. A string or piece of fishing line is attached to themed point of the bend in the hook. The free end is held tightly. The shank of the hook is depressed to free the barb and the string is yanked parallel to the shank while application of pressure is maintained. Depending on the situation it is possible that the removed hook will get loose so keep other people away from the path of removal.

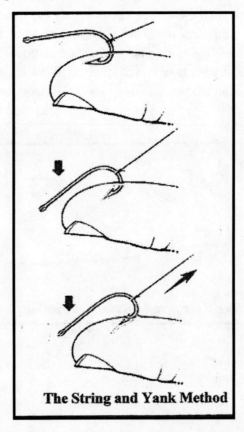

The String and Yank Method

The "Advance and Cut" method is normally used for hooks that are more deeply imbedded into the skin and for larger hooks. Two specific techniques are involved here, the first for single barbed hooks and the second for multiple barbed hooks.

Both techniques of the advance and cut methods are illustrated below: the point of the hook is advanced through the skin for single barbed hooks. The barb is cut off and the hook is backed out.

The technique for multiple barbed hooks is different. The eye of the hook is cut off and the hook is advanced through the skin and removed in the same direction as the point is advanced.

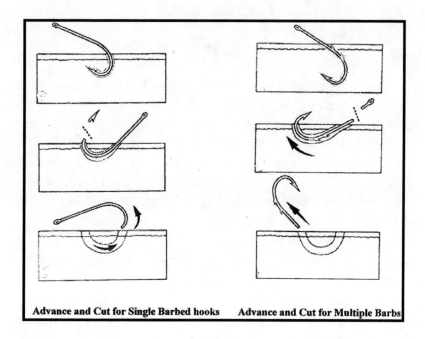

Advance and Cut for Single Barbed hooks   **Advance and Cut for Multiple Barbs**

In every case of hook removal, the wound should be examined after the hook is removed to insure that there is no residue in the wound. The wound should be cleaned thoroughly and protected with the application of a bandage. If the hook was deeply imbedded or you suspect significant damage or the possibility of infection, the wound should be examined by a doctor as soon as possible.

SOME DEVICES HELP YOUR FISHING EXPERIENCE

Since the beginning of recorded time, man has been using fishing as a means of supplying food and sustenance for his survival. The earliest known fishermen were of course, confronted with different obstacles than we face today. Their fishing spot was limited to their ability to move around and was usually confined to a few areas close to where they lived. They did not spend much time "looking around" for a good fishing spot they simply picked an area and hoped that a fish would come along.

Today things are very different, helped along by advances in both knowledge and technology, we not only have the means to move around and cover much more area in our fishing waters but we have some very sophisticated equipment that is available to us at affordable prices, to help in the task of finding fish.

Several studies have concluded that in most fresh water bodies, 90% of the fish are concentrated in 10% of the water area. The secret to a successful fishing experience is therefore to find the area of those concentrations. Fish locations are effected by several conditions including bottom structure, vegetation growth, water clarity, water temperature, sunlight, wind and most important the availability of food. The last of these items, food availability, is perhaps the most important of all of these factors. Food takes many forms for the different type fish but most prevalent among the food sources are the living creatures that also reside in the same waters, namely the small fish, plankton and insects. So, if we can find these food sources we will also be more likely to find the game fish. Sonar devices such as fish finders can help us find the food and the fish. Throughout this book I have tried to keep all of the discussions toward the basic end of their spectrum. I need to get a little more detailed in this chapter because we are surrounded today by technology that is readily available at reasonable prices to move our fishing strategy to a higher level.

The use of sonar to find things under water has been a practice for many years. The technology was developed and found it greatest use during the second world war when it was used to locate enemy submarines and other ships. The equipment at that time was bulky and cumbersome compared to today's sport fishing versions that can often be held in one hand. It is worth some space here to help understand Sonar and how it can be a useful tool for a better fishing experience.

Sonar is short for Sound, Navigation and Ranging. A sonar system, no matter how simple or complicated consists of four major elements, a transmitter, transducer, receiver and display. Simply describing its operation, electrical signals are generated in the transmitter and sent to the transducer where the electrical signals are converted into sound waves or sound impulses. These sound impulses are sent down into the water in a controlled beam from the transducer several times every second. Any object that comes into the beam deflects the beam back to the transducer where it is converted back into electrical impulses and sent to the display unit. Knowing the speed that sound travels in water permits the equipment to determine the distance of the object from the transducer.

Significant among the technical factors that need to be understood is the shape of the signal that is transmitted down into the water. The beam that leaves the transducer is small at the transducer and gets wider as the beam goes further into the depths of the water. The beam therefore takes the form of a cone with the widest portion at the bottom of the lake or pond. His is illustrated in the sketch shown below. Precise areas can be calculated but for this tutorial it will suffice to say that at the most popular transmission angle which is 20 degrees, the beam covers an area about one third the depth of the water. If the water is 30 feet deep then the area covered will be a circle with a diameter of about 10 feet. This is important to understand because in the context of a lake or pond this is a very small area compared to the total surface area of the water.

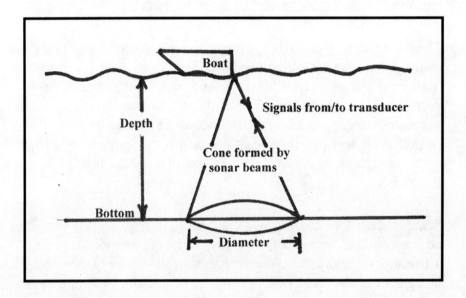

For more effective interpretation of your sonar images it is also necessary to understand how the fish images or arches are created. Again I will keep this description simple, referring to the illustration below.

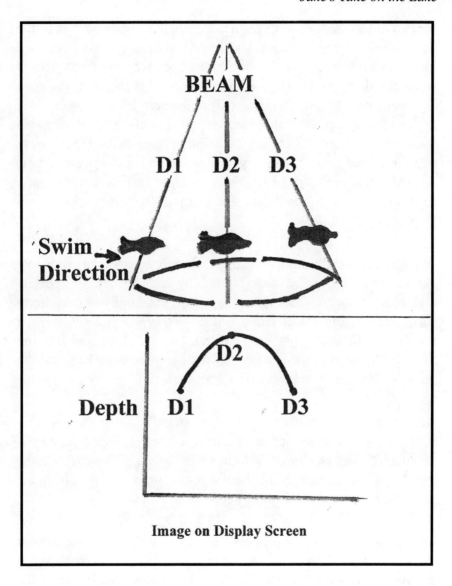

Most fishermen understand (because the sonar instruction manual tells them) that a fish image on their sonar screen is usually represented by an arch. To get this arch display there must be relative movement between the fish and the boat as the fish comes into the cone for viewing. As the leading edge pulse of the cone signal strikes the fish, a display pixel is turned on and sent back to the transducer. This signal is represented by D1 on the illustration. As the boat passes over the fish or the fish swims through the cone, the distance between the transducer and the fish decreases a little so the pixel transmitted back to the transducer indicated a shorter distance from the boat. This is represented by D2 on the illustration. When the center of the cone is directly over the fish, the first half of the arch is completed. Since the fish is now closer to the boat the signal is also stronger and the image is therefore thicker on the display. As the fish moves away and out of the cone, the reverse happens and the complete arch is created. This is illustrated as D3. For simplicity I have shown only three signals where in fact there are hundreds that make up an actual display arch.

The concept is fairly simple but there is rarely a perfect situation that allows the concept to be exercised exactly as described. The perfect arches that are usually shown in the equipment handbooks are rarely seen. As an example, if the fish does not swim directly through the center of the cone the arch will not be perfect. Fish swimming through the edge of the cone would not be in the cone long and the reflected signals would be shorter and weaker.

Keep in mind that arches require movement between the boat and the fish. If the boat is stopped and the fish is resting in the cone area, this may appear as a horizontal line on the display. This may also be true is the boat is moving but the fish is swimming in the cone in the same direction and at the same speed as the boat.

You might recall viewing an old war movie where a seasoned boat captain is leaning over the shoulder of a young sonar operator asking the young man to interpret what he is seeing and hearing from the sonar equipment. Understanding the theory of the sonar device, you can now appreciate that just like the movies, you as the fisherman need to get practice interpreting what you are seeing on your display. With a little practice you can become a much smarter fisherman resulting in bigger and better catches.

Nearly all sonar devices available today come with very detailed instructions on their use, so detailed that you may even get confused and give up. To simplify your sonar device experience I offer two important suggestions: First and foremost, for your initial use, leave the device set at its factory settings. These setting were established by the designers as the points where the equipment has shown its best results and these settings seem to work best for most units under most boating and fishing situations; Second, don't use the fish ID capability but learn to interpret what is being displayed on the raw data screen. The fish identified and fish alarm are nice gadgets that impress you with the equipment capability but more often than not it will simply drive you crazy with false alarm signals. The fish ID can alert you when fish are present but if you learn to interpret what you are looking at on the screen you will have a much more rewarding and less noisy fishing experience.

My experience with sonar fishing devices has taught me that a proven piece of equipment like a sonar device never lies and it is consistent. Every time the sonar sees a 5 pound fish in the same position in the cone that is moving at the same speed, the image is exactly the same. If you understand your sensitivity and color settings (if you have a color unit) and you never change these settings you will eventually be able to interpret the density or approximate weight of the fish in the cone, the type of fish that is being shown, how many are around, what they are eating, how deep you need to fish and how fast your speed should be. With all of this information, how can you fail to catch fish?

I have conducted more that two years of experiments and tests on my home lake that included taking digital camera photos of sonar screen images, making notes of what I saw and then recording and photographing the fish that were caught immediately after seeing the image. My boat is also equipped with a portable under water camera that on occasion I have used to verify the type of bait fish that I have identified on the sonar screen. I have also run tests on my rig weight and the trolling speed of my boat and I have a chart on my boat that tells me exactly how deep my bait is for the trolling speed that I am using. This information was discussed earlier in this book. With this information I can predict with reasonable accuracy how long after the fish is seen on the screen that the hit will come. You too can make these measurements and acquire this same expertise. Just imagine how shocked and impressed you fishing partners will be when you tell them that they can expect a hit in about 30 seconds and it actually happens as you predicted. Knowing where the fish are and their relative depth, you can slow down or speed up your boat speed to put the bait right into the strike zone of the fish that you see on the screen.

To help you in this learning experience I have taken from my library of data and photos, several pictures that I have taken of typical images that you might see on your sonar screen. I have the sensitivity on my two boats set at about 75% to eliminate the clutter and noise. Although the units on each of my boats used for these tests are color units, this book does not permit me to show the color images so I will concentrate discussions on the non color images and therefore the discussions will be kept to only a few of the capabilities of this type equipment namely: bottom conditions; food types; feeding habits; depth settings and fish species recognition.

USING SONAR TO SCOUT THE BOTTOM

Bottom structure is a very important factor for determining where the fish will be in any water body. I have discussed this in detail in an earlier chapter. If you find yourself on a strange lake or in a new section of a familiar lake, your sonar device is your best friend for locating the more ideal fishing spots because even when traveling at relatively high speeds, which you might do when scouting a body of water, you can mentally map the bottom to locate the areas that may be good feeding grounds for the big game fish. These areas will often be where the bottom has structure or has significant depth variations such as would be the case for drop offs, shoals or underwater islands. Of course when traveling at high speeds you will have to deal with the water burble effect which adds noise to your display in the form of dots of black. They may look like fish but at high speeds this is only interference.

In the sequence of three photos that follow, scouting the bottom is simply demonstrated. The first photo taken at slightly more than 31 miles per hour quite clearly shows the overall contour of the bottom. At this speed the contours are exaggerated because we are covering a large area in a short time. The steep drop offs are visible and these areas would potentially be areas where schools of bait fish would hide and therefore where the game fish would be feeding.

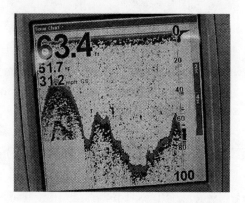

As the speed is reduced to about 5 miles per hour as shown in the second photo, the noise disappears, the bottom structure stretches out still further but vegetation and fish now cone into view.

The third photo in this sequence becomes clear at a speed of about 4 miles per hour. All interference is gone and vegetation and bottom growth becomes visible. There appear to be no fish in this photo but keep in mind that at a depth of 22 feet we are only looking at an area of about 8 feet on the bottom.

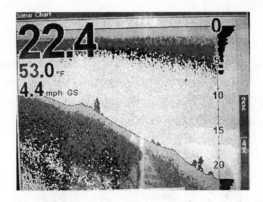

Cruising the waters as described above can present a fine picture of what lies beneath the surface and will point to the best potential fishing areas based on bottom features only.

FINDING THE FOOD SOURCES

You have certainly learned by this point that finding food is the primary mission of the game fish so another important function of your sonar is to find and identify the sources of food. Earlier in this book I discussed several types of live bait fish, for purposes of this discussion I will concentrate on two types, herring and shad but the types are not really important except when we discuss game fish feeding habits.

Small bait type fish will by habit move around in schools. Schooling is actually an instinct for insuring safety. Since the small fish are always prey for the larger game fish. They group into tightly crowed schools for self protection. These schools are easily recognized on any sonar unit.

Herring like colder water so they will almost always school on or near the bottom where the water is the coldest. If a water body has springs feeding it, these springs will attract the herring because of the colder water. The photo shown below is a large school of herring tightly packed together near the bottom of the lake. This school is about ten feet thick and represents thousands of small fish. This type of image would certainly indicate a good potential feeding spot for any game fish that are in the waters in question. Finding a school of bait like this would suggest that you stop and fish around the school for the predators that will eventually come along.

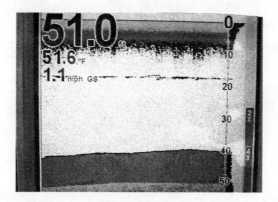

To give equal time to the other species of bait fish in my home lake, the photo below shows a school of shad. Notice that shad will school at any level in the water column and not necessarily on or near the bottom. Nearly every type of game fish like shad as a meal and finding a school like this is cause to stop and begin the search for the predator game fish.

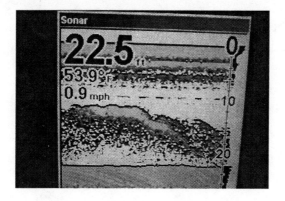

FEEDING HABITS

Having now found the food source it helps to understand the feeding habits of the game fish. Most predator game fish will approach a bait school from the edges and from beneath the school and they will pick off their meal from the outer most fish in the school. The photo below is a good illustration of this. In this case bass and perch are shown feeding from the outside edges of the small school of shad. Since the school has not scattered we can assume that there is not a large group of hungry fish attacking the school of bait. If these were stripers attacking the bait school as we will see in later photos, the school of bait would be breaking up.

The photo below shows another small group of bass that has broken away several bait fish from their school and the bass are feeding higher in the water column. The bait that have remained schooled are still grouped on the bottom of the lake.

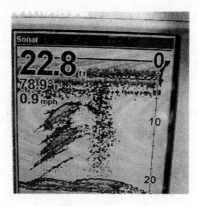

Earlier in this book I described the use of birds and their habits as a tool for locating the game fish. The above photos illustrate why in some lakes where the bait fish populations are changing, the birds are finding it harder to locate their food.

On Lake Norman as an example, shad were the main source food for the stripers for many years. The stripers would attack the schools of shad from the bottom edges and drive the shad schools to the surface. The fish parcels that remained were easy pickings for the gulls having been driven to the surface.

In recent years since herring were introduced into the lake, the herring school near the bottom so the stripers attack these schools from the top edges and the schools are not driven to the surface but the feeding takes place near the bottom of the lake. In these situations there are no parcels that rise to the surface and no food for the gulls. In this situation the absence of gulls does not indicate the absence of stripers but only that the stripers are not feeding on shad.

YOUR BAIT DEPTH SETTINGS

Whether trolling, drifting or casting, the depth of the bait fish and more important the depth of the game fish is critical knowledge for your equipment settings. I have mentioned earlier that I have run several tests to measure bait and rig weight at various boat speeds against the depth of the bait at these speeds. This permits me to know exactly where my bait is in the water column. Let's see how this information assists me in the fishing experience. The photo below shown a school of herring on the lake bottom and also shows some bass feeding above the school. The bass are lying at about 20 feet depth. Since I know that I want to put my bait slightly above the bass and with my existing rig I am trolling at about 12 feet of depth, this sonar image tells me that I need to slow down my troll to below 1 mph in order to drop my bait closer to the strike zone of the bass. In this case I did reduce the boat speed to .8 mph and caught two nice largemouth bass about 30 seconds after I saw this image.

Even if you do not see the game fish on the sonar image but the bait schools are visible you can estimate the speed increases or decreases that are necessary to get your bait at or near the top of the school of bait. Remember that game fish almost always attack their prey from below so you want to have your lure or bait above the game fish.

RECOGNIZING THE GAME FISH SPECIES

I have mentioned in the descriptions above on several occasions, the specific fish species that were being shown on the sonar screen. You are certainly curious how I knew those species. Again, it was from running test and keeping logs for nearly two years recording the photos with a digital camera and recording what was caught immediately after viewing the images. Since my sonar units are both color units it was also possible to estimate size and weight from the color tunes on the return images. I have learned as an example that for my specific sonar units, if the images have heavy red or heavy yellow center markings, the fish are very dense and their weights are more that 3 pounds. By the repeated recording of this information I can estimate the fish weight by the thickness of the center color lines of the fish images. This is far more difficult to accomplish for non color units but it is still possible with regular practice except that it is the gray and black tones that you will interpret and not specific colors.

Game fish species also relates very closely to the fish weight and density. If I see a small group of game fish appearing to be in the 2 or three pound range and they are feeding from the edge of a bait school I will assume that they are bass and not stripers. If I see a fairly large group of game fish showing densities around weights of ½ to 1 pound, I assume that they are perch. If the fish image is feeding near the bottom of the lake I assume that it is a catfish.

I will use two photos to illustrate how I determine fish species. The photo shown below is of a small group of largemouth bass in the 1 and 2 pound range (based on the catch). They are feeding quietly off of the edge of a school of herring that are resting on the bottom of the lake. There are two groups of game fish both containing about five or six fish.

The last photo in this series is what I call the striper fisherman's dream. Striper images are unlike almost any other fish. If you happen to come upon a large group of stripers like this, the frenzy of their feeding is immediately obvious and you can be assured that if you adjust your bait depth properly you will be in for a few minutes of sheer panic with multiple strikes from the stripers. Because of the lack of color here the weight of the fish is not obvious but with the color photos and repeated practice I can estimate that these stripers are all about 4 to 5 pounds in weight. This type of image will almost always produce multiple strikes but be aware that these types of schools do not stand still and as fast at they appear, they will also disappear.

My library of photos and fishing logs contain hundreds of photos like those shown. Most normal fishermen will not collect this many records or photos but I have included them to illustrate that with practice and persistence, you can learn to make sonar image interpretations that will make you a smarter fisherman or woman and your sonar equipment will certainly make your fishing experience more exciting.

WHICH SONAR DEVICE TO BUY?

I have been asked on many occasions to recommend a particular brand of sonar device to purchase. I always try to stay away from discussions of brands and I usually remind the person asking that type of unit to buy will vary with the type of fishing to be done and of course your level of affordability. A person who only occasionally goes fishing does not need the same capability as does the fisherman who goes out two or three day a week. There are some items that are more important than others to be considered when buying a sonar device.

Most sonar devices operate at frequencies between 192 and 200 KHz. There are some that operate at 50 KHz but these are normally limited to deep salt water applications. Target definition is better at the higher frequencies. A 20 degree cone angle is the most common for typical fresh water applications. Although you will never have occasion to measure it, cone angle is measured by finding the depth at which the signal strength is half of what it was at the transducer. At this depth (known as the –3db point) the spread of the beam is measured and that is the cone angle.

The pixel is the mark made when the sound beam hits the target and is reflected back to the transducer. The more pixels that hit the target, the better the image on the screen. This is called resolution. The higher the pixel count on the screen the better the picture. Screen size is also an important consideration. In general (especially when you are getting older) the larger the screen the better the viewing is. Power is also important. When comparing units, the higher the power the better the unit quality but remember nothing comes for free, as the features improve, the cost will also increase.

Color or non color to many fishermen is only an issue of cost. To me it is more than that. A properly set up sonar will present much better interpretation capability if the display is in color. Some of the interpretations that were made in the previous discussions could not have been made without a color image. The density and weight of the fish as an example is much more difficult to predict without color images. A fisherman who only occasionally goes fishing can probably get by with a non color unit.

How about GPS? This is also a personal preference item but since many higher priced units come equipped with GPS capability, some fishermen have the capability and have paid a higher price for it when they really never need or use it.

GPS (Global Positioning System) is possibly the most amazing invention to have occurred in our lifetime as an aid to navigation. As a pilot and aircraft owner I depend very heavily on the capabilities of my GPS. As a fisherman however I use this capability almost exclusively for measuring boat speed and rarely if ever for navigation. Most lakes are not large enough to require GPS for navigation. On some of the nation's larger lakes such as the Great Lakes, GPS would probably be a necessity but on most of the smaller lakes it is not required. If I had the choice of color or a GPS add on I would always choose the color screen.

In all of my previous discussions I have used boat speed as a critical indicator. For boat speed I need a GPS. There is equipment that will present speed without the GPS but it is not common. If speed is the only item that leads you towards a GPS capability, keep in mind that there are small portable hand held GPS units that can be purchased at very reasonable prices that will provide you with speed indication.

For the occasional fisherman, there are also portable, battery operated sonar units that are available for under $200. The primary value of the portable units are for bottom indication but for that data the portables are fine. Color portable units are now beginning to enter the marketplace and their prices will eventually make them available to more fishermen.

How about price for the better capability units? It's difficult to discuss price because the technology in the electronics industry in addition to the continual growth in competition keeps the price of good equipment from rising and more important often drives the cost down. Today (2006) it is possible to purchase a fine non color unit with GPS capability for less than $400. Color units of good quality range around $500-$600. If you are inclined to buy a unit with all of the bells and whistles be prepared to hold on to your wallet but remember that the big money units might not help you catch any more fish.

TELLING THE STORY

Hopefully as you read through this book you had a chance to make many practice fishing trips and hopefully the things that you learned here helped you make some fine catches. Or maybe you were already an experienced fisherman and just read this book to sharpen your techniques. Whatever the case there is a very important part of the fishing experience that is yet to be addressed and that is the telling of the story of the fishing experiences that you have had. There have been some light sides of many of the experiences that we have shared in this book and maybe there were even some tongue in check portions. It is in that spirit that I choose to conclude the book with some advice on how to wrap up your fishing experiences by learning how to tell the fishing story.

Do you ever think about the fact that when you were fishing alone and came home to relate to your wife or a friend what happened to you that day, the one pound Bass ended up a two pounder, or the three fish that you caught turned into four. Well that's not really unusual, it happens to all of us. You see, when you spend a lot of time on or near the water and when you are alone with your thoughts during those times, there is a damp mist that rises from the surface of the water that you breath deeply and as you breath the mist it creates a virus in your brain called the "amplification virus" which changes your perspective on the things that happened to you that day. Your mouth wanted to say that it was a one pound Bass but you brain made you say two pounds. Your mouth wanted to say three fish and your brain made you say four. Doctors have found only one cure for this virus and the cure seems to work best when you take someone with you fishing, and the cure works best if that person did not catch anything. When you're in that person's presence the one pounder stays one pound and the three fish remain three fish. How about that!

An amazing medical discovery. Sometimes, it has been discovered, that the cure works less than desired if the other person is also an experienced fisherman and he or she also caught some fish. Under these conditions the virus seems to spread to the second person rather than curing your illness. Researchers are working on this problem and I suppose that some day a complete cure will evolve but until then lets try to learn how to live with the virus in a manner that gives us the greatest enjoyment in life.

Not only should you learn how to deal with the "amplification virus" but you need to practice your poetic adjustment when you relate your experiences to others. That's the choice of the words that you use and the level of excitement that you exhibit when you tell the story. Let's see how these two factors need to play together.

You went out in your boat for 8 hours alone. The weather was fine and there was no wind to speak of. You pulled in to a local diner on the lake for lunch and after lunch you actually dozed off for a while to re energize your body. After your snooze you caught a ½ pound Bass that you found had been wounded by another fisherman and had actually caught itself by accident on your hook and was hooked in the side. You didn't even need your net for that fish; you just lifted it into the boat by the line. After hours of trying you finally caught a 1-pound Blue Channel Catfish that stung you when you were taking it off of the hook. With little other success you tied your boat to an overhanging limb near shore and fished for Bream and caught a couple of small sunfish before you fell asleep from boredom.

Now you arrive home and your wife and two kids are waiting for you for dinner. Their standard question, how was your day? That question is like the magic word that is used to put a person into a hypnotic spell, you are suddenly struck by the "virus."

I had a great day dear, you reply. No one on the lake was catching fish but I got my share. You know I am a catch and release fisherman and I never keep my fish but if I did I would have had at least one that

I may have had mounted. It was a six-pound, 26 inch Largemouth Bass that hit my pole so hard that I nearly lost the pole before I could get to it for the retrieve. It was big and strong and it fought real hard but, you know, I can handle fish like that and after a 20 minute fight I finally got him into the boat.

I forgot my lunch so I went all day without any food or water and I am hungry and thirsty and I'll probably hit the sack early tonight. Maybe you could fetch me a beer? Early in the afternoon I snagged a huge catfish, at least 10 pounds. I thought about keeping this one to show the kids. You know you really have to be careful taking those cats off the hook because they can sting you seriously if you don't know what you are doing so I decided to get him back into the water as quickly as possible.

Fighting that big Cat was really tiring but I stuck it out and sure enough I caught a few good sized Crappie before I decided to call it quits for the day. I fought the wind all day long. The waves on the lake were actually white capping when I was fishing but with my experience that was not a problem. It was really a great day of fishing, I should have taken you and the kids with me, you would have had a ball but being as it is I think I'll just kick back and enjoy this beer.

This is called, "telling the story" virus and all. If you had been in a group of other men fishermen the virus might have given you a few more adjectives like, I caught a "bunch" or "tremendous fighters" or maybe "the biggest one broke my line off." There is a whole dictionary of "virus words" and someday I think I'll write a revision to that dictionary.

This type of virus is very common among fishermen and hunters especially when they are together re hashing old stories. The numbers always get bigger, the sizes and weights get larger and of course the monster always gets away. This is the fun part of fishing, the part that stays with you, the part that gives you the material for telling tales to your grandkids years later. This is the virus that you should never be ashamed of and probably should never try to cure. Telling the story is like the dessert that goes with a meal or the fine Cognac that tops a great feast. This is what drives all fishermen and makes us believe with a passion that we might have a bad day at work or even a bad day at home but we will never have a bad day of fishing.

SAVING YOUR TROPHIES

The use of the term trophy these days is coming to have less and less meaning as schools and clubs and providing trophies to young kids just for showing up. In the sport of fishing however a trophy catch becomes a matter of preserving the event and the memories of the day, providing a visual reminder of the occasion of the catch, the fishing partners present and the excitement of the final fight. A trophy fish does not mean that the fish caught represents any State or local record but rather that is was a personal best or represents an unusual or memorable situation.

There are many areas of the US and Canada where it is illegal to take home the larger fish so having a fish mounted in the traditional fashion is often difficult. Many fishermen, on the other hand, do not want to keep the larger breeder fish but want to return them to the water to maintain the growth of the species. These "catch and release" fishermen like myself often want their catch preserved for their memory or to take up a prominent place in their trophy room. Like just about everything else in life a solution has come along that satisfies everyone's needs and it is reproduction taxidermy or the art of creating an exact replica of your fish with nothing but a photo and some measurement references. I have found that using this technique I can have my larger catches reproduced to fit into specific spots in my trophy room. My feeling is that the huge monsters that represent State or local records are often too big to fit comfortably into my house but with this technique available to me I can wait to catch the one that is exactly the right size for me and have it reproduced to fit in the spot that I have selected for it. I have found that the price of the mounting is about the same a the old method of skin mounting but the new reproduction mounts last a great deal longer and retain their natural color and beauty for a very long time. I have been using reproduction taxidermy for more than ten years now and not one of my mounts has lost even the slightest amount of beauty or color.

I have become so excited about this new method of preserving the memories of the unusual catch that I decided to invite a very skilled artist in this field, who also does all of my mounts, to write a section of this book to describe the work that he does and show you some of the work in progress and the results. The remaining information in this section of the book was contributed by;

Kevin Liska

American Fish Taxidermy

Cookeville, Tennessee

Licensed as a Taxidermist in 1976, Kevin Liska pursued a BA degree in Environmental Studies from Northland College in Ashland Wisconsin. He received a MBA from Tennessee Tech University and he has published several research papers on environmental stewardship and in 1991 he was a national leader creating one of the first classes on environmental marketing and management taught at a business college.

With a lifelong interest in environmental education and conservation, Kevin's artistic interests evolved to a focus solely on fish replicas. With a passion for fish painting and creating realistic fish replicas, Kevin created American Fish Taxidermy as a family studio that custom paints fish from anglers photographs.

Over time Kevin has painted more than 60 different species of fish for anglers, schools, museums, governments and organizations. Kevin is now using his artistic skills to create the nation's first fish museum dedicated to the catch and release angler. The American Fish Museum will be opening in Livingston Tennessee and will showcase fish replicas, offer educational exhibits, and recognize anglers and guides who participate in catch and release fishing. Please enjoy Kevin's description of his creative artistry in the following paragraphs.

Fish replicas can be traced back to the early 19ᵗʰ Century. During the early days, commercially available blanks created considerable interest particularly with saltwater anglers who quickly recognized that fiberglass replicas were the only option for large, greasy sailfish. During the early 21ˢᵗ century, industry leaders like Ron Reynolds, Dennis Arp and Mike Kirkhart employed innovative techniques to cast superior quality fish replicas that reached beyond the classic saltwater options

As taxidermists embraced these new replicas, leading craftsmen continued to cast additional high quality fish specimens to create what taxidermists enjoy today as a wide assortment of detail, realistic fish blanks. A fish blank as the word implies us a fiberglass cast of an actual specimen with the mouth interiors, eyes, fins and seams unfinished. The taxidermist adds considerable value by modeling and painting with artistic creativity and technical skill to bring what started as a white, fiberglass shell back to life, to the point where it can nearly swim off the wall, bringing back memories for years to come for the angler and others who glimpse the trophy.

The photo below (top) shows my daughter Katie holding a blank 48 inch Striper blank and the (bottom) finished replica.

The population of conservation minded anglers continues to increase, and digital cameras contribute to capture the fisherman's trophy in "living color" the number of sportsmen opting for a custom painted fish replica continues to increase. In turn, more fish will be cast and the general inventory of fish blanks will grow. Interestingly, many sportsmen will comment with surprise on the current inventory of quality replicas available in almost every fish size and shape. The most requested species is the Largemouth Bass. Throughout the entire taxidermy industry, a quick count of available Largemouth replicas would yield several hundred blanks from 2 inches up to the current world record of 36 inches. When selecting a replica blank. I limit my choices to the top three replica craftsmen in the industry. Of course my judgment of quality is based on my evolving style of painting, but nevertheless a count of Largemouth Bass blanks from just the top three replica craftsmen will still yield an assortment of 80 different fish sizes and positions. A similar analysis for a Rainbow Trout will yield 122 options from the top three suppliers. The photos below show three views of a common Largemouth Bass cast with the bass in the swimming or "S" left turn with the mouth open and cast gills.

Less common species like Chinook Salmon will yield a nice assortment of 34 different sized replicas from the same leading craftsmen. However, there are species like the Chinook or King Salmon whose looks will vary considerably depending on the geographical location and time of the year the specimen is caught. In such cases the angler counts on the taxidermists experience to properly choose the correct fish. The King Salmon from Alaska's Kenai River will vary considerably in shape and texture from the same size Great Lakes fish, or even a similar size west coast fish. The same is true for Steelheads, Brown Trout, Rainbows and Coho's. The variance can also be seen in Smallmouth Bass which show shape differences among fish caught in rivers, reservoirs, lakes or the Great Lakes. In the case of Smallmouth, we will even see dramatic color variances from brass, to brown, to green.

Taxidermists prefer to pick the turn and style based on measurements and general fish characteristics. But there are more choices available than just left and right. Surprisingly, where a customer might shy away from a certain turn because of a room corner or other site specific characteristic, positions like "S' or swimming styles offer fish positions that look slightly out from the wall displaying very convincing lifelike positions that are effective from almost any viewing angle even if the fish is not looking directly into the room. In the two photos below I am holding a finished "S" Muskie in the top photo and a swimming Northern Pike in the bottom photo.

Habitats can add significant value over fish just displayed on the wall. Habitats available in the industry can vary from plastic rocks to elaborate encased coffee tables. My favorite habitat is made from natures own weather-worn driftwood artistically dressed up by intertwining pieces and adding natural reeds, dried flowers, lily pads or willow branches. For fish like Smallmouth Bass, special taxidermy flat rocks made from polyurethane can be custom painted and dressed with moss and natural branches to complement the fish replicas and add interest to a room. Driftwood and habitat photos are shown below. The perfect driftwood can complement any fish replicas. Most driftwood can be improved by the addition of dried reeds and other natural materiam.

Shelf habitats are really fun to build as they open the option for the taxidermist to work with a new medium by using artificial water sculptured from 2-part clear epoxy resins. Frequently a cedar wood slab can be router out, painted blue and filled with the artificial water. After tossing in a couple quartz rocks and green duckweed the display looks unique and natural. Adding lily pads contributes to any artificial water habitat. The water shelf habitat shown below is a very convincing presentation and is as much fun to design as it is to view.

If a rocky habitat is desired, I'll start with a butternut base, add a 12 to 16 inch, 2 inch diameter winter birch branch, and saturate the base with about 1/8 inch of Elmer's glue followed by several handfuls of quartz pebbles. A freeze dried crawfish will complement the lifelike display and match up nicely with the brassy tones n a Smallmouth bass.

By choosing the perfect driftwood with a slight depression filled with artificial water a shelf habitat can be converted into a fantastic dual habitat by adding driftwood to the middle back. The customer can choose to display the fish as a shelf or move it to the wall after a few years. Any habitat can be spruced up by adding bait fish or crawfish. The photo below shows a Largemouth Bass chasing a small bluegill bait fish.

Like replicas, fish eyes have evolved with amazing lifelikeness. Early eyes were clear flints with black pupils simply painted in basic colors. Later, eye specialty companies added hand painted realistic eyes that captured veins, tones and other lifelike details. During the last several years, Dan Rinehart Supply added eyes captured from digital photography magically fused to a specially shaped glass offering a truly unique fish eye. This new eye actually captures the species unique shape as well as the color. I recently mew a fishing guide who had Dan on an eye photographing exhibition. The guide noted how enthusiastic and passionate Dan was about photographing fish eyes. Dan's resulting line of Aqua-eyes contributes to today's modern, lifelike replicas.

Like the evolution and innovation of new fish eyes, experimentation with various fiberglass resins and new alternative fin techniques has also contributed to a better lifelike replica. Traditionally, fins were cast using material and techniques that yielded thicker rigid fiberglass. In the late 20th Century, very realistic fins were cast out of hot glue material. These fins were thin, flexible and transparent. Although these transparent fins were almost perfect duplicates of the real thing (almost too thin for commercial use) they were hot and cold sensitive. Fish shipped in freezing temperatures would frequently arrive with broken fins as the frozen fins would become brittle and easily break if the package was dropped or experiences any bump or shock. Recently these fins were replaced with a superior, clear fiberglass resin and offers great quality and solid durability. Further adding to fin realism, recent taxidermy conventions and trade publications have offered seminars documenting techniques to custom mold fins allowing for great artistic expression. In summary, fins are an important part of recreating a fish that is lifelike and looks like it could swim away.

The best fish replicas are cast fresh, undamaged specimens by skilled craftsmen who have logged hours to learn the techniques and tips that produce great blanks. The original molds are used over and over again to produce blanks ready for the taxidermist to add value and artistic beauty. Most molds are cast with fiberglass using a variety of techniques. The outer layer of the blank is formed with a gel coat which captures incredible detail from the mold. For example if a piece of hair was laid across the fish as the mold as made, then the gel coat would show the hair in the final blank. Some companies use a form of acrylic instead of fiberglass. This style blank performs equally as well as fiberglass. Surprisingly, even though the fish blanks are made one at a time, companies employing quality manufacturing processes have contributed to consistently producing outstanding blanks for the fish replica industry and shortening the traditionally long lead time once the taxidermist places the order.

Great fish start as simple, white fiberglass blanks. I imagine that working on a high quality fish blank can be like playing a great round of golf. For the taxidermist, crafting and painting a quality fish is really a fun, satisfying sport. I've completed fish that look so real that I can't help but stare over and over again in amazement.

This rarely mounted gar shown below will hold its unusual beauty for many years

Top molds have a few common characteristics: 1) natural lifelike positioning, 2) accurate face detail, 3) cast interior mouths, 4) realistic and appropriately placed fins, 5) exceptional scale detail. A very lifelike museum quality custom painted Striped Bass is shown below.

To illustrate a work in process the photos below my hands skillfully trimming and preparing a 44 inch Muskie. This is the first step in the reproduction process.

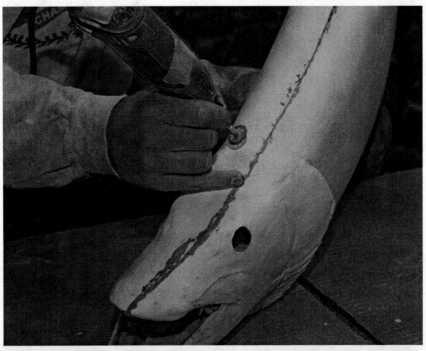

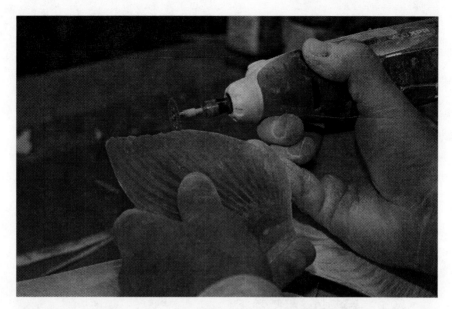

Working with a quality replica, the taxidermists completes the final modeling around the seams, mouth, eyes and fins. Fish are carefully cleaned and prepared for painting. In species like trout, pike and salmon, teeth are individually hand sculptured by steady and patient hands. I find that my teenage son with his young nimble fingers can master this small sculpturing better than my older fingers. The photo below (left) shows my son Luke molding fins into a 44 inch Muskie and (right) my son Sam sculpturing the teeth of a 38 inch Chinook. These actions are the second step in the process.

Step three is the final painting and sealing and this is where the artist in me is really permitted to show. The photo below shows me painting a 48 inch Striped Bass.

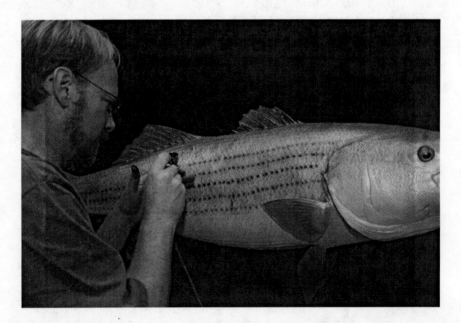

I've studied and watched several fantastic fish artists learning and combining techniques from the collective group. Interesting tips that have helped me become a better fish taxidermist include the following: Dennis Arp's technique of randomly painting fish markings avoiding the logical left to right repetitive method. Mike Kirkhart's creative angles-turning the fish on the side or as needed to catch the scale details just right. Mike Orthober's use of finger waxes to create the perfect salmon face or special tips to capture the unique yellow/ gold markings on walleyes. Ron Reynolds detailed paint charts and numerous tips. Perhaps overall, the best advice I ever received from my first taxidermy lesson over 30 years ago was taught by the classic Northwestern School of Taxidermy. Finish every mount, no matter what it looks like during the process-study it, learn from it and improve. The Smallmouth Bass shown below is a good example of a fish combining techniques of the industries best teachers.

A critical comparison of replicas vs. skin mounts will show the strength of modern custom painting replicas. While the Fishing Hall of Fame in Baraboo, Wisconsin, I photographed a great comparison. The saltwater room had a side by side display of Tarpon. Both fish looked to be several decades old. The skin mount showed classic grease bleeds, broken fins, paint chippings, and form distortions as the skin was wrapped round a less than perfect fit manikin.

While the replicas would be considered inferior to a similar six foot Tarpon like the fish that I had recently completed. It still was a clear winner over the skin mounts. Consider now a modern, custom painted tarpon complete with a full cast of the actual fish mouth interior, super detailed fins, accurate eyes and topped with a high tech 2-part automotive clear coat finish. The six foot Tarpon shown below exactly matches the detail of the real fish.

The actual painting process starts with pre coats of various silvers, pearls, and gold's followed by darker misting to highlight individual scales and enable the white fiberglass to gain depth. This pre coat process is a critical component of the replicas color base. Whenever I catch a fish whether a bluegill or a once in a lifetime Cobia, I find myself studying the various color tones and depth exhibited by Mother Nature. The more fish I paint the more convinced I have become that the realism comes from this important foundation that allows the transparent colors to suspend and really shine to their true potential.

With the base in place, additional pearls and silvers are added with care to angle the airbrush letting scale edges catch sparkles and pigments. Airbrush techniques allow nearly every possible option needed from the lines and width of a needle to gradients covering the width of a life-size Striped Bass. The excitement really starts as we add additional layers of color following proven paint charts for the species at hand.

The old saying that no two guppies are the same carries over to most fish species. With careful inspection of photographs, details can be seen that makes each fisherman's trophy a unique project. Color phase variations are made as the various layers are added. A Brown Trout might receive more or less yellow ochre in the belly, Striped Bass more or less bronze gold in the cheeks. As the fish comes to life, the stripes, spots and facial details are painted in. During this time, careful attention to photographs and other references is key. Since during stress several detail markings often become non-existent, the artist must know the species markings and make appropriate adjustments. For example the vermiculations on a Largemouth bass can fade out completely on some photographs.

What's really neat about catch and release taxidermy, is that with accurate species reference material and detailed photos of the actual fish caught and released, the taxidermist can come very close to recreating the anglers individual fish. Anglers' photographs provide the detail to make that fish unique and accurately reflect the fish that was landed.

Understanding how the taxidermist uses photos is especially important to providing "picture detail" valuable for recreating that special trophy. Wildlife artists know, from industry studies, that fresh caught fish do not display dominant color patterns. These frightened fish show generic color patterns with subdued highlights. This is caused by the production of adrenaline and other hormones caused by stress that result in the general lightening of the fish when it is pulled out of the water. In contrast, exhaustion and fish death causes a darkening of the fish base color.

Fish photos are useful to study geographic and seasonal color phases. Good photos help identify patterns and positions of spots and stripes. Close up shots highlight other fine points like scale detail, iridescent shimmers and facial tones. Wildlife artists use many references in addition to the fisherman's actual photos, these might incuse: observations of live fish, taxidermy industry reference photos and videos, sports magazines, mounts at national competitions and their own files and experiences.

If you have the opportunity to catch a personal trophy, here are a few tips that will help the taxidermist recreate "your fish".

1. Always reposition with sunlight over the photographers shoulder shining directly on the fish.

2. Be prepared to take several but remember that the fish is being stressed while it is out of the water.

3. Make the fish the subject and let it fill the frame.

4. Try sitting or squatting holding the fish horizontally where it fills the frame. This is especially effective for kids who can't hold up a heavy fish.

5. Rotate the fish to photograph the upper side/back detail as well as the middle side detail.

6. Split the fish into thirds taking close ups of the head, middle section and tail section.

7. Know that the taxidermist is looking for detail and color phase that will supplement their experience and many other references.

One of the most priceless rewards for a taxidermist is to see the expression on the face of a customer who sees his trophy reproduced for the first time. One of my most excited and enthusiastic customers was Matt Miller shown below.

Matt landed this 28 inch Largemouth in a central Florida lake called Brick Lake. His facial expression before he released the big fish showed his excitement but I understand that when he opened the box containing the replica his excitement was almost uncontrollable. Matt will relive this catch many times over and by returning the monster fish to the lake, he gains the additional incentive of trying again next year to catch the fish when it is even larger.

If you have any questions about this form of taxidermy, fell free to contact me by e mail at <u>Kevin@americanfishtaxidermy.com</u>. Or look me up at my web site at <u>info@americanfishtaxidermy.com</u>.

Now it's Up to You

I started this book on a quiet May morning waiting for the sun to rise. This was to represent a fisherman being born into the world of the joy of fishing. Throughout the book I have tried to progressively submerge you into a mixture of the technical aspects of fishing blended with the sometimes harsh realization that most of it just makes practical sense. It doesn't take a deep understanding of brain surgery to know when you have a headache. Similarly it doesn't take a deep and detailed knowledge of every brand name of fishing equipment to understand the basic elements required to enjoy the sport of fishing. I have sometimes gone into more detail than may have been necessary to illustrate a point but some basic knowledge of the science related to the sport will enhance your ability to reason out a given situation to develop a fishing strategy that will work for you.

What you do with this information is a matter of your choice. You need to select the equipment that feels good to you. You have to pick the fishing spot that fits your needs best. You will be the one to decide just what kind of a fisherman you are going to be. Your hands and your head now hold the secrets for your future enjoyment of this marvelous sport.

I was on the lake the other day on a beautiful February afternoon in North Carolina. The temperature was a balmy 65 degrees and we had suffered with a very light southerly wind all day. The temperature was unusually warm for this time of the year and the 51 degree water temperature had kept several species of fish very active and aggressive. I had adjusted my plan for the afternoon to accommodate the warm day and my success was reflected by the empty bait well in my boat. It had been a good three hours of fishing but more important it had been another good day in my life. As I looked to the west and saw the sun about to set over the horizon, I said aloud to myself again today as I say at the end of every fishing day, life doesn't get much better than this!

ACKNOWLEDGEMENTS

1. Illustrations and some minor content of the section on Fish Biology was provided by The Florida Fish and Wildlife Conservation Commission (MyFWC.com) Sketch by Duane Raver Jr. Modified by John Cimbaro.

2. Some fish photos courtesy US Fish and Wildlife Service National Image Library, Wildlife Service Extension USFWS https//dis.gov

3. The Chapter on Catch and Release fishing was provided by: Kevin Liska, American Fish Taxidermy, 420 Maddox Road, Cookeville. TN 38501 info@americanfishtaxidermy.com

4. Computer production and editing assistance provides by Maureen Croes and Susan Jankowski.

5. Advice, encouragement and cooperation was provided on a continuous basis by my wife, Mary Lou.

REFERENCES

The following list of books and articles is a complete listing of sources that were used to gather corroborating data. It was the authors intent to have at least one validating source for each significant item of data included in this book. In no case was a significant amounts of data taken from any source without permission to do so and in those cases the source reference is included in the acknowledgements.

On Internet sources where no date was included on the subject material, it can be assumed that the reference was used in 2005 or 2006.

- Fishing new Waters by Paul Crawford- www.bassdozer.com

- Holding Bass Right by Ralph Manes—www.bassdozer.com

- Beginning Night Fishing by Tom Lester—www.bassdozer.com

- Fishing Ethics by C.A Johansen—Stripersonline.com

- Fish Ecology, Fangs, Fins, Mouth and Eyes-Project Oceanography, 1999

- Stocking Bass In Lakes, Guide to Freshwater Fishing, Ronnie Garrison, Aboutfishing.com

- Lake Murray Stripers by Eric Bumgarner, June 1986 reprint, www.striperchasers.com

- Do You Know Your Catch, Maine Dept of Nat resources, Maine. gov

- Fly Fishing At A Snails pace, www.aquahabitat.com

- Bass Basics For Beginners, by Charles Stuart, www. bassdozers.com

- Secrets of Fishing, Vince Travnichek, 2005, www. conservation.state.mo.us

- Hooks In Or Out, by Ralph Manns, www.bassdozers.com

- It's A Walleye Wind by Bernie Schnieders, www.fishontario. com

- Return To freshwater Fishing, Spotted Bass, Iowa dept of Natural Res.

- Fishing Is Fun For Everyone, by bob Schmidt,US Fish & Wildlife Service,www.pueblo.gsa.gov

- Those Spotted Bass, Steve Quinn, 2005, www.fisherman. com

- The Choice Between Spinning and Casting, by Ronald F. Dodson, www.bassresource.com

- Spotted Bass, ESPN Outdoors, www.espn.go.com

- Youth Fishing, Washington Dept. of Fish and Wildlife,http:// wdfw.wa.gov

- Smallmouth Bass by Gerald Wickstrom, 1994 South Dakota Dept. of Game Fish And Parks.

- Michigan Dept. of Natural Resources, www.michigan. gov, data source for Brown Bullhead, Lake Sturgeon, Lake Whitefish,Muskellunge, Walleye, Smallmouth Bass.

- Smallmouth Bass, Staff Cornell Univ. www.dnr.cornell.edu

- Fishing Species, Smallmouth Bass, Fishing Guide To Canada, www.pvisuals.com

- Life History Notes, Flathead Catfish, Ohio Dept of Nat. Res. www.phiodnr.com

- All About Fishing, Catfish Fishing, www.aa.fishing.com

- Channel Catfish, Life History and Biology, Southern Region Aquaculture Center, Texas Agricultural Extension Service.

- Channel Catfish, Discover The Outdoors, www.dto.com

- Blue Catfish, Texas Parks and Wildlife Commission, www. tpwd.state.tx.us

- Blue Catfish In Alabama, www.outdooralabama.com

- Farm Raised Channel Catfish, University of Florida Extension Service, IFAS July 1992.

- Channel Catfish, Fishing Resources,www.landbigfish.com

- Walleye Fishing by John Vance, 1998, Outdoor Fishing Walleye, www.execulink.com

- Fish Species Information, Walleye, www.walleye.ws

- Casting Principles, Outdoor Texas, www.outdoorstexas.com

- Earth, Water, Lakes, Reservoirs, 2005, US Geological Survey, US Dept. of Interior.

- Safe Fish, Wisconsin Dept of Natural Resources, www.wiscinsin. gov

- White Bass, Life History Notes, Ohio Dept. of Natural resources, www.dnr.state.ohio.us

- Northern Pike, Biology and Identification, 2002,Minnesota Dept. of Natural Resources, www.dnr.state.mn.us

- Blue Catfish, The Free Dictionary, http://encyclopediathefree dictionary.com

- Fishing Blue Catfish, Outdoor Alabama, www. outdooralabama.com

- Catfish Biology and Identification, Flathead Catfish, Minnesota Dept. of Natural Resources, www.dnr.state. mn.us

- Entry on Flathead Catfish, Texas Parks and Wildlife Commission, www.whusoo.org

- Flathead Catfish, The Virtual Aquarium, Virginia Fish and Wildlife Information Center, www.cnr.vt.edu

- Flathead Catfish, Information Paper, Penn. Fish and Boat Commission, www.sites.state.pa.us

- Channel Catfish, National Fact Sheet, Ontario- Great Lakes Area, Fish and Habitat Management Program, www.dfo. mpo.gc.ca

- Walleye, University of Wisconsin Sea Grant Program, Wisconsin Dept. of Natural resources, www.dfo.mpo.gc.ca

- Fish Anatomy, Florida Fisheries Commission. http:// Floridafisheries.com

- Lakes and Ponds, March 2006, Mid Atlantic Integrated Assessment,US Environmental Protection Agency, www. epa.gov

- A Quick Course in Ichthyology by Jason Buchhein, www. marinebiology.org

- Pennsylvania Striper Jackpot by Ken Schultz, 2005, ESPN Outdoors, http://espn.go.com

- The Spectacular Striped Bass, www.arkansasstripers.com

- Stripers- Temperate Bass, http://myfrnc.com

- The Spectacular Striped Bass, by Jerry L. Moss, Outdoor Alabama, www.outdooralabama.com

- Hybrid Striped Bass, Biology and Life History, by Ronald G. Hodson, University of NC Sea Grant Program. Southern Region Aquaculture Center, North Carolina State University.

- Striped Bass, Species Profiles. Mass. Division of Marine Fisheries, www.mass.gov

- Striped Bass, ACE Basin Species Gallery, South Carolina Dept. of Natural Resources, www.csc,noaa.gov

- White Perch, Aquatic Nuisance Species List, www.kdwp. state.ks.us

- White Perch, Life History, Maryland Dept. of Natural Resources, www.dnr.state.md.us

- White Perch, New Jersey Dept. of Environmental Resources, Division of Fish and Wildlife, www.state.nj.us

- White Perch, Exotic Aquatics on The Move, www.iisgcp. org

- Is it a Bass or a Perch, Exotic Species, Ohio Sea Grant College Program, Ohio State Univ. grant NA90AA-D-SG496.

- White Perch, Fish Identification, Maine Dept. of Natural Resources, www.state.me.us

- Wildlife of The Alligator River, The Yellow Perch, www.carolina. com

- Outdoors Fishing Perch, 2006. www.execulink.com

- Crappie & Crappie Fishing, April 2004, PWD BRT3200-178, Texas Park and Wildlife Commission. www.state.tx.us

- Crappie Fishing Tips, 2005, http://fifi.essortment.com

- Fishing For Crappie by Jim Wahl, Iowa Dept. Of Natural Resources, www.iowadnr.com

- Crappie Fish a Springtime Favorite, April2002, Ohio Dept. of Natural Resources www.oneilloutside.com

- Fishing Black Crappie, Colorado Division of Wildlife, http://ndis.nrel.colostate.edu

- Bluegill Information, 2006, Michigan Dept. of Natural Resources, www.michigan.gov/dnr

- Northern Pike, Minnesota Dept of Natural Resources, www.dnr.state.mn.us

- Northern Pike Identification Characteristics, Michigan Dept of Natural Resources, www.michigan.gov/dnr

- Northern Pike, Essox lucius, R Lefevre, 1999, http://animaldiversity.ummz

- Northern Pike, Fishing Online, www.pvisuals.com

- Freshwater Fish Temperatures by Louis Bignami, www.finfishing.com

- Lake Temperatures and Fish, The Essential Guide to Fly Fishing, 1998 Clive Schaupmeyer.

- Code of Angling Ethics, Outdoor Alabama, www.outdooralabama.com

- Fishing Etiquette, www.fintalk.com

- Live Bait For Bass by Captain Jerry Sloan, www.cyberangler.com

- Ecology of Lakes and Ponds, www.combat-fishing.com

- Alewife and Blueback Herring, www.dnr.state.md.us

- The Lure of Live Bait, Scott Campbell, www.iglou.com

- Facts About Herring, Mike Laptew Reference Library, http://artnflies.com

- On Line With Jay Yelas by Hart Davis, www.bassresource.com

- What's My Line, Russ Bassdozer, www.bassdozer.com

- Braided Vs. Mono by Nick Ruiz, www.bassdozer.com

- Buyers Guide, Hooks by Justin Hoffman, www.bassdozer.com

- Hook Styles Explained by Jaiem Fleishmann, www.artsnf.com

- Texas Rigs by Jim Reanean, www.bassresource.com

- The Texas Rig by Deitz Dittrich, www.catcherman.com

- Fishing tips, www.fishmitchell.com.

Books Referenced

- Familiar Birds of The Sea and Shore by Simon Perkins, National Audubon Society, Alfred A Knoph Inc. Pub.

- In-Fisherman, 100 Best Freshwater Fishing Tips, The editors of In Fisherman, Harper Perennials. Pub.

- Lives of North American Birds by Kenn Kaufman, Houghton Mifflin Co.

- The Anglers Guide To Fish, Ian Wood, editor, DK Publishing.

- The Freshwater Angler, Fishing For Catfish, Creative Publishing International.

- Fishing Tips. www.fishmitchell.com/custom/fishing.

LaVergne, TN USA
29 March 2011
221926LV00001B/68/A